Buckler's Hard

Buckler's Hard

a rural shipbuilding centre

by A J Holland

 Kenneth Mason

By the same author
   The Teaching of History (with others)
   The Age of Industrial Expansion
   Ships of British Oak
   Trade and Communications
   Our Exbury

© A J Holland 1985, Revised 1993

The right of A J Holland to be identified as the author of this work has been asserted in accordance with the Copyright, Designs and Patents Act 1988

British Library Cataloguing-in-Publication Data
A catalogue record for this book is available from the British Library

ISBN 0-85937-398-3

Published by
Kenneth Mason Publications Ltd
Dudley House, 12 North Street
Emsworth, Hampshire PO10 7DQ

Printed and bound by
The Cromwell Press Limited,
Broughton Gifford, Melksham, Wiltshire

Contents

Illustrations

Foreword

The Abbey and the Manor of Beaulieu have attracted their historians over the years. But the story of the shipbuilding village of Buckler's Hard, on the lower reaches of the river, has not been told in detail on the basis of widespread research. This gap has now been filled, and Alec Holland is the obvious person to fill it. Head of History, and then Deputy Head Master, of King Edward VI, Southampton until 1979, and Curator of the Buckler's Hard Maritime Museum since its foundation, he has the qualifications, and as the reader will find, the qualities, for the task. His earlier book on Hampshire shipbuilding in the days of sail, 'Ships of British Oak', gives him the background from which to relate a strictly local to a wider scene; and from his knowledge of original sources, in public and private archives, he has written an authoritative survey – and unobtrusively corrected earlier mistakes.

Buckler's Hard has never been very much larger than the main street down which we look today. But it was the home of a yard which, thanks mainly to the energy and skill of one man, the master shipwright Henry Adams, built more vessels for the navy over a period of 80 years, including Nelson's favourite ship *Agamemnon* and two others also present at Trafalgar, than any other of the private Hampshire yards. The village however was not founded for that purpose, but rather as an entrepot for trade, notably for sugar to be imported from the West Indian island of St Lucia by the Duke of Montagu under royal grant. What, one may wonder, might have happened if that venture had succeeded; if the French had not at once taken the island as they did, and put paid to the hopes? Would a substantial, and growing, 'Montagu Town' have been established? And would it have survived into the next century, rivalling its commercial neighbours? What might have happened if it had then declined, under the limitations of a small river? We might have a scene very different from the single broad street that we now see.

That scene, or something very like it, and the life of the village, were settled in the decades following the great French wars. As early as 1831 a visitor found 'all . . . quiet as the grave, no sound of axes or hammers, no shouts of active men'. Buckler's Hard and the river were entering on the slumber of what Alec Holland has called their 'Rural Retreat'. The changes, to the life though not the appearance of the village, have come more recently, under the pressures of our own times. The author discusses them, and also the future they have provoked. But it is as an historian, not a prophet, that I have studied and enjoyed the book and welcome it as an account, steeped so clearly in knowledge and affection of a river and a hamlet which, in their interest and beauty, are among the most remarkable in England.

John Ehrman

Acknowledgements

AS WITH ALL AUTHORS my debt to others is great, and cannot properly be conveyed in print. First I am most grateful to Lord Montagu for giving me the opportunity to write for publication the results of more than 20 years of research. H E R Widnell began the mammoth task of discovering and collecting the manuscripts extant in Palace House. Alan Bartlett, over a period of eight years, brought order to the collection, and produced a comprehensive catalogue. In addition, Alan Bartlett most generously gave me the benefit of his knowledge of source material, and saved me many months of hard labour. Corinne Evans not only typed the first draft, a heroic task in itself, but also helped me with the muniments in Palace House when the mantle of H E R Widnell and Alan Bartlett was assumed by me. Then, Ann Matthews had the task of typing the 'revised' version. Also, I am most grateful to those who believed in the value of this publication, and especially to John Ehrman, Graham Carter, and Kenneth Mason.

Finally, my gratitude is due to family and friends, who have given me the peace of mind to forget the present and to allow me to live in the past. With the completion of this book, the future of Buckler's Hard must inevitably replace the present.

1 Buckler's Hard on the Beaulieu River

THE BEAULIEU RIVER, 12 miles long, has only three small settlements on its banks. The siting of two of them is geographical: Beaulieu grew up close to the Abbey at the bridge crossing nearest to the sea; Lepe hamlet developed at the entrance to the river. The third, Buckler's Hard, was almost an accident of history. It was an instant creation as a 'new town' in the 1720s; flourished as an important naval shipbuilding centre for a hundred years; then became a sleepy backwater for another hundred before developing into the popular tourist attraction of today.

Those who arrive by sea enter the Beaulieu river off Lepe where shipbuilding also took place in the 18th century. After a long westward beat, the seafarer passes Need's Ore Point into Fiddler's Reach, where the hulls of newly-launched ships anchored en route for Portsmouth. Sea banks now keep high tides out of the meadows between Need's Ore and Gin's where the river winds past Lord Henry's oyster beds, the site of the Mulberry building in 1943-44, past Gilbury Pier on the Exbury side, until Buckler's Hard comes into view.

Most visitors, however, come by car, along a road from Beaulieu still in the same location as in the 18th century. The wide village street, running north towards the river, is flanked by terrace houses, most of which are more than 200 years old. Across the river the ancient oaks of Exbury serve as a sylvan backdrop to its rural peace.

Buckler's Hard is a time capsule, largely preserved as it was 200 years ago, but is not a typical village. Part of the Manor of Beaulieu, it is the maritime centre of the river. The village of Beaulieu, the metropolis of the river, contains the residence of the owner, the church, the shops, the policeman, and the school.

Buckler's Hard is, and always was, a specialist outpost and, in common with the Solent waterways, enjoys the natural advantage of a double tide, a secondary high water. The flood tide takes six hours coming in then, after a gentle fall, there is a second high tide, not quite as high as the first, some two hours later, followed by a period of slack water for about an hour. Then the ebb sets in, and low water is reached in just two and a half hours. This secondary high water has three major advantages. First, as mariners prefer to proceed upstream on a flood tide, there are more hours of flood than of ebb. Secondly, there is a relatively current-free period of about three hours around high water, and six hours out of every 24. Thirdly, the fast ebb has a scouring effect on the river bed, which minimises silting. In addition, the sluice on the mill dam at Beaulieu has the effect of scouring the upper reaches of the navigable part of the river. Ships drawing up to five feet can proceed upstream as far as Buckler's Hard at any state of the tide; at high water there is a depth of between two and three fathoms. Between Buckler's and Bailey's Hards the river is navigable only for about eight hours each day, whilst the last mile from Bailey's Hard to Beaulieu can be navigated solely at high water. Buckler's Hard is thus the most suitable site for maritime enterprise on the river.

There the river bank is profuse with rice grass (*Spartina townsendii*) a hybrid development of the late 19th century, which has helped to prevent erosion. At low tide much of the river reveals considerable expanses of mud or saltings where the spartina acts as an aesthetic cover. Buckler's Hard is unusual in that there are considerable deposits of gravel near the bank giving firm ground for landing. The term 'hard', common in the south of England, means such a natural landing place rather than one artificially created. The origin of Buckler's possibly derives from the Buckle family who appear in Beaulieu parish registers from 1668. But the Buckles played no part in the development of the village, though they probably used the hard for commercial purposes before 1720. When the village was created in the 1720s its official name was Montagu Town, but this soon passed into disuse with a return to the former popular name. It was sheer coincidence that in the 19th century Frederick Buckle, having no previous connection with the hamlet, became the tenant of the Master Builder's House.

The identification of Buckler's with a family is consistent with other place-names on the river. Bailey's Hard is named after a

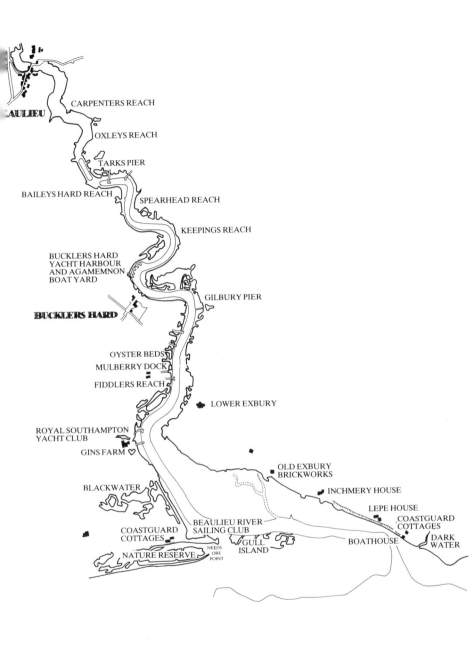

CARPENTERS REACH

BEAULIEU

OXLEYS REACH

TARKS PIER

BAILEYS HARD REACH

SPEARHEAD REACH

KEEPINGS REACH

BUCKLERS HARD
YACHT HARBOUR
AND AGAMEMNON
BOAT YARD

GILBURY PIER

BUCKLERS HARD

OYSTER BEDS
MULBERRY DOCK
FIDDLERS REACH

LOWER EXBURY

ROYAL SOUTHAMPTON
YACHT CLUB

GINS FARM

OLD EXBURY
BRICKWORKS

BLACKWATER

INCHMERY HOUSE

LEPE HOUSE

COASTGUARD
COTTAGES

BEAULIEU RIVER
SAILING CLUB

COASTGUARD
COTTAGES

GULL
ISLAND

BOATHOUSE

DARK
WATER

NATURE RESERVE

NEEDS
ORE
POINT

- Sketch map of the Beaulieu river, showing the principal places mentioned
  in the text

15

family of tenants of Beufre or Bouverie Farm in the 17th century, although the modern name had to establish itself in competition with the more ancient Bouverie Hard. The inventory of Nicholas Bailey (1681) shows that he owned an eighth share in the 'good ship *Providence*'. Carpenter's Dock, less than half-a-mile from Beaulieu, is also named after 18th century leaseholders and not after an occupation. Braces or Braziers Key is probably named after Robert Bracey, a 16th century tenant,[1] and, again, has no occupational significance.

The name of the river on which Buckler's Hard stands is now firmly established as Beaulieu although before the foundation of the Abbey in 1204 it was known as the Otter. Gradually the tidal part of the river became known as Beaulieu Haven, with the upper reaches still anonymous as late as 1570, when the Lepe Admiralty Court described it as 'the river that goeth up from Beaulieu Haven towards Iplie in the Forest'. Then, the term Beaulieu river was applied to its whole course. However, 17th and 18th century Navy Board clerks, and even Henry Adams, the famous Buckler's Hard shipbuilder, invariably wrote the name as Bewley. This phoneticising of proper nouns, for people as well as places, was common in England until the standardisation of spelling in the 19th century. Matthew Paris' map of circa 1250 show Beauli for the Abbey site, but it is always Beaulieu in ecclesiastical documents. In the early 19th century some antiquarians followed the lead of Camden's *Britannia* of 1806 by referring to the river as the Exe, a common generic water noun in the south of England. The name was later popularised by Sir Arthur Conan Doyle in *The White Company*, a story about the Hundred Years' War in which the main characters are Hampshire folk. This 'new' name was doubtless welcomed by the people of Exbury; even as late as the 1920s some of them felt aggrieved that their rivals in Beaulieu had stolen the name of 'their' river. However, the case for calling the river the Exe lacks foundation. Exbury is derived from the saxon burh or fortified place, (which is a common place-name in various forms — bury, borough, or burg), and from the original saxon fief whose name is spelt variously as Hurkere, Ekere or Ykere. The creek upstream of Inchmery House is known as the Exbury river, and one of its tributaries is called St Catherine's Creek after the patron saint of Exbury Church. Although from the 1720s Buckler's Hard became the most important commercial port on the river, there were other landing and loading places. Beaulieu had a wharf near the mill where, as late as the early 20th century, coal for the electricity station was unloaded. From 1805 Carpenter's Dock, near Beaulieu, was used as an outlet for bricks and timber. The ordnance survey map of 1810 shows Carpenter's Dock as a shipyard, but this is an error. Brace's Key, on the western side, was a minor hard used for grain. Bailey's Hard, the first site for naval shipbuilding on the river, was the 'port' for the important brick-works which operated from 1790 to 1930. Below Buckler's Hard, Gin's was much used by farmers, a continuation of its monastic function. Gin's stands at the confluence of the tributary which runs from Hatchet Pond into the main river; the name derives from the latin *ingenium* as the monks erected a device for loading and unloading ships there. No suitable hard existed between Buckler's and Gin's due to the marshy nature of the bank, epitomised by the name Clobb derived from slob or sloppy ground. Below Gin's is Need's Ore the nearest landing point to the river mouth on the western side, and the station for the revenue cutter until 1922.

• Bailey's Hard. The first Beaulieu river man-of-war was launched there in 1698. One hundred years later a brickworks was established there, and one of the kilns has recently been restored. Minesweepers were fitted out there during the 1939-1945 war

On the opposite bank from Buckler's Hard stands Gilbury Hard, thus known in the 18th century. The present hamlet of Lower Exbury was once the village of Exbury, whilst the present village of Exbury was known first as Gilbury and then as Upper Exbury. Exbury Point, opposite Gin's, was used by Lower Exbury farm, while St Catherine's creek was used as the entrepot for the brickworks there and is still known locally as Brickyard Creek.

Lepe, at the mouth of the river, was the usual departure point for the Isle of Wight. It was normally spelt Leap or Leape until the 19th century, perhaps denoting a landing place where one could leap ashore. Alternatively, the name Lepe may come from the Latin *lapis* (stone) or *lapidosus* (stony), which accords with the topography. The suggestion that it marked the terminus stone (*ad lapidem*) of a Roman-Saxon road to Totton is another possibility.

Buckler's Hard is part of the Manor of Beaulieu, a land unit with the Beaulieu river on the east, the Solent on the south, and the New Forest on the west and north. In 1204 Cistercian monks were given what was then part of the New Forest by a royal charter, and during the next 300 years the abbots of Beaulieu acquired more land. The monastic period saw the creation of Sowley Pond, made in 1270 by building a causeway which held back the waters of two streams outside 'the King's wood of Suthle'.[2]

A more important legacy of the monastic period were the river rights. Successive abbots claimed the ownership of the river bed, and the rights of flotsam, jetsam, and lagan (ie items which lie on the bed of the river), ownership of the foreshore to the high water mark, right of wreck, and shooting and fishing rights. The lords of Exbury were forced to pay rent to the monks for the weir which was situated at the mouth of the Dark Water at Lepe. The abbots also guarded jealously their right to control all fishing in the river, a restriction which local inhabitants found hard to bear. Successive abbots had to counter the claims of Southampton to control the river. Southampton had admiralty jurisdiction over the coastal region from Hurst Point and Lymington in the west, to Langstone and Portsmouth in the east. These rights, defined in 1324, were reaffirmed in 1451 when the mayor of Southampton was given the title of Admiral of the Port. He had the right to collect local customs, could lay claim to all wrecks within the defined port, and had jurisdiction over fishing. But the abbots of Beaulieu had already been granted some of those privileges over the Beaulieu river, and refused to surrender them to Southampton. Whilst the

Admirals of the Port accepted the exemption of the Beaulieu river from their jurisdiction in flotsam, jetsam, lagan, wrecks and fishing, the vexed question of local customs remained. In expecting exemption, the monks had some reason on their side; ecclesiastical houses were usually immune from secular taxation and, as the burgesses of Southampton were exempted, the Abbot of Beaulieu could expect the same treatment. Friction between Church and State is a constant theme of medieval history; the local story is a microcosm of wider issues. H S Cobb, editor of the *Local Port Book of Southampton 1439-40* [3] states that 'Beaulieu may . . . have been exempt from the levy of local customs, since it is not mentioned in the Port Books'. It may be that the reaffirmation of the rights of Southampton in 1451 by Henry VI strengthened the claims of the town, as there are occasional references to Beaulieu Abbey trade in the Port Books for 1469-71. [4] But the monks were largely successful in preserving their autonomy of the river, this benefitting later lay owners. The present rights of Lord Montagu derive directly from those held by the abbots of Beaulieu, through King John's charter.

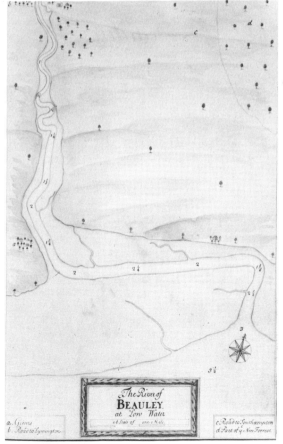

• Map of the Beaulieu river in the Commissioner's Report of 1698. The original, which is in colour, is in the British Library. Gin's is shown too far to the south, but the purpose of the map was to show the depth of water. The figures denote fathoms

When Beaulieu Abbey was dissolved in 1538, ownership passed to Thomas Wriothesley, later created the first Earl of Southampton. Wriothesley became the proprietor of the Beaulieu river, with all the rights so jealously guarded by the monks. Eventually, in 1673, due to the marriage of the youngest daughter of the fourth and last Earl of Southampton to Ralph Montagu, ownership passed to the Montagus of Boughton, whose descendants have been the owners of the Beaulieu river for more than 300 years. During the last century, the manor of Beaulieu, including the river, was given as a wedding present by his father the fifth Duke of Buccleuch to Lord Henry Scott, later the first Baron Montagu of Beaulieu.

The Wriothesleys can be credited with the development of the local iron industry. Sowley Pond, created by the monks for fish, became the site of an ironworks, started in about 1600 by the Earl of Southampton.[5] As the Wriothesleys also owned Titchfield Abbey, the plan was to have ironworks in both places. Although the two properties became divided in ownership in 1673, with the marriage of Ralph Montagu to the Wriothesley heiress, the tradition of commercial connection continued, Sowley's blast furnace being used for the production of pig iron, while the forge at Titchfield produced wrought iron. The ironworks at Sowley were in use throughout the 17th century and were to prove of considerable advantage to the shipbuilders of Buckler's Hard in the next century. This industry, which had a prelude in the 1690s at Bailey's Hard, was to be the most important economic activity on the river from 1690 to 1815, leading to the development, though not the inception, of Buckler's Hard.

References

[1] Beaulieu Muniments
[2] A B Bartlett, *The Iron Works at Sowley* (unpublished, Beaulieu Muniments)
[3] H S Cobb (ed) *Local Port Book of Southampton 1439-1440* (Southampton 1961)
[4] D B Quinn (ed) *Port Book of Southampton vol 1 1469-1471* (Southampton 1937)
[5] A B Bartlett, *op cit*

2 The advent of naval shipbuilding

BUCKLER'S HARD was not the first site used for shipbuilding on the Beaulieu river. Until 1690, it took place in Beaulieu itself. Documentary evidence is almost non-existent, but Edward Shish was a shipwright in Beaulieu, building and owning small craft, until his death in 1640. The exact location of his yard cannot be determined, but only a small area of river bank would have been required. Shish is an unusual surname, and a John Shish was Master Shipwright at Deptford in 1686, when he was criticised harshly by Samuel Pepys. However, as yet, no link has been found between that John Shish and Edward Shish of Beaulieu. The Beaulieu river can claim some vicarious part in shipbuilding on the Hamble river, for the Wyatts of Bursledon bought Beaulieu timber between 1667 and 1772.

The start of naval shipbuilding on the Beaulieu river was brought about by national and international events rather than by local causes. The accession of the Protestant William III and Mary in 1689 led to a fundamental change in foreign policy. France, hitherto Britain's ally against the Dutch, became Britain's main enemy; during the years from 1689 to 1815, a period of 126 years, Britain and France were officially at war for 65 of them, and in a state of 'cold war' for most of the remainder. There was a need for the development of royal dockyards more convenient for aggressive or defensive naval action against the French coast than those on the Thames. Accordingly, Portsmouth dockyard, founded during the reign of Henry VII, was expanded rapidly during the 1690's. This development was to have a significant effect on the Beaulieu river, for Portsmouth needed timber and other materials. At the same time, at Devonport, Plymouth, a new

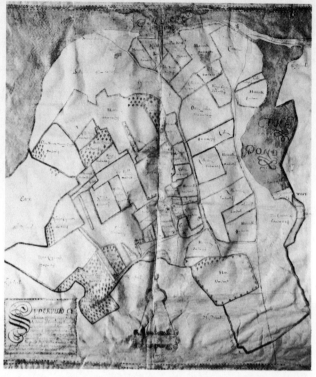

- Map of Lepe, 1640, owned by Maldwin Drummond of Cadland. The pond and the mill can be seen upper right. The latin inscription, bottom left, refers to the manor of Stone, as Cadland was then called

dockyard was founded which also became a customer for Hampshire timber. There was even a suggestion that a third royal dockyard should be established on the south coast, and in 1698 a commission was appointed to enquire into the possibility. Its members were Edmund Dummer, Surveyor of the Navy; Thomas Willshaw, Comptroller of the Storekeeper's Accounts; with James Conoways and William Cruft, both masters of Trinity House. They began work on 4 July 1698, and studied 18 possible sites on the south coast, including some in Hampshire. The report, dated 19 November, 1698 was concisely worded, and embellished with beautiful maps — a copy of the Beaulieu river map can be seen in the Maritime Museum at Buckler's Hard [1]. There the Beaulieu river entry read,

Beauly. *Is a river of somewhat less consideration in degree than Bussleton (ie Hamble river). But of large in draught, good tides, and fair depths at low water. Tis about four miles from the mouth of it, to the Toune of that name. Tis also convenient for building small ships. One of the 4th rate hath been built about a mile below it at a place commodious and safe.* [2]

By comparison, Lymington was described as 'a place more short and scanty in the accomodations to be found in Beauly river'. The Commissioners' conclusion and advice was that no further dockyard should be established between Dover and Land's End. But, as the report shows, the naval connection with the Beaulieu river had already been forged, and the first man-of-war built, the *Salisbury*, a fourth-rate of 48 guns, built by the Herring brothers.

The naval disappointments of 1690, and especially an engagement with the French off Beachy Head, led to the government's tax on beer and spirits to raise £570,000 for the building of 27 ships for the Navy. The royal dockyards could not cope with this unprecedented building programme, so that the Admiralty, with some reluctance, gave contracts to civilian builders. Whilst the Admiralty decided policy, it was the Navy Board, established by Henry VIII, through one of its principal officers, the Surveyor of the Navy, which was responsible for the design and construction of ships. The Surveyor of the Navy from 1692 to 1699 was Edmund Dummer, a relative of the Dummers of Stoneham, near Southampton. The Navy Board designed the ships, and the civilian builders were expected to build the hulls to these specifications. Usually, the fitting-out of the ships with masts, spars, and rigging, and with much of the ironwork was done at a royal dockyard. The ships were classified by 'rates', which denoted the number of guns and the number of men; the largest were called first-rates, and fourth-rates had, in the 1690's, from 40 to 59 guns. Ships of the same rate had the same keel length, overall length, extreme breadth, and depth in hold. They were also classified as of a certain number of tons burthen, which was, in the 1690's, arrived at by the formula,

$$\frac{Breadth \times \frac{1}{2}\ breadth \times length\ of\ keel}{94}$$

Civilian builders obtained contracts by offering their services to the Navy Board, who would need to be satisfied that the builder had a suitable site, a labour force, and materials. The price was fixed at a certain sum per ton and payment made in instalments as each part of the construction was completed, not in cash, but in government bills. In effect these were a promise to pay when parliament voted the money, so that the contractor had to hold off his own creditors, or to sell the government bills at less than their face value to a broker, should the payment from the Admiralty be delayed. In general, therefore, the civilian shipbuilder needed some capital at the outset.

When the expansion programme began in 1691, John Winter obtained a contract to build a third-rate in Southampton, as did William Wyatt of Bursledon. Between 1691 and 1698, nine naval vessels were built at Southampton and five on the Hamble river. Richard Herring, who was to be the first Beaulieu river shipbuilder, was a Southampton man who was foreman shipwright for William Wyatt at Bursledon. When the latter died in 1694, Herring continued to work on naval contracts for Wyatt's widow. Then, in 1696, Herring obtained a contract to build a 48-gun ship on his own account, at just over £7 per ton. Thus, Herring was undertaking a £5,000 venture, the equivalent of about £500,000 today. On the signing of the contract he would have received £1,000, with further instalments as the work proceeded. Richard Herring then had to find a site. The Wyatts were busy on the Hamble river, while Winter and Parker were occupying sites in Southampton. Herring's original intention was to build on the Isle of Wight, but Joseph Nye came from Kent to Cowes, and was building the *Poole* there. Herring needed a site removed from other builders, to avoid competition for men and materials. He entered into negotiations with Ralph, third Baron Montagu of Boughton, a Privy Councillor and intimate friend of William III. Montagu agreed to lease a site on the Beaulieu river, the whereabouts of which are still a matter for conjecture. The site was either at Bailey's or Buckler's Hard, with the evidence pointing towards the former. There are no extant records of the location through leases, and most documents refer to the site as 'Bewley', meaning somewhere on the river. A Navy Board Official, writing on 17 January 1698, referred to the ship as being built at 'Buckley's Hard in Buley River'.[3] Though this may have been meant at Buckler's Hard, it could equally have been a rendering of Bayley's Hard, or even Boeufre's Hard (the old monastic name), by a clerk writing at a distance from the operation. As Buckler's Hard later became famous for its shipbuilding, historians assumed that this was the natural site for Herring's activities. But the more probable site is Bailey's Hard. On 27 February, Richard Herring informed the Navy Board that he intended to build 'at Bayley's Hard'.[4] Intention does not prove actuality. But the Commissioners of 1698 reporting on the Beaulieu river stated that 'one of the 4th rate hath been built about a mile below it (ie Beaulieu) at a place commodious and safe'.[5] It is hardly conceivable that the Commissioners who

24

conducted so accurate a survey could have meant Buckler's Hard, two and a half miles from Beaulieu, especially as Bailey's Hard is almost exactly one mile from the village. Moreover, a pictorial estate map dated 1718 [6] shows the hinterland of Buckler's Hard as completely afforested, whilst access to Bailey's Hard appears feasible. It is known that Herring had to cut a path from the Hard through the woods to the road,[7] but no path is shown in the 1718 map, near Buckler's Hard, whilst it is possible to interpret a line running from Bailey's Hard towards Curtle as a path. A tradition that the first naval building on the Beaulieu river was at Bailey's Hard was current among some of the local inhabitants as late as the 1920's, so it may be that, for once, local lore was correct. On the evidence, Bailey's Hard must be given the honour. Certainly it had all the requisites for a suitable building site for Herring. It was reasonably distant from other merchant builders; it was sheltered from the prevailing westerly winds; there was a depth of two fathoms at high water; the bank was hard enough to take building blocks; accessible timber was close at hand; Sowley Pond was near for iron work; the soil, rich in loam and clay, was suitable for brickmaking; on the opposite bank was Brace's key and there was already a hard in existence at the site. The village of Beaulieu, only a mile away, could be reached by Herring's workmen, who needed lodgings. The site was well up the river, and was a difficult target for any French privateer. It was still close enough to Portsmouth with whom constant communication was necessary.

- Buckler's Hard, when it was a 'rural retreat'

While there is little documentary evidence on the building of Herring's *Salisbury*, a picture of the project can be built up if he is regarded as typical of his time. Herring was to use Bailey's Hard for a single contract, which would occupy him for about two years. Shipbuilders did not erect buildings for such ventures, for obvious reasons. Thus, little can be gained by an archaeological exploration of Bailey's Hard.

Having agreed a site, Herring's next task was to assemble a work-force, and to ensure that his men were not impressed into the royal service. On 26 February 1696 he wrote to the Navy Board asking for exemption from impressment for 40 shipwrights, eight pairs of sawyers, 15 labourers and two timber hewers.[8] Such a labour force could not have been drawn entirely from Beaulieu; most of his men would have come from other parts of Hampshire, and afforded lodgings in Beaulieu. After cutting a rough path through the woods, the immediate task was to dig or erect saw-pits. Then, using local timber, keel blocks were cut and laid on the river bank immediately above the high-water mark. On those, the keel of the ship was laid, whilst a staging of posts was erected round the vessel as it was built. A mould loft was not necessary; Herring would mark out the lines of the ship on a scrieve board, placed near the site, using a sharp knife. Ironwork was done by a Portsmouth blacksmith, who put up a temporary forge and other workshops in the grounds of Beaulieu Abbey.

Herring needed timber, all of which was to be found near the site. English oak (*quercus robur*), with its strong grain and high density, was used for the frames and the stem and stern pieces. Elm could be used for the keel and keelson, as well as for parts of the masts. Beech, for thickstuff filling, also grew in abundance. This timber was bought by Herring from Lord Montagu, and felled by manor workmen.

So Richard Herring began to build the *Salisbury*, a fourth-rate of 48 guns, of 682 tons burthen, 134 feet long, with an extreme breadth of 34 feet. Then, in January 1697, he died whereupon his brother James took over the contract.[9] But James Herring was soon in financial difficulty, and by January 1698 work was at a standstill, with the uncompleted ship abandoned. Herring's workmen had left the site due to arrears of pay. At a time when their skills were in high demand, they could hardly be blamed for deserting their employer. Herring owed Baron Montagu for timber, and perhaps also for arrears of rent. As a safeguard against these debts, the landlord took possession of the site and the uncompleted vessel. Herring was being pressed by the Navy Board to complete the ship, but he was unable so to do. There followed a series of meetings between Baron Montagu's solicitor, Thomas Dummer of Stoneham and Navy Board Officials. On 3 March 1698 the latter reported an agreement whereby, *his Lo(ordshi)pp would not interrupt the dispatch of said Shipp nor the launching and receiving her for the King but hopes his Lo.pp having an assignment of Herring's bills We will order the said Bills to be alter'd into his Lo.pp name and paid him when they come in due course.* [10]

Later that year, men and materials were sent from Portsmouth dockyard to complete her. *Salisbury* was one of the four sister ships launched in the region that year: *Worcester* was built at Northam by Robert Winter, *Jersey* at Cowes by John Nye, and *Dartmouth* in Southampton by James Parker.

The *Salisbury*'s career was undistinguished. In 1702 she was part of the force under Sir John Munden, Rear-Admiral of the Red, sent to Corunna to intercept a French convoy to the West Indies. In the following year she was captured by the French who retained her name but when she was recaptured by Byng's squadron she was known as the *Salisbury Prize,* as a new *Salisbury* had been built in 1707.

Her building was symptomatic of the changes then taking place in Beaulieu. There was a deliberate attempt to foster enterprises other than farming, and the ubiquitous Edmund Dummer, Surveyor of the Navy until 1699, was at the centre of them. He was acquainted with Ralph, first Duke of Montagu whom he probably persuaded to invest money in the iron industry. The blast furnace at Sowley still worked in association with the forge at Titchfield, both leased by Roger Gringoe. Duke Ralph financed the building of a forge at Sowley, so that it became a complete ironworks. This, together with repairs to the furnace, was effected at a cost of £2,000. Another of Dummer's contacts, Henry Corbet, a blacksmith from Portsea, contracted with the Portsmouth commissioners to supply iron to the Dockyard in May 1700. In June he took up the lease of Sowley, and of Palace Farm. On the site of the old Abbey Church, Corbet put up a range of buildings including a blacksmith's shop, foundry house, moulding house, plumber's and carpenter's shops. But the ambitious Corbet was soon in financial trouble, and by 1701 he was indebted to Ralph Montagu and Edmund Dummer in the sum of £4,249 13s 3d. In December

• An aerial view from Gins to Need's Ore

1701, Dummer took over the enterprise, and agreed to pay Corbet £500 a year as manager. By 1711 Dummer was also in financial straits, his other business interests having failed. His son, Thomas Dummer, himself a contractor of ironware to the Navy, took over his father's debts, and operated Sowley until 1717. In the 'Dummer' period, Sowley produced about 300 tons of iron each year for Portsmouth Dockyard. Thus, a further connection between Beaulieu and the Navy had been forged.

After the launching of the *Salisbury* on the Beaulieu river, no further naval shipbuilding occurred there until the 1740s, apart from some small boat building by James Herring until 1703 or so.[11] By about 1720, apart from traffic in timber and iron, the river was in the commercial doldrums; but a bold scheme to make it an important artery of commerce was being planned.

References

[1] British Library Additional MSS 33279 (Sloane 3233)
[2] *ibid*, p 141
[3] Public Records Office Adm 1/3583
[4] PRO Adm 106/489
[5] British Library Sloane MSS 3233
[6] Beaulieu Muniments
[7] J P W Ehrman *The Navy in the War of William III* (Cambridge 1953) p 72
[8] PRO Adm 106/489
[9] PRO Adm 106/506
[10] National Maritime Museum, Greenwich *Sergison Papers* 39
[11] Beaulieu Muniments, Account Books

3 Montagu Town

BUCKLER'S HARD, which was to become one of the most prominent of the private shipbuilding sites in the 18th century, owes its foundations to a scheme far removed from the shipwright's trade. In 1709 John, second Duke of Montagu (1689-1749), inherited the manor of Beaulieu from his father, Ralph. Duke John was the son-in-law of Sarah, Duchess of Marlborough, the holder of many royal offices and honours, a Fellow of the Royal College of Physicians, a Fellow of the Royal Society, a keen agriculturist, a generous philanthropist, and an imaginative entrepreneur. 'John the Planter' conceived the idea of founding a colony in the West Indies, to produce sugar there, and to import that valued commodity through a new port to be built on the Beaulieu river.

In the early part of the 18th century colonial enterprise was fashionable; Europeans sought possessions in the warmer latitudes for the tropical and semi-tropical goods that could be produced there. Duke John's interest was drawn to the West Indies where many islands, formerly claimed by Spain, were then contested by Britain and France. By the Treaty of Utrecht, signed in 1713, five West Indian islands — Dominica, Grenada, Tobago, St Vincent and St Lucia — had been declared 'neutral' by the contestants, as ownership rights could not be agreed. Duke John asked George I for a charter for the proprietorship of St Vincent and St Lucia, and on 20 June 1722 the King granted the Duke the two islands, with the title of Governor and Captain-General.[1] The choice of the two islands held some dangers, for the few English settlers there braved a climate unsuitable for Europeans, and were wholly dependent upon the Royal Navy for protection against the French and Spanish. St Lucia was but some 30 miles from the

French island of Martinique; the nearest English base was on Barbados, three times the distance. However, some risks had to be taken. The islands decided, Duke John then had to choose a site for the new port on the Beaulieu river, to be known as Montagu Town. Its concept had a sound basis. In Beaulieu the Duke had a large amount of timber, an ironworks at Sowley Pond within easy distance, and the privileges of a free port inherited from monastic times.

● John, second Duke of Montagu (1688-1749), the founder of the Buckler's Hard. He married Mary Churchill, youngest daughter of the Duke of Marlborough, the hero of Blenheim. John had the reputation of a practical joker, but also was a man of many talents. He was a Fellow of the Royal College of Physicians, and was called 'the Planter' because of his interest in forestry. His father, Ralph the first Duke of Montagu, became the owner of Beaulieu through marriage to Elizabeth Wriothesley, daughter of 4th Earl of Southampton. Ralph built Boughton House in Northamptonshire and Montagu House in Bloomsbury. All three properties were inherited by John, who, therefore, had little time to spend at Beaulieu

Choice fell on Buckler's Hard, then merely a landing place, lacking wharves or quays, with the trees of Dungehill Copse reaching to the water's edge. Almost certainly there were no houses in existence at Buckler's Hard, as none is shown in a rent schedule for 1718. Thus, the new port was to be an original creation, and not an extension of an existing village. The site was wisely chosen as Buckler's Hard, two miles below Beaulieu, was accessible at all states of the tide; the river there was wide yet sheltered from the prevailing westerlies by Clobb Copse. It was also one of the few places on the river where the hard gravel bed stretched to low water mark. Moreover, there was a spring near the site to supply the new town's drinking water.

Duke John made discreet enquiries about the extent of Southampton's jurisdiction – remembering the many frictions which had arisen in the past. He wrote confidentially to his steward, *Enquire of Burgess or Troughton if they know how far the privileges of the Port of Southampton extends and how far it interferes with the trade at Bewley, and if one could get a charter – and what would be the proper encouragements, but let them not mention it to any body – the Southampton and Lymington people might be allarmed at it and might prevent anything of that kind should it prove feasible.* Simultaneously, the Duke asked for enquiries to be made regarding the rights of the manor of Exbury, recently acquired by Mitford. There is no record of the replies, but presumably all was well, as Southampton, Lymington and Exbury offered no opposition to the scheme.

The project was conceived: now to put it into practice. Having ensured there were no legal bars to establishing a port on the Beaulieu river, the Duke began to assemble ships and stores for the founding of the West Indies plantation, and appointed Captain Nathaniel Uring as deputy-governor and expedition leader. An obvious choice, Uring was an experienced mariner who knew the West Indies intimately. He was born in Walsingham, Norfolk in about 1682, the son of a retired mariner who fired his son's imagination with his stories. Nathaniel Uring left home in 1697 for London where he learned the rudiments of navigation. After voyaging by collier from London to Newcastle and back, he joined the *Swift*, en route for Barbados. Although captured by the French, Uring and the rest of the crew were put ashore at Penzance. In 1698 and 1699 he saw service in the West Indies and North America, where he contracted smallpox. On his return to Britain, he joined Herring's *Salisbury*, aboard which he took part in Sir George Rooke's action off Copenhagen. Uring left the *Salisbury* in 1701 and, after a voyage in a slaver, joined the 96-gun *St George* as a midshipman. From 1702 to 1707 he was the master of packet boats to the West Indies, followed by voyages in other ships to North America and West Africa. When the war ended in 1713, he endured life ashore for just over a year before returning to sea. In 1722, at the age of 40, he was to set out on the last of his adventures.

The planting of a new colony in those days was like transporting a new town overseas: materials, food and people all had to be taken across the Atlantic. This inventory of the expedition can be seen in Buckler's Hard Maritime Museum,

Ship	Tons	Officers	Indentured servants
Elisabeth	130	3	9
Charles and Free Mason	200	13	108
Griffin sloop	90	3	48
Little George	100	8	30
Adventure	200	13	141
Hopewell	250	11	89
Leopard	190	loaded at Boston with horses fram'd and live cattle	

The first six ships were loaded in London with 1,460 barrels of beef and pork, flour, pease, oatmeal, butter, cheese, beer, rice, brandy, tobacco, coals, and candles. The seventh vessel, the *Leopard*, was sent in ballast to Boston, Massachusetts to take on board 40 sheep, 30 wooden house frames and 50,450 feet of board (less than one and a half inches thick) and plank (between one and a half and four inches thick). As trouble was expected from the French, the expedition was equipped with 56 cannon, 1,163 muskets and bayonets, and two machine guns. The last-named were the invention of James Puckle (1667-1724), a Sussex lawyer. His invention, patented in 1718, had a revolving block to hold seven or nine bullets. He specified that round bullets should be fired against Christians, and square bullets against the infidel Turk![2] Unsurprisingly nothing came of this invention; the two prototypes were not fired. However, their presence on board are indicative of Duke John's willingness to experiment with new ideas. These guns have been preserved, and one can be seen today on display in Buckler's Hard Maritime Museum.

There were no government-assisted passages in those days; the indentured servant arrangement was common in the late 17th and early 18th centuries, by which the workman agreed to serve his employer for a number of years, usually five, without pay, in return for a free passage to the colony, and free board, food, and clothing during the term of the agreement. Thus, the indentured servant was practically a slave until his five years were completed. During the previous century, volunteers came forward during the initial settlements in North America and the West Indies. But by 1722, more was known about the inhospitable climate (for Europeans) of the West Indies, and the appalling death-rate. So it is probable that the majority of the 425-strong labour force were conscripted from the prisons or from the pauper population. No keen and loyal pioneers with a mission these, but a sullen force of unwilling settlers, with a sprinkling perhaps of volunteers, in a hopeless situation in their native land, with dreams of becoming landowners in a new world of opportunity.

St LUCIA 1722

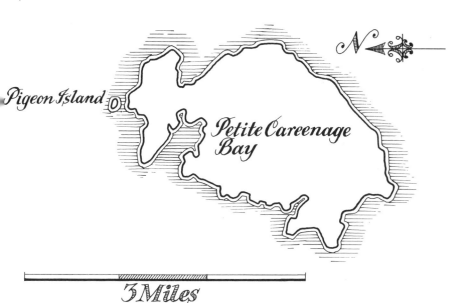

Captain Uring left London on 22 August 1722 for Portsmouth where he met Captain Humphrey Orme, master of HMS *Winchelsea*, a 36-gun fifth-rate, which was to act as convoy escort. The *Charles and Free Mason* had left ten days earlier for Cork, in Ireland, while *Elizabeth* sailed to St Kitt's (St Christopher's), an English possession in the Lesser Antilles. The remaining transports, followed by Uring on 10 September, set out for Cork where some of the indentured servants escaped and were not recovered. At the end of the month, the expedition sailed for Madeira, where water and food were taken on board. This was the usual sea-route at that time, sailing south in order to catch the trade-winds, thus minimising the length of the Atlantic crossing. Uring arrived at Barbados, the nearest British possession to St Lucia and St Vincent. The *Elizabeth* reached Barbados from St Kitts, and the *Leopard* from Boston. In Barbados, Uring bought horses, pigs, turkeys, ducks, chicken, and cows, as it was not practicable in those days to keep live animals during the long Atlantic crossing. He also obtained supplies of vegetables, rum, sugar, corn, and tobacco.

Uring had decided beforehand, with the concurrence of Duke John, that the colony should be planted on St Lucia. He sailed for that island on 15 December 1722, arrived two days later, and anchored in Pigeon Island Bay. But the soil there was sandy and barren, and the anchorage poor, so he sailed south to Petite Careenage Bay on 17 December. Meanwhile, Captain Orme arrived in *Winchelsea* with some disturbing news. In Martinique a proclamation had been read in the name of King Louis XV, claiming that St Lucia was a French possession. Uring's expedition was ordered to leave within 15 days, or 'be driven off by Force of arms'.

At Petite Careenage Bay Uring found water-places, and as the name suggests, beaches suitable for hauling up the ships and careening them. 'Careening' meant more than just cleaning the hulls of the weed growth of a long voyage through tropical seas; in those days of primitive hygiene, the ballast and the bilges soon became dirty, and it was common practice to 'disinfect' ships, usually with vinegar, after a long sea voyage. However, as the land around the harbour was hilly, Uring was still unsure if the site was suitable; nevertheless 50 men were landed to cut down trees and prepare for building. Having sailed further south, without finding a better spot, Uring returned determined to plant the new colony in Petite Careenage Bay. His main worry was defence against attack. However, he decided to build a fort and place batteries of guns on the south side of the harbour, which he named Montagu Point, now the site of Vigie airport and Coalpot restaurant near Castries Harbour).

The new colony existed less than a month. On 19 December the Union Jack was hoisted on Montagu Point, the settlers toasted the health of King George and Duke John, the Council were sworn in, and the unloading of stores began. On Christmas Day a large cow was killed and roasted, the only leisure which the settlers had in their short stay on the island. A week later the French had landed 1,800 soldiers on St Lucia, and on 7 January Uring was given seven days to get out.

● Uring's base on Petite Careenage Bay. After long ocean voyages, wooden sailing ships needed to have barnacles and other marine growth taken from the hull. Ships were dragged up on to a beach; and the cleaning operation was known as "careening"

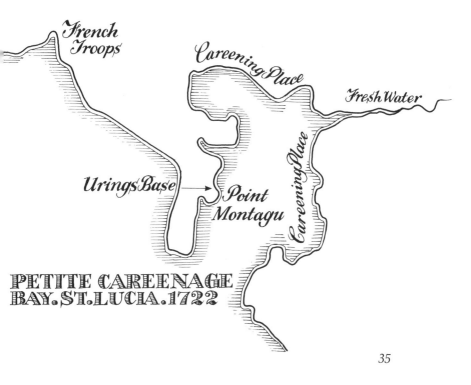

French Troops

Careening Place

Fresh Water

Urings Base

Point Montagu

Careening Place

PETITE CAREENAGE BAY. ST. LUCIA. 1722

So began the sad task of re-embarking the stores, completed on 14 January. The wooden fort was fired, the flag pulled down, and Uring set sail for Antigua, arriving on 19 January. He intended to plant a colony on St Vincent. On 11 January, Uring had sent the *Griffin* there in order to carry out a thorough survey. On 31 January, *Adventure* arrived at Antigua from England with a letter from the Duke of Montagu giving Uring permission to retire from St Lucia and to transfer the project to St Vincent. *Adventure*, whose passage had been delayed by storms, also brought a further 150 indentured servants. But the plans for a settlement on St Vincent were not carried out. On 10 February 1723, the French governor of Martinque wrote to Uring warning him that he would be driven off that island should he attempt to plant a colony there. On the same day, *Griffin* returned from St Vincent with an unfavourable report. Uring now abandoned the project. The stores were unloaded in Antigua, and the indentured servants released in that island. What happened to the 'settlers' can only be conjectured: but there was no contractual obligation for Uring to return them to Britain, and they would have had little difficulty in entering the service of employers in Antigua. Uring spent a year in Antigua selling stores and equipment as best he could before returning to England in 1724. This was the end of Uring's seafaring. He died in 1742, at Falmouth, leaving some £7,000 to his relatives.

The Duke of Montagu had lost £10,000 over the venture, a fortune in those days, but although the plantation of the new colony had failed, the creation of Montagu Town at Buckler's Hard had already begun. The trees of Dungehill Copse stretched almost to the water's edge, so that the foundation of Montagu Town could be compared with the creation of a new housing estate today. The land sloped towards the river unevenly, and one of the first tasks was to cut down some 20 acres of woodland, to clear the way for a wide street, and to shift earth and gravel in order to effect a uniform slope. Today's visitors to the village can stand at the top of the street, and see the results of this work, all performed by manual labour. The work was supervised by Michael Hobbs, probably late in 1724.

One of the earliest tasks was the building of a quay for the new town.[3] This entailed the erection of wooden posts and boards projecting into the river, and filling in with earth and gravel, so that ships could moor alongside. Some of the surplus materials from grubbing the slope were used in the work. The building of the quay, to be 18 inches above the level of high water springs, was done by Miles Troughton and the Edwards family and was completed in 1727, though it had to be raised still further as a freak tide washed over it in January. This original quay was not a success. Within ten years it had sunk four feet, and a considerable rebuilding was undertaken. Sixty-two piles, some 20 feet long, were placed on the outer side, after tons of earth and gravel had been poured in as a foundation. Miles Troughton had been the Duke of Montagu's mining agent in Furness, Lancashire, before coming to Beaulieu as a resident. He was one of a partnership of four running the ironworks at Sowley, lived at Keeping Farm, and played a prominent part in the Montagu Town project. The Edwards family were timber merchants and general contractors from Twyford, a small village between Winchester and Southampton. Some of the timber for the quay was supplied by Michael Hobbs, of Eling, whose men also grubbed out the vista.

• Plan of Montagu Town, showing its intended wide streets and squares. The inset designs show the sea-water baths, which were never built. The original is in the Bodleian Library, Oxford

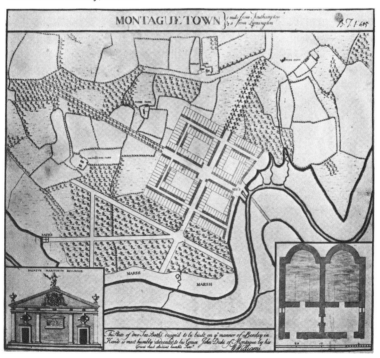

Joseph Wyatt, a timber merchant from Hardley, near Fawley, and whose brother, James, was later to be a shipbuilder at Buckler's Hard, was also engaged in some work on the quay in 1726.[4] Others were engaged in building streets, to link Montagu Town with the road from Beaulieu to St Leonard's, digging ditches, and fencing the boundary of the new town. Many a local craftsman must have been grateful to Duke John for his enterprise and patronage. In addition to the quay, Troughton and Edwards were engaged to demolish the stone fulling millhouse at Beaulieu, and to use the materials to build a storehouse and counting house at Buckler's Hard.

The new town needed houses, built to a plan. A prospectus of Montagu Town, a copy of which may be seen in the Maritime Museum at Buckler's Hard, was issued. The concept was of a wide street, running at right angles to the river. A symmetrical pattern of blocks of houses, in squares, was to be developed, with a wide street as the focal point. The main street, shown on the plan as 80 feet wide, which is what it is today, was to be used for fairs, markets, and general concourse. By accident rather than design, the wide street was useful to shipbuilders who needed to cart timber to the launchways later in the century. The amenities of the town were to include a chapel, an inn, and salt-water baths; an aesthetically pleasing drawing of the latter was shown as an inset to the town plan. A high wall, presumably for protection against a French invasion, was to be built at high water mark on the riverside, inside which were to stand large storehouses for sugar, and a large open space as a market.

It was not the Duke of Montagu's intention to finance the building of the new town himself. As the ground landlord, he would be able to obtain an income from ground rents. Habitation was to be encouraged by offering attractive terms to those willing to build houses at Buckler's Hard. As early as 1722 a prospectus map had been issued (a copy is displayed in the Maritime Museum) which praised the advantages of the Beaulieu river and of the manor of Beaulieu. The 'proposals' for settlers in the new town were, *For the greater Encouragement of Trade in the said Harbour, any Merchant, or other Person, that is willing to settle there, may, upon Application to his Grace the Duke of Montague, have a grant of a Piece of Land, 170 feet in Depth, and 40 feet in Front, at the Yearly Ground Rent of 6s 8d only, and So proportionable according to a greater or Less Quantity of feet in Front.*

That every House may have a Close of Land belonging to it, in the Neighbourhood (if required) of Two Acres, at the Yearly Rent of 13s 4d.
That the Front of all Houses be built entirely with Bricks.
Three Loads of Oak-Timber will be allowed Gratis, for every House to be built.
The aforesaid Grants to be made for 99 Years if either of three persons nominated shall so long live, without paying any Fine for the same.[5]

These terms were most attractive; the rental demand was but a fraction of the 'rack' or economic rent; three loads of timber, with each load about 40 cubic feet, was the equivalent of a gift of about £35; whilst the last clause gave exemption from a fee for a lease renewal by an heir for three generations. However, the great influx into the new town did not materialise.

By 1731, only seven houses had been built, five of them at the expense of the Duke.[6] While it is impossible to identify the first houses to be built they were probably those nearest the river, with superior houses on the western side; on both sides, there were gaps between the houses, later filled by additional dwellings. For example, the present numbers 78 and 79 were built after number 80 and 77. Building began in 1725, and continued throughout the next three or four years. Although some timber and bricks came from the Manor of Beaulieu, considerable quantities were landed at the new quay,[7] from Southampton, Lymington and the Isle of Wight, again affording local employment. The Duke did not himself attend to the detail of the initial building, but he visited Beaulieu several times between June 1723 and August 1729, and the work was done to his instructions.

The first house to be built, probably on the eastern side, was for a blacksmith, John Froud,[8] who opened a blacksmith's shop there. By the mid 1730's, Froud had left Buckler's Hard, presumably because the new busy seaport had not materialised. Three houses, probably on the western side, were built by Miles Troughton, at the Duke's expense, at a cost of £600,[9] and were occupied by Salt Officers. In those days, salt was obtained by the evaporation of sea-water in salterns, one at Gins, one at Park and another at Exbury Point, on Mitford's land. All began operations in the late 17th century, and made a modest contribution to the manufacture of salt. The Solent as a whole, centred on Lymington, was an important salt exporter, the main supplier of that commodity to Portsmouth and Devonport dockyards, and to the whole of the south coast. Salt was used not only for making food palatable, but to cure skins; as a medicine against scurvy and gum diseases; as a flux in glass-making and metal smelting; as a glaze in pottery; and to preserve fish. The salt tax was imposed in 1694 and, apart from a brief period between 1730 and 1732, salt remained an excisable commodity until 1825, when it was abolished by William Huskisson, long after its French equivalent, the hated *gabelle*, had been swept away by the Revolution. In 1789 the duty was 10s (50p) a bushel, and the English paid an average of 3s a year. Salt Officers were required to be present when the proprietor of a salt pan removed or sold any salt, to supervise the weighing, and record the amounts. The Salt Officers, a service separate from the excise men, were the lowest rank in an organisation headed by five commissioners in London who received the then princly emolument of £500 a year. The Salt Officers were paid £40 a year to perform a most unpopular task, often before sullen and silent proprietors. They were not allowed to serve in their birthplace, and they were moved every four years or so to minimise the chance of corruption. This meant that they had difficulty in obtaining a house, and there were frequent complaints of exorbitant rents. The new town, therefore, helped to solve a

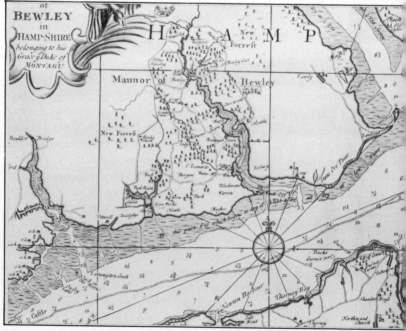

problem, as a new Salt Officer could occupy the same house as his predecessor. In 1732 there were 438 Salt Officers in the whole of the United Kingdom, and the presence of three of them in Buckler's Hard underlines the importance of the Solent region. There was always at least one Salt Officer (and more usually two) resident in Buckler's Hard until 1825. In the first years of the new town, their houses suffered from flooding, and a gulley was dug to drain away the water.

A fifth house was built by Edward Fry, a Beaulieu carpenter, but he died and his widow occupied the house as a tenant. Another was built by Alexander Morris, a bricklayer-builder from Beaulieu, but there is no evidence that the house was for his own use and was probably occupied by Philip Sone. Sone came from Northamptonshire in 1706 to be the vicar of Beaulieu, which living he combined with the office of steward of the Manor of Beaulieu. He lived in the Domus, the traditional residence of the parson until 1724 when he had to find another house as Thomas Burman started a brewery in or near the Domus. Philip Sone's son, another Philip, was rector of Warkton and Scaldwell, two parishes in

• **Prospectus Map of Montagu Town, issued in 1724 to attract merchants to settle there. The prospectus stated that Buckler's Hard had a quay 100 feet long, and 80 feet wide, with a depth of water of 18 feet. Buckler's Hard, it was claimed, was more advantageous for trade than Bristol or London, as ships could sail out of the Beaulieu river when the wind was in the east or the north. Despite the offer of a cheap rent, and free timber, Montagu Town never became a reality. The original is in the Bodleian Library, Oxford**

41

Northamptonshire, near Boughton House, the advowsons of which were held by the Duke of Montagu. Sone was also chaplain to the Prince of Wales, as well as to his patron, the Duke of Montagu, but spent much of his time in Beaulieu, directing the ironworks at Sowley.[10] As Philip Sone II married Miles Troughton's daughter, it was perhaps natural that Sone should look for a house in the new town of which Troughton was the principal developer. Further, as the provision of a house for Sone was the responsibility of the Lord of the Manor, the new town, where houses were needed, was an obvious choice. The seventh house probably on the eastern side was occupied by Richard Scanes, who was described as 'the watchman'. Although there were changes in tenancies in the 1730's, there is no evidence of further building. In 1740 a house at Buckler's Hard was demolished by James Elcock, in three days.[11] Presumably, the new town, almost 20 years after its conception, contained only six houses.

So ended the Duke's dream. The St Lucia expedition had failed, and in the treaty of 1748 which ended the war of the Austrian Succession the island was declared neutral and the Duke's proprietorship lapsed. The new town on the Beaulieu river, occupied by three tax-collectors, a widow, a night-watchman, a blacksmith and a retired parson, was apparently a failure. But not all was wasted. What had been done was to lead, not to the fame of Montagu Town, but to the development of an important centre of naval shipbuilding, under the original name of Buckler's Hard.

References

[1] N Uring, *A relation of the late Intended Settlement of the Islands of St Lucia & St Vincent* (London 1725)
[2] G M Chinn, *The Machine Gun,* Vol I (Washington D C 1951) p 17; W H B Smith, *Small Arms of the World* (Pennsylvania 1955) p 92; H L Blackmore, *British Military Firearms 1650-1850* (London 1961) p 239
[3] Beaulieu Muniments: *Estate Papers 1723-30*
[4] *ibid* 11/133
[5] Bodleian Library Oxford: *Prospectus for the founding of Montaguville*
[6] Beaulieu Muniments: *Estate Papers*
[7] *ibid:* 8/38, 10/9, 10/79, 10/89, 11/46, 12/44, 14/83, 17/63, 18/68
[8] H E R Widnell, *The Beaulieu Record* (Pioneer 1973) p 105
[9] Beaulieu Muniments: *Estate Papers*
[10] A B Bartlett *op cit*
[11] Beaulieu Muniments Vouchers 1721-63

4 The return of the shipwrights

IN 1739 BRITAIN was again at war, with Spain, and the conflict widened in 1742 into the War of the Austrian Succession, with France once more the main enemy. Although the war was lamented by Walpole, it was welcomed by the shipbuilders. Again the demands of the Navy could not be met by the royal dockyards alone and the building of ships under contract by civilian builders had to be resumed. The Thames was still the most prolific centre for naval building, but the shortage of sites there and the development of Portsmouth dockyard caused some London builders to look towards Hampshire. In the 1740's George Rowcliffe, a Southampton man, built under contract at Northam, on the river Itchen. When he died, in 1746, his yard was occupied by Henry Bird, a famous London shipbuilder. Robert Carter, also from London, was building for the crown at Chapel, near the mouth of the river Itchen.

This burst of naval building was to lead to the return of the shipwrights to the Beaulieu river but, unlike those in Southampton, the entrepreneurs were Hampshire men. Those who undertook naval contracts can be called either 'shipbuilders' or 'master shipwrights'; there was no official distinction between the two terms. However, there were two distinct types of entrepreneurs. First, there were those who were trained shipwrights, who were skilled craftsmen in their own right, and who were willing and able to work on the project alongside their men. Many such a master shipwright had received his initial training as an apprentice in a royal dockyard, had risen in the King's service, perhaps to the status of quarterman, or as an overseer supervising naval contracts in merchants' yards. Other master shipwrights had learned their craft entirely in the merchants' years and, in time of war, built for the navy instead of the private owner. Secondly, there were shipbuilders who were capitalists; who had the money to rent or own a yard; who had the business expertise to carry out a contract, but had limited practical skill. Such men had a diversity of financial interests, as timber merchants, shipowners, traders, or as owners of farmland, inns and houses. When the boom years of naval shipbuilding ended, they were not ruined, as they were able to engage in the business pursuits of peacetime. They were also financially stronger than the ambitious master shipwright, and were less liable to become bankrupt during a contract. Whatever their origin, the contractors needed courage and versatility. They needed to be literate as they had to negotiate contracts, keep accounts, pay bills and men. They had to find their own labour force, and buy all the materials. Arranging timber supplies alone was an exercise in logistics which needed a cool head. They had to find a building site, erect temporary buildings, and ensure that the work progressed on schedule. Naval contracts contained a penal clause to ensure the punctual completion of the ship. If the launching was late without just cause, a deduction or 'mulct', to use the contemporary word, was made from the final payment. The mulct was usually 25p per ton if the launching was less than one month late, and 50p per ton for each month thereafter. If, therefore, a ship was launched three months late, the mulct amounted to about 10% of the total price, a sizeable proportion of the profit. The Navy Board adopted a humane attitude to late launchings: difficulties due to the weather or supply of timber, or in obtaining sufficient workmen were accepted as reasonable excuses, and the mulct was waived. However, in order to prevent shoddy work done quickly in order to complete the contract in time, the final payment was withheld until the new ship had been inspected by naval officials. If the latter gave the ship 'a perfect bill', the payment was made; if not, deductions were made for any rectification which had to be done by dockyard labour.

The first shipbuilder at Buckler's Hard was not a trained shipwright, but a capitalist entrepreneur named James Wyatt, who obtained a naval contract in 1744. Despite the assertion by many authors that 'the firm of Wyatt and Co were attracted to Buckler's Hard from Bursledon', it was not so. Wyatt was a very common surname in Hampshire, and not all of that name were necessarily related. The Wyatts of Bursledon, who built ships there in the 1690's, were not engaged in the industry by 1744, nor was there a male Wyatt of that name left from that family.[1] James Wyatt was the younger brother of Joseph Wyatt, a prominent and respected businessman of Hythe. Joseph Wyatt was a timber merchant, maltster, and shipowner who lived at Hythe until his death in 1757. In 1719 Joseph supplied boards for the gate of Beaulieu Church;[2] in 1726 he did some work on the quay during the building of Montagu Town.[3] He supplied Portsmouth dockyard with timber and treenails between 1744 and 1746, in association with Moody Janverin, a Hamble shipbuilder: he and Janverin had a timber yard at Eling. In 1752 he sold a small transport vessel to the Navy Board, but he was not the builder of the ship.[4] He is buried in Dibden Churchyard, next to his brother James, (there was no parish church in Hythe then), where there is a magnificent tombstone engraved with figures of a ship and his four children. He was a man of fair substance: some of his land was well-timbered, some was good farmland. His property included Ashlett Mill, a large house in Hythe, a house near Hythe called 'Racketts', Newhouse Farm in the Manor of Beaulieu (as a tenant), Gore Farm, and many other parcels of land in Hardley, Fawley and Lymington.[5] Joseph Wyatt was able to act as a financial cushion for his younger brother.

James Wyatt was also a timber merchant and used, among others, the quay at Buckler's Hard from 1735 onwards. In 1739 he supplied the Duke of Montagu with a considerable quantity of nails for £24 11s 7d.[6] When war was resumed, he was busily engaged in the supply of timber and treenails for Portsmouth dockyard.[7] Then, in 1744, he obtained a contract to build a 24-gun ship, the *Surprise.*

James Wyatt's choice of Buckler's Hard was a natural one. He was known by, and had had dealings with, the site's owner, the Duke of Montagu; he was also acquainted with William Warner, the steward of the manor. The landlord was anxious to inject some form of activity into the stagnant new town, and Wyatt's rent, at £5 per annum, was a very fair one. Buckler's Hard was near enough to Wyatt's home for him to commute daily, on horseback, either through Beaulieu, or by horse to Gilbury and then crossing the river by ferry. Thus, Wyatt did not have the additional expense of renting a house at Buckler's Hard. The uniform slope, or vista, artificially made some 20 years earlier, afforded the right angle of declivity for the building blocks; the river had a depth of more than two fathoms, yet was not too wide; thus, posts could be erected on the opposite bank before a launching, so that guiding ropes could be attached to the stern of the ship. The wide street gave storage space for large pieces of timber, as well as good access from the site which was sheltered from the prevailing westerlies. There was even a new quay in good repair. But, above all, it was surrounded by oak and elm owned by the Duke of Montagu. Timber in the royal forests, including the New Forest, was reserved for the royal dockyards. A civilian builder could not obtain his timber from the New Forest, so its proximity to Buckler's Hard was no asset. Shipbuilders had to rely on the great trees from the private estates which had escaped the woodman's axe. Trees for compass timber needed to be about 100 years old, and in accessible places. In order to build a ship of 100 tons, about 75 oaks and elms needed to be felled. The civilian builder, unable to obtain supplies from the dockyards or the royal forests, had to ride about the countryside finding his own timber. Wyatt, therefore, like Herring before him, was assured of a supply of some of his needs from his landlord, the Duke of Montagu. As well as the manor of Beaulieu, there were other large estates in the neighbourhood. William Mitford, the grandfather of the historian of Greece, had bought Gilbury, on the eastern bank of the river, in 1718. The land in Fawley, Holbury, Hardley, Langley and Hythe was owned or leased by lesser gentry, whilst the manor of Marchwood passed to Sir William Oglander during the 18th century, as did the manor of Dibden to the Harris family (the Earls of Malmesbury). Also the ironworks at Sowley was near at hand. In 1744, the year in which James Wyatt signed his first naval contract, the Duke of Montagu was Master General of Ordnance. Also, Miles Troughton, by then advanced in years, made an agreement with John Coulson of London, under which the latter would cast guns at Sowley, and instruct Troughton's grandson, Philip Sone III, in all the arts of ironwork.[8] The ironworks at Sowley were in need of repair, and it was probably due to the inception of shipbuilding at Buckler's Hard that, in a new lease, given to Philip Sone in 1746, the Duke of Montagu agreed to give £400 for the building of a new furnace and an air furnace, for an addition of 5% to the £40 annual rental.[9]

James Wyatt, the capitalist contractor, needed the skill of a practical partner. This he found in John Major, a shadowy figure who was perhaps an admiralty official, who had acted as overseer for the Navy Board on civilian contractors.[10] Major was still resident at Buckler's Hard in 1747 when his baby son, James, was christened at Beaulieu. In the register, he was described as 'Mr Major, a shipwright.' As usual, the Navy Board appointed an overseer to supervise the contract. The man chosen was Henry Adams.

Henry Adams, who was to become the most famous of all the Buckler's Hard shipbuilders, was appointed on 24 August, 1744. He was born in Deptford in 1713, the son of a shipwright Anthony Adams. Like his father before him, Henry entered into a ship-wright's career at the royal dockyard at Deptford, starting as an apprentice to the then first Foreman of the Yard, Benjamin Slade, in 1726.[11] In those days shipwrights, as for most skilled trades, had to serve a seven-year apprenticeship, so that they were not fully qualified or full wage-earners until they reached the age of 21. One of the many restrictions on apprentices was that they were not allowed to marry until their apprenticeship was completed. As Henry Carey wrote in *Sally in our Alley* . . . 'But when my seven long years are out Oh, then I'll marry Sally' . . . The idea behind this was to prevent young men falling into the poverty trap of becoming parents before they could afford the expense of a wife and family. As an apprentice, Adams began at a daily rate of 1s 2p, rising to 2s 1p per day at the end of his apprenticeship in 1734. He then served a further ten years in the royal dockyard at Deptford before accepting the position of overseer at Buckler's Hard. The practice of the appointment of overseers for naval contracts in the merchants' yard began not later than 1692; the overseers were paid by the Admiralty, and they were sent to supervise a particular contract, at the end of which the overseer would resume his duties at the royal dockyard from which he had been seconded. The appointment of overseers usually went to comparatively junior men, and such posts were not universally popular with the labour force. It entailed long periods from home, living in lodgings in strange surroundings, for a wage, in the 1740's, of 30s a week. Presumably Henry Adams was motivated by ambition. He was aged 31, unmarried, had served in the dockyard for 18 years, where both his father and his brother, another Anthony, were shipwrights. The decision to go to Buckler's Hard must have been a difficult one. Henry had to leave his family, his friends, his place of birth, and the secure routine of the dockyard. There was considerable resistance on the part of many shipwrights when the

Admiralty tried to persuade them to transfer to Portsmouth from London. Stories were put about that the Hampshire coast was fog-ridden and unhealthy, and that the waters were infested with wood-eating sea-worms. Buckler's Hard, an obscure hamlet on the Beaulieu river, would have been a journey into the unknown. But, after two years, with valuable experience gained, Adams could return to Deptford with a greater chance of promotion. He was not to know that, when he left his native Deptford, he was migrating to a place in which he was to remain until his death in 1805.

Thus, the men were assembled to begin the first naval vessel at Buckler's Hard; James Wyatt, the timber merchant capitalist: John Major, his co-partner; and Henry Adams, the naval overseer. The building went smoothly, and the 24-gun *Surprise* was launched in 1745. Wyatt had by then signed a second contract, the building of an 18-gun ship, the *Scorpion,* which was begun in 1745 and launched in 1746. The *Scorpion*'s dimensions were 276 tons, gundeck 91ft 2in, keel 74ft 11½in, breadth 26ft 4in, depth 12ft. She took part in the famous expedition to Quebec, led by Wolfe in 1759, and three years later was lost in the Irish Sea. With the completion of these two contracts, James Wyatt's brief career as a shipbuilder came to an end; presumably he found his timber merchant's business less exacting, and less risky. However, he had pioneered the shipwright's craft at Buckler's Hard and, with some difficulty the Duke's agents were able to find another builder.

Wyatt's immediate successor was John Darley, a Gosport shipwright, who had served an apprenticeship in the Portsmouth dockyard, and who married Ann Woodman of Bishop's Waltham in 1742. Between 1744 and 1746 he was engaged in the building of two 24-gun naval sloops, the *Tavistock* and the *Kingfisher* at Gosport.[12] Darley was not rich; like Herring and unlike James Wyatt, he was a master craftsman, with slender financial backing. Moreover, he was prone to misfortune. During the building of the *Tavistock* he fractured a leg 'whilst carting a piece of Keelson', and his brother, Samuel, had to finish the contract for him. In 1746, Darley took over Wyatt's lease at Buckler's Hard at £10 per annum, having obtained a contract to build a 44-gun ship, the *Woolwich*. The construction of such a vessel required a larger labour force than the two smaller ships built by Wyatt. Also, Darley, unlike Wyatt, needed accommodation for himself and family at Buckler's Hard. It is probable that he lived in what was to be known later as the 'Master Builder's' house. Whatever the house, it needed repair, and Darley engaged Alexander Morris, the Beaulieu builder who had built one of the original houses in Montagu Town. In addition, Darley employed Morris to build a mould-loft, with two dwelling units on the ground floor. Whilst Herring and Wyatt had managed without a mould-loft, Darley needed one, as the ship he was building was larger. A mould-loft had obvious advantages over an open-air scrieve board; the former was under cover, could be worked at by candle-light, and the moulds could be chalked on the floor more quickly and more accurately than scrieve-knife carving. In addition, Morris built for Darley a kiln to be used for 'stoving' or bending plank timber.[13] Darley also had constructed four sawpits and a joiner's shop. All in all, a proper shipyard was developing at Buckler's Hard. Morris' bill, rendered in 1746, was for £24 16s 10d, of which Darley paid £12 9s 0d on account. Morris was more fortunate than Philip Sone, of Sowley ironworks. In 1746 Darley received £31 worth of iron bars and cast iron plates and the account had not been settled in 1748, when Darley went bankrupt. Personal misfortune was added to professional problems; his young son died in April 1748. Like Herring before him, Darley had an uncompleted ship on the stocks, and the Duke of Montagu again had to impound the ship as collateral against debts, which included payment of rent. Darley's dues to Beaulieu people amounted to £154 9s 11d at the time of his bankruptcy. The following list of Darley's debts give an illustration of the complexities confronting shipbuilders,

William Beeston, for valuing the buildings at Buckler's Hard between His Grace and Mr Darley	10s	6d
Thomas Cleeves for leadwork and glazing and painting the new house	£20 17s	3d
Alexander Morris (the residue)	£12 7s	10d
Robert Bull, cash disbursed for Mr Darley	£ 8 19s	4d
Stephen Barnes, for bran and flour	£11 12s	10d
William Ingram, for bricks, tiles and lime	£29 16s	0d
Joseph Amsbury, for carriage of timber	£ 3 2s	8d
Bottley Brackstone, for Darley's son's board and schooling	£ 7 3s	0d
John Hooper, for saddler's work	11s	5d
Thomas Eads, for shoes	£ 1 12s	2d
Thomas Hayter, for malt and barley	£ 5 16s	0d

Stephen Purse, for carriage of timber	£ 7 1s 10d
James Wyatt, for laths and nails used for building	
the moulding house	£ 4 10s 2d
Charles Reade, for nails etc	£ 3 2s 0d
Philip Sone for iron	£31 3s 4d

Additionally, there were other debts amounting to £6 3s 7d, making a total of £154 9s 11d. The Duke of Montagu paid these debts, all to local people. In return, Darley's trustees assigned to the Duke the mould-loft, the four saw-pits, the stove kiln and the joiner's shops, which were valued at £155. In effect, the Duke of Montagu bought back the shipyard appointments, including the house containing the mould-loft, which had been built by Darley.

Meanwhile, the ship remained uncompleted. The Admiralty solved the problem by asking Moody Janverin, who was building a ship at Lepe at the time, to complete Darley's vessel. This Janverin did, and the 44-gun *Woolwich* was launched in 1749 at Buckler's Hard where Darley remained until the launching, acting as foreman on the project. Darley received £2,380 from the Admiralty on completion and then left the village. Thus, of three Beaulieu river shipbuilders to date, two, Herring and Darley, had suffered financial difficulties.

Whilst Darley was suffering misfortune at Buckler's Hard, Moody Janverin was successfully building ships at the mouth of the Beaulieu river at Lepe. He lived at Hamble House, in the village of Hamble and made a living by repairing small craft and supplying timber to Portsmouth dockyard in association with Joseph Wyatt of Hardley. He built two small 14-gun brigs on the Hamble in 1745, in which year he obtained a contract to build the 50-gun *Greenwich*. As the site on the Hamble was not big enough for this vessel, which had a length of 117 feet, and as shipbuilders were engaged in naval contracts at Bursledon, Cowes and Southampton, Janverin decided to build the *Greenwich* at Lepe. The use of Lepe can be accredited to a Navy Board official, Thomas Ernle. In 1744 the Navy Board was seeking new sites near the royal dockyards, and in that year Ernle visited Lepe and reported that it was 'very commodious for building Ships of war of any rates',[15] and asked that it be surveyed. Subsequently a favourable report was given, and Janverin was encouraged by the Navy Board to build there.

Lepe, then an inconsiderable hamlet, had been used from time to time for repairs. Apart from an inn, on the site of the present

Lepe House, and two or three houses, there was no other settlement nearer than Lower Exbury, Cadland and Langley, all a mile away, which could have afforded some accommodation for Janverin's workforce. A crude sketch, inaccurate in other respects, drawn by Luttrell in 1785 shows the site where Gipsy Lane is today, ie to the west of Lepe House. There was sufficient depth of water there at high tides, a hard gravel beach, with mud below the high water mark. Gipsy Lane was sheltered from the extremes of the south-west winds by the mud-banks on the port hand of the Beaulieu river. However, a more probable site was one to the eastward of Lepe House, where there was deeper water, a hard stony beach, and gravel cliffs which overhung the beach, useful for lowering large timbers down to the site. The disadvantage of a site there was the lack of shelter from south-easterly and south-westerly winds.

Janverin had to create the site at Lepe which he did at a cost of £700. This initial expenditure, which he was able to sustain, shows the contrast between Janverin and Darley: the former had sufficient capital to undertake a major enterprise. Janverin's men erected a wooden mould-loft, blacksmiths' shops, storehouses, and saw pits. Then they cut the large building blocks and began work on the ship. The contract did not go smoothly. Bad weather, and especially high winds from the south, caused many delays in the unloading of timber from the hoys. Then some of Janverin's workmen contracted the ague; at one time as many as 12, a quarter of his workforce, were laid low. He was unable to get replacements 'as there were several other ships of war building in the neighbourhood'.[16] The *Greenwich*, 50-guns, was launched in April 1748, six months late but Janverin was released from the mulct, which would have amounted to some £500. He then began work on a 28-gun ship, the *Fowey*, which was launched at Lepe in 1749 and the *Woolwich* at Buckler's Hard in the same year. Janverin received £3,570 for his share in building the *Woolwich*, compared with Darley's £2,380. In 1749 Janverin returned to Hamble where he continued shipbuilding until his death in 1766. His magnificent tomb can still be seen in Hamble Parish Church. After him, Lepe was not again a shipbuilding site until Henry Adams used it between 1763 and 1765 for the *Europe*.

Meanwhile, Buckler's Hard was burgeoning as a shipbuilding centre. While Janverin was completing Darley's *Woolwich*, another naval vessel was being built at Buckler's Hard. Henry Adams, the

Navy Board overseer, had become a shipbuilding contractor. Adams' decision may have been influenced by his marriage, on 8 May, 1747, to Elizabeth Smith. The ceremony took place at Brockenhurst, and the parish register describes Adams as 'of Deptford' and his bride as the daughter of 'Mr Smith of ye Parish of Bewley'. Later in that year, when Darley ran into difficulties, the Duke of Montagu's steward helped Adams to set up as a contractor. The landlord needed a tenant to succeed Darley; Adams had impressed with his skill and honesty, but although he had little financial means, his wife's family were comparatively wealthy. Many years later, Adams gave his own account of his involvement in shipbuilding at Buckler's Hard. In 1781, when he was objecting to an increase in the rent for the shipyard, he wrote, *I came here from London in the year 1744 Being apointed by the Navy Board to Survey some Ships Building here. Which after two Persons had fail'd in Executing (One of them having become a Bankrupt) was prevail'd on to discharge myself from the Government Service, in order to undertake the carrying On the Business of Ship building here, Being promis'd by his Grace the late Duke of Montagu, that I should always have Ships to build, If any were wanted for his Majesty's service, and that as the Ground I was to occupy for Building and laying Timber was all waste Ground, only made use of as a Common for the Houses here, I should only pay five pounds a year . . . But as all the Groundways had been taken up and every preparation for ShipBuilding taken away and sold by the Assignees of the person that failed, I was oblig'd (at a very great expence) to lay down New Groundways and make every preparation for building Ships . . .*[17]

This letter, even allowing for Adams' prejudice on his own behalf, shows that the officials of the Manor of Beaulieu made promises to Adams. Duke John was to use his influence to obtain naval contracts; Adams had to pioneer a new building site, and to build concurrently with the completion of Darley's ship.

On 14 March 1748 Adams obtained a naval contract signed on his behalf by his father Anthony, and leased part — but not all — of the shipyard site at Buckler's Hard, for Darley's trustees were still in possession. Adams left the royal service after 22 years, and in Deptford Yard records for September 1748, he was described as a 'contractor in merchant yard' and 'Prick'd out of Wages'.[18] It is probable that Henry Adams lived at Buckler's Hard initially in a house leased by his father-in-law, who was also the lessee of a part of Clobb Farm: Beaulieu records show a house at Buckler's Hard in the name of William Smith from 1745 to 1748.[19] It is also probable that Smith was able to help Adams with some capital. If so, it proved a good investment. Adams obtained a contract to build a 24-gun sloop, the *Mermaid*, 533 tons burthen, with a keel-length of 96ft 10in, extreme breadth 32ft 2in, and depth in hold 10ft 2in. She was launched in 1749, the same year as Darley's *Woolwich*. The building of both ships was supervised by White, Adam's successor as overseer.

Darley and Janverin left Buckler's Hard in 1749, but Adams remained and took over the whole of the shipyard and the tenancy of the Master Builder's House. It is paradoxical that, at a time when no shipbuilder was able to sustain a shipbuilding business in Southampton, Adams was to found a firm at Buckler's Hard which was to last almost a hundred years.

References

[1] A J Holland *Ships of British Oak* (David & Charles 1972) p 98
[2] H E R Widnell *Beaulieu Record* p 80
[3] Beaulieu Muniments Accounts 11/133
[4] PRO Adm 95/12
[5] Prerogative Court of Canterbury Herring 143
[6] BM Accounts
[7] PRO Adm NB 106/1000; 106/1021
[8] A B Bartlett *Sowley Ironworks* pp 19-20
[9] *ibid*
[10] NMM Greenwich NB *letters* vol 130 25/10/1745
[11] PRO Quarterly Pay Lists of the King's Dockyards vol 517
[12] PRO Adm NB 106/989 and 95/12
[13] Beaulieu Muniments
[14] *ibid*
[15] PRO Adm NB 106/989 dated 10/12/1744
[16] PRO Adm NB 106/2184
[17] PRO 30/8/153
[18] PRO Adm NB 2976
[19] Beaulieu Muniments Overseers' Accounts

● Buckler's Hard from Gilbury, 1776. This watercolour is owned by Lord
Redesdale, whose ancestor William Mitford was then lord of the Manor of Exbury.
Wooden sheds can be seen in the shipyard, but there were no ships being built.
The vessel in the foreground is loading or unloading cargo

5 Henry Adams: the fight for survival

WHEN HENRY ADAMS' first naval vessel, the *Mermaid*, was launched at Buckler's Hard in 1749, the war of the Austrian Succession already had been over for a year. As always, the return to peacetime meant an end to naval contracts in the merchants' yard so that, to survive, the shipbuilder needed merchant contracts or other interests. There was some truth in the old saw about shipbuilders, 'Seven years living lavish, seven years on the parish.' Henry Adams was in a precarious position. The shipyard appointments were still primitive; he was not yet an established shipbuilder so that contracts for the repair or building of merchant vessels had to be sought; nor had he yet developed other business interests, such as timber or farming. Further, John, second Duke of Montagu, the originator of Buckler's Hard had died in 1749 when the estate passed to his two daughters, Isabella, whose husband Edward Hussey was later created the first Earl of Beaulieu, and Mary the Countess of Cardigan. Duke John's intention was that the younger daughter, Mary, should control the estates, and pay her sister a moiety. But Isabella took legal action, and as a result the manor of Beaulieu was to lack the firm control of a dynamic resident landlord. This was unfortunate for Henry Adams, who had left the security of the royal service in the hope that his landlord would be able to obtain contract work for him. For him, the years from 1749 were to be a question of survival. He was not to know that the Seven Years' war would begin in 1756, and that he had only a few lean years to endure. As always in the case of an absentee landlord, the steward became of prime importance. Fortunately for both Henry Adams and Beaulieu Manor, there was continuity in that office; William Warner became steward in 1734 and remained so until his death in 1765 when his son John succeeded him. William Warner had married first Anthonetta, daughter of Thomas Burman of Smallbridge Hall, Suffolk.

Burman had come to Beaulieu in order to start a large-scale brewing industry in the Domus building, as a consequence of another of Duke John's schemes. The Manor had paid for extensive alterations to the building, and for the building of vaults adjoining it. The business did not develop as it had been hoped, but one consequence of the venture was the marriage between the young steward and Burman's daughter. When Anthonetta died, Warner then married Ann Ingram, whose father had run the Beaulieu Brickyard. Warner, as well as acting as steward, ran Palace House and the brickyard in his own right with some business acumen. Later, Henry Adams was to marry his daughter Anne, after the death of his first wife.

● Nelson's baby clothes, now in the Maritime Museum at Buckler's Hard. It was customary in those days to preserve a child's christening garments. This set is not complete, but they really were Nelson's!

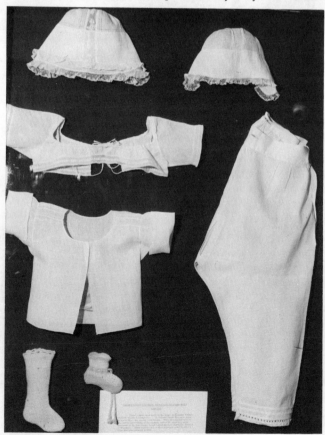

Warner can be credited with persuading Henry Adams to remain at Buckler's Hard but in January 1751 the future looked bleak for the houses were in need of repair and there was no shipbuilding work. Adams indeed was considering a return to the royal dockyard at Deptford as a quarterman! But Warner was instrumental in obtaining for Adams a contract to build two busses, herring fishing vessels.

For a century there was nationwide disquiet over the decline of the British fishing fleet. Other Europeans, notably the Dutch, caught the bulk of the white fish, especially herring, then abundant in the North Sea. In those days no international agreements regarding territorial waters existed: in general the sea was a free for all. Dutch fishermen followed the herring shoals south from Scotland to the South Foreland according to the season, curing their catch on English shores, to the disquiet not only of fishermen, but to those who saw in a thriving fishing fleet a necessary naval reserve. In 1748 the House of Commons set up a committee to enquire into the state of the herring and cod fisheries.[2] In the following year a group of merchants sent a petition to the House of Commons asking for an organisation to be set up for British Fisheries, and offering to put up capital of £600,000 if the government would give a subsidy. In February, 1750, the committee reported favourably to the Commons, and an Act of Parliament was passed later in the year, 'for the encouragement of British White Herring fishery', establishing a joint-stock company to be called the Society of the Free British Fishery. Frederick, Prince of Wales became the Governor of the Society, and visited Beaulieu, Buckler's Hard and Gilbury later in the same year. Frederick's visit may have been coincidental, but it may also have been connected with the new Society. Four Southampton men were subscribers to the new Society in 1750, the most important of whom was Richard Taunton, the founder of Taunton's School, Southampton, who invested £5,000 in the venture. Taunton supervised the building of the first two herring busses, both at Southampton, and he was probably instrumental in persuading the burgesses of Southampton to make Frederick, Prince of Wales a Freeman of the Borough. Joseph Sibrell of Hamble and Robert Fabian of Eling both obtained contracts to build a fishing buss. This local involvement in the Society of the Free British Fishery must have given Henry Adams some grounds for hope.

William Warner served Adams well. He asked William Folks, the Duchess of Cardigan's London agent, to persuade the Society of the Free British Fishery to give Adams a contract for two busses and he obtained permission from the owners of the Manor for Adams to obtain all the necessary timber from Beaulieu, including six elms to be taken from the lanes, and a considerable quantity of compass oak. This enabled Adams to tender for the building of the busses, which were 66ft long with a beam of 16ft, at the competitive price of £6 10s a ton.[3] Henry Adams' father Anthony, still working in the Deptford dockyard, represented his son at the final signing of the contract. The two fishing vessels were completed by September 1753, on time. William Folks deserved the 12 bottles of claret which Adams sent to him in London in July of that year for this work was good for Beaulieu as well as for Adams. The venture afforded employment, and on 18 August 1752 Adams took on Isaac Mitchell as an apprentice shipwright at a premium of £25.[4] In the same year one of the houses on the east side of the street in Buckler's Hard opened as an alehouse, with widow Palmour as its first landlady. The inn was called 'The Ship', also the name of an inn in Beaulieu village at that time.

● **The Ship inn, Buckler's Hard, which opened in 1752, the oldest of the village's two ale-houses. It is now a private residence**

Henry Adams had survived by a narrow margin. He was to outlive the Society of Free British Fishery — for the Society foundered within 20 years of its inception. Meanwhile, he had obtained a contract to build a small transport for Portsmouth dockyard. Such vessels were used by the Royal Navy to carry stores and materials, including timber, between the dockyards. The vessel built by Henry Adams, launched on 3 July, 1753, was the *Lion*.

Adams had survived for four years, but by the end of 1753 there was no work for the shipyard; and, in November, he had the misfortune to lose his four-year old daughter, Ann. There was a proposal to convert the blacksmith's shop into a dwelling house which was completed by 1755. Also, the mould-house, which had been built with a loft in the upper storey, with two tenements beneath it, was converted into two dwelling-houses, and the oven was repaired.[5] It appeared that Buckler's Hard's short career as a shipbuilding centre was at an end. The economic depression affected the whole of Britain from 1752 to 1755; so that local reasons for the plight of Buckler's Hard should not be sought. Beaulieu inhabitants, disturbed by the incidence of unemployment and the increase in the poor rates, petitioned the co-owner of the Manor, the Countess of Cardigan.

The year 1755 was the turning point of the trade cycle nationally. In the Spring Henry Adams negotiated with the Navy Board for another contract. The House of Commons had granted the sum of £100,000 in 1754 for the building and repair of ships, and contracts were again offered to the merchants' yards. On 6 June, Adams obtained a contract to build a 24-gun ship at £7 19s 6d a ton;[7] as Moody Janverin, of Hamble, received a contract at the same time, the Navy Board clerk who wrote that Adams was to build 'at Bussleton on the Bewley river' can be forgiven. So Buckler's Hard entered a new and vigorous phase in its history. The contract obtained by Henry Adams was to tide him over until the outbreak of the Seven Years' War in 1756. However, Adams' ship was disappointingly small; he had hoped to persuade the Navy Board to give him the task of building a 74. This new class had 74 guns on two decks instead of the 80-gun three-decker which had proved rather cumberous. The 74 became the utility ship-of-the-line, the building of which became both prestigious and profitable. In December, 1755, Adams was again in London, with hopes of obtaining a contract for a 74 and again he was disappointed.[8]

However, one small ship was better than none, and Buckler's Hard came to life once more. Snooks was appointed by the Navy Board as Overseer for the contract, and the *Kennington* was launched on 16 April 1756, with these dimensions: keel 88ft, beam 30ft 4in, depth in hold 9ft 8in, 430 tons burthen. Under this contract, Adams also had to supply the masts and spars,

	Masts	Spars
Main	24yds 20ins	21yds 1in
Main top	13yds 34ins	14yds 32ins
Main gallant	8yds 8½ins	10yds 3ins
Fore	21yds 17ins	18yds 4ins
Fore top	7yds 24½ins	13yds 26ins
Foregallant	17yds 27ins	9yds 33ins
Mizzen	11yds 17½ins	19yds 30ins
Mizzen top	15yds 11ins	10yds 35ins
Bowsprit		16yds 1½ins
Cross yackyard		15yds 35ins
Flying jib boom	10yds 31in	

Even a small 24-gun ship required almost 300 yards of mast timber.

On the completion of the *Kennington,* Adams secured further contracts due in part to the influence of the Earl of Cardigan, who lobbied Lord Anson on the matter. One was for the rebuilding of the 28-gun *Lyme,* built at Deptford in 1748. Rebuilding was quite common at that time, as wooden ships were liable to warp, to rot, and to become ravaged by the tropical worm, although often costing as much as the original construction. Nevertheless the Navy Board considered such expenditure worthwhile as some of the original materials could be saved. The *Lyme* was back in service in Portsmouth dockyard by January, 1757.[10] In addition to this work, Adams also obtained a contract to build a 28-gun ship, the *Coventry,* at £9 5s a ton.

Henry Adams had weathered the economic storm; now he had sufficient confidence in the future to persuade his younger brother, Anthony, to join him. Anthony Adams, born in 1716, was three years younger than Henry, and had spent his working life as a shipwright in the Deptford dockyard. He left the royal service on 6 August, 1756, and migrated to Buckler's Hard with his wife and three children; he died in 1761.

In October, 1756, a naval officer inspected the *Coventry* and wrote as follows in his diary, *Wednesday the 13th went on board the*

Commys'rs yacht and turn'd down through Spithead and as far to the westw^d as about Two mile below Cows, where the Yacht was brought to an anchor opposite Leap at the mouth of the Bewly River and from thence about ½ past 3 proceeded in the Barge up the River to Buckler's Hard where Mr Adams is Building the Coventry of 28 Guns by Contract, which is about 4½ miles above Leap got there about ½ past 4 took a view of the said Ship, found the Walls and the Bottom about ½ plank'd up, Timber of the Frame in general white young sound Timber, planks wrought Irregular, and badly pay'd to which appear'd to be from want of care in Dubbing the Timber Several of them being furr'd which should have been let out, and One Frame in the loff of the Starboard Bow too slack or rather ye Timber on each Side of him wanted to be beat away to fetch him Hawse piers very waivy and sappy in so much that nothing could be done but takeing the Two Middle pieces on each side out.

Overseers and Officers from Portsmouth who Inspect the said Ship much in fault to Suffer a Certificate to be given for the payment seing such deficiencys and bad work, the Overseer should never be employ'd again on any Other Ship his name is Snooks.

The work displeased came away angry about ½ past 5 . . .[11]

The officer had a thoroughly disagreeable day, as the wind and the tide were contrary at Lepe, and men had to row the barge from Buckler's Hard to Southampton which was reached at 9pm.

While these criticisms were doubtless accurate enough, such harsh terms on work done in the merchants' yards were not unusual. Many naval officers and Navy Board officials were antagonistic to any building effected outside the royal dockyards, and the Admiralty made scapegoats of the merchants when faced with awkward questions in the House of Commons.

Two months before the *Coventry* was launched on 20 May, 1757, for which contract Adams received £5,435, he had signed another contract to build the 32-gun *Thames*.[12] Unusually, the builder was not only to supply masts and yards, but also furniture and stores, and all to be completed in eight months. Further, the ship was to be built largely with foreign oak.[13] The strains of war were telling on the capacity of Portsmouth Dockyard. Contract terms were,

'Hull measures 646 13/94 at £9 7s 6d a ton

with masts and spars	£6461 7s 6d
Furniture and stores	£3184 8s 0d
	£9645 15s 6d

[14]

61

Meanwhile, Adams had obtained a contract to build another 32-gun ship under fortuitous circumstances. The Admiralty decided to build ten such vessels similar to *Coventry*, of Scots pine, or 'fir' as it was then called colloquially, because of a shortage of oak and elm. All merchant builders on the Thames were asked to attend a conference on 2 May to discuss the proposal, but only four attended. Only one was willing to consider such a contract, and the proposal was scrapped.[15] On 26 May, the Admiralty decided that the ships should be built of oak, seven to be laid down in the royal dockyards, and the remaining three in merchants' yard. One ship was given to Stanton and Wells, the second to Inman, another Thames builder, and the third to Henry Adams. Adams' ship was the *Levant*, to be built at £9 5s a ton in ten months, or at £9 a ton in 12 months.

Both ships were launched in 1758, the *Thames* on 10 April, and the *Levant* on 6 July. For the latter Adams received £5,423, and for the former £9,645, considerable sums in those days. Adams travelled to London in July in order to persuade the Admiralty to give him yet another contract. In this he was unsuccessful, but in 1759 he was given the task of building a small timber hoy for Portsmouth dockyard. That vessel, named the *Hayling*, carried four guns, and was 67ft long; she was launched at Buckler's Hard on 1 April, 1760.

Although there were no further launchings of naval vessels at Buckler's Hard between 1760 and 1773, the future of the village and of Adams was not in the balance. At Buckler's Hard, more houses were erected as a direct consequence of Adams' naval building in the late 1750s. In 1757, at his own expense, he constructed three small tenements to house some of his workmen and was charged an annual rental of £1 6s 8d by Beaulieu.[16] The renewed shipbuilding activity also led in 1757 to the restoration of a blacksmith's shop where John Edwards plied his craft while John Hewett, having succeeded widow Palmour at the Ship Inn, was also lessee of a house and shop in the village, another indication that the community was growing. Hewett's lease of the shop was shortlived, however, for by 1763 Henry Adams was the lessee. It was common practice in the late 18th and early 19th centuries for the employer to own a shop in isolated communities. Much has been written emotively about this practice, but its origins were soundly based: there was a need for such shops, but their small turnover attracted few volunteer shopkeepers. Also, there was a shortage of coin, so that the joint role of both paymaster and receiver enabled some employers to circumvent the problems of monetary supply. There is no evidence to suggest that Adams was an unscrupulous 'tommy-shop' owner. In any case, by 1789, at the latest, the shop was being run by Joseph Wort. In many settlements similar to Buckler's Hard, the main employer was often the landlord of the ale-house, a good means of collecting small coin. At Buckler's Hard, Adams had no connection with either The Ship or the later New Inn. By 1763 Buckler's Hard comprised 15 houses, with Henry Adams the principal lessee. He held the shipyard, the Master Builders' House, and four tenements, in addition to the shop, and some land at Clobb Farm and Dungeon Coppice, for which he paid a total of £16 19s 8d a year in rent. Of the other tenants in 1763, Joseph Barnes was a timber merchant related to the Wyatts of Hardle. He fades from the rentals after 1767, by which time Henry Adams was himself engaged in the timber trade.

While Henry Adams flourished as a shipbuilder, his private life was not without sorrow. In May, 1757, his wife gave birth to a daughter, Elizabeth, who died six months later, and then, two years later, died herself. There were no surviving children of the marriage, and on 13 November, 1760, Henry Adams married again. His second wife was Anne Warner, daughter of William Warner, the steward of the manor of Beaulieu, and the sister of John Warner, who succeeded his father in that office. Henry Adams, then 47, took a young bride of 22, who was to be the mother of his seven children. His first wife had seen him overcome his early difficulties, but she was not to witness his later fame. During the 19th century, several inhabitants of the Master Builder's House 'saw' a ghost on the stairs and in one of the bedrooms. Ellen Smith, daughter of Lord Montagu's river bailiff, who lived in the house in 1901, described a visitation as follows, 'a lady fair and rather nice looking, with such a sad face and light eyes which seem to say help me . . . it is a sad face in grey dress, light hair, about 28 or 30'. Who else but Elizabeth Adams, née Smith?

In 1761, Henry Adams' brother Anthony died also, at the age of 45, leaving a widow, two sons and a daughter. The bereaved family remained at Buckler's Hard, to be cared for by Henry Adams and his young wife. In 1763 Henry Adams engaged his two nephews, Anthony and William, then aged 18 and 16 respectively, as apprentices. They were later to play an important part in helping to run the shipyard, with Anthony as a partner and a supplier of timber. Anthony took over Clobb and Purnell Farms in 1790, until his death in 1814; William returned to Deptford.

The year 1761 saw the birth of the first of Henry Adams' seven children, a daughter, Martha, who was baptised on 31 August, but died in March of the following year. But by then, Henry Adams was about to enter an exciting period of his life.

References

[1] Beaulieu Muniments: Steward's letters 22/1/1751
[2] J W Horrocks, More About the Tauntons, in *Hampshire Advertiser*, 12/5/1928; R P Challacombe and H Spooner: *History of Taunton's School* (Southampton 1968) pp 10-12
[3] BM Steward's letters 14/3/1752 and 28/3/1752
[4] PRO Register of Apprentices 19/51 p 51
[5] BM Audit Memoranda
[6] BM 15
[7] NMM Greenwich NB to Adm Vol 150
[8] BM Steward's letters 11 and 15 December 1755
[9] NMM Greenwich MSS POR/A
[10] PRO Adm/NB 106/1119
[11] *Notes and Queries*, No 65 (12th series) 24 March 1917, Journal of an unnamed naval officer
[12] PRO NB Minutes 2566: and Adm/NB 106/1119
[13] PRO Adm 95/84
[14] PRO NB/Adm 106/1119
[15] NMM Greenwich NB/Adm Vol 155
[16] BM Steward's letters

6 Henry Adams: the years of expansion

BY 1760 HENRY ADAMS had built seven small ships for the navy; now he was anxious to build one of the new 64s. On 4 January, 1762, he obtained a contract to build such a vessel, to be called the *Europe,* at a cost of £15 8s a ton, or a total of £22,389 4s 6d[1]; the builder was to receive eight instalments of £2,200 and the remainder on completion. But, the Navy Board insisted that the ship should be built at Lepe rather than Buckler's Hard which they considered too small. Adams described the situation 20 years later, *The Navy Board not Admitting any large Ships to be built so high up the River, thinking it impossible to launch them or to gett them down the River, I was therefore oblig'd to hire a piece of Ground at the entrance of this River (called Leap) of a gentleman that own'd the Estate on the other side of the River; For which I paid ten Guineas a year, On which I built a 64-gun Ship; and could have built five or six sails together, having near 40 acres of Ground to lay Timber on, which was included in the above rent . . .*[2]

Thus, Henry Adams, while continuing to lease the shipyard and some houses at Buckler's Hard, also became the lessee of land owned by Mitford of Exbury. The exact site of the building of the *Europe* cannot be stated with certainty: nor was it necessarily the same as that used by Moody Janverin in 1748 and 1749. It is probable that the ship was launched near the present 'coastguard cottages', where small cliffs could be used for lowering materials on to the site. Work began on the ship in 1762, and she was launched — with some difficulty and damage — on 21 April, 1765. *Europe* carried 64 guns, had a keel-length of 130ft 9ins, a gun-deck of 159ft, a breadth of 41ft, and a burthen of 1,369 tons. With her launching, Lepe's brief career of a shipbuilding site came to end.

The *Europe* was also the last of the men-of-war launched in Hampshire during the Seven Years War, which ended in 1763 with the Treaty of Paris.

During its building at Lepe, Adams continued to live at Buckler's Hard. In November, 1763 for Hutchinson Muir of London, he contracted to build two merchant ships at Buckler's Hard with a keel length of 77ft 6in, extreme breadth of 27ft 6in, and depth in hold of 11ft 10in. He received £900 on signing the contract, and a further £3,600 in instalments during the building, which was completed by the end of 1764.

● **Henry Adams (1713-1805)**

In 1763 Adams further extended his business interests by entering a partnership with two London shipbuilders, William Dudman and William Barnard. Dudman (1719-1772) had been an apprentice shipwright at Portsmouth dockyard, had worked at Plymouth and Woolwich before serving in the Deptford royal dockyard as an overseer; he owned houses and land in Portsmouth.[3] William Barnard, a member of an Ipswich family of shipbuilders, served his apprenticeship in the Deptford yard at the same time as Henry Adams. Dudman and Barnard had formed a partnership to build ships for the East India Company at the Nova Scotia Dock in Ipswich. Then, in 1763, they obtained the lease of a shipyard at Grove Street, Deptford, owned by Sir Frederick Evelyn. Thus Hampshire connection was renewed as the yard, near the Victualling House, had been originally constructed by John Winter, a Southampton shipbuilder, in 1704.[4] The two partners moved from the comparative remoteness of Ipswich to the heart of the shipbuilding industry, near the sites of the great firms of Wells and Wests, close to the headquarters of the East India Company, and near the royal dockyard at Deptford. Here was an attractive prospect: an opportunity to build East Indiamen in peacetime, and naval contracts in time of war. They had the offer of the lease for 30 years, but they needed a third partner and Henry Adams was invited to join, to take one-third of the profits, to supply timber and other materials from Buckler's Hard, and to inject working capital, an indication of the profits which Adams had already made. He had become a wealthy man in just over a decade by constructing seven small ships for the Crown.

Adams was attracted to the proposition, as large men-of-war could be built at Deptford, which he was unable to do at Buckler's Hard. So began a profitable but uneasy business partnership which was not dissolved until 1792, on the expiration of the lease. During those decades numbers of large men-of-war were built in Deptford; so that 'ships built' lists often contain errors of location, as not all 'Adams ships' were built at Buckler's Hard. For Henry, the partnership entailed frequent visits to Deptford during those 30 years, when he often combined this business with appointments at the Navy Board Offices. He was 50 when he entered into the partnership, an age when most men begin to reduce their commitments, but the Deptford business secured his life in Buckler's Hard, as he was no longer dependent on his enterprises there for a living.

Meanwhile, his life was enriched by the birth of a son, baptised as Henry on 31 October, 1764. Henry junior went to Wadham College, Oxford, took holy orders and was later vicar of Beaulieu. In 1765 Henry senior's father, Anthony, retired from the Deptford dockyard, aged 77, after 63 years as a shipwright there. He came to Buckler's Hard old and wizened and with a crippled left arm, to spend the rest of his days with his son until his death in 1773.

In February, 1766, Ann Adams gave birth to a second son, named Balthazar, an unusual forename common in the family of Mrs Adams' mother Mrs Warner who was a Burman, a Dutch family who had come to England in the 17th century. In November, 1767, a third child, Edward, was born. Balthazar and Edward were later apprenticed to their father, and eventually inherited the shipyard. Three sons were followed by twins, Lucy and John, born November, 1770, and two more daughters, Mary Ann, January 1774 and Elizabeth, April 1777. Buckler's Hard, formerly Montagu Town, had almost become Adamsville.

From 1765 to 1771 Henry Adams, in common with other Hampshire shipbuilders, obtained no further naval contracts. None was to be had, as Parliament was unwilling to vote the money for the proper maintenance of the Navy during peacetime. Adams was able to survive, and indeed to thrive, because of the diversity of his business interests. In 1768 he had the unusual task of building a small flat-bottomed boat in sections. The pieces were taken by road to Merstham, in Sussex, where the boat was used to explore an underwater lake (until as late as 1911!). Adams expanded his enterprises by becoming a timber merchant which was to entail a considerable amount of travel and organisation.

In the 18th century, timber merchants obtained their produce not only from their own locality, nor even from surrounding counties, but from all over Britain. Merchants preferred to see timber 'in the round', and spent the months of January and February travelling on horseback to inspect it. The buyer might offer a price to the owner as a private sale, but more often public sales took place in the late Spring. Then the merchant had to arrange for the carting of the timber, usually drawn by horses in tandem, to the nearest water transport. In addition, sawyers and woodmen would be employed at the felling site, cutting off the 'lop and top'. When the timber eventually arrived at the timber merchant's yard, more sawyers had to be employed to fashion the timbers. This labour force of carters and sawyers expected

68

fortnightly payments, whilst the timber merchant may have to wait for months, or even years, for a return in his capital. The would-be timber merchant needed money to make more money.

Henry Adams had several advantages. He had spare capital to invest; he had a roomy site at Buckler's Hard for the storage of timber; some accessible compass timber was close at hand; as a shipbuilder he knew what was required; Portsmouth dockyard was in the neighbourhood as a potential major customer; he had a labour force; and, above all, he had energy and business acumen. Adams became a major supplier of timber to both Portsmouth and Plymouth dockyards, selling to them not only compass timber, but frames and knees already fashioned, together with vast quantities of treenails, or wooden pegs. The Navy required timber in peacetime as well as in war, as ships were in constant need of repair. Thus, the suppliers of timber were not as susceptible to the violent fluctuations of demand as were the shipbuilders. Timber was the main material needed for the construction, not only of ships, but of houses, bridges, fortifications, furniture, tool-handles, wagons, farm implements, gates and fences. It was a commodity almost as essential to the 18th century economy as is oil today. Adams was to continue to take an interest in the timber trade for the rest of his career, and he became an acknowledged expert on timber preservation.

Although not all Adams' timber was shipped from Buckler's Hard, his participation in the trade inevitably meant the laying down of timber yards in and near the village in excess of the demands of the relatively small shipyard. In addition to timber stocks near the river immediately downstream of the shipyard, known as the East Timber Yard, a larger area to the south-west of the village, known as the West Timber Yard, was used later. Additional saw-pits were constructed in both yards, where not only was timber cut, but treenails were also fashioned by Adams' sawyers ranging from the standard 12 - 36in long.

The year 1768 saw Henry Adams particularly active as a timber merchant. In January and February he was in London, where he negotiated the sale of 100 loads of plank to Portsmouth and Plymouth, followed by a further consignment,

Oak Plank 3in 50 loads, 2½in 40 loads, 2in 10 loads.

Oak and Elm Board 12,000 feet.

Treenails of 36in - 4,000,, 33in - 4,500, 30in - 5,000, 27in - 5,500, 24in - 6,000, 21in - 7,000, 18in - 10,000, 15in - 9,000, 12in - 9,000. Total 60,000 [5]

This extract from a letter written by Henry Adams typifies the vast quantities involved. Later in the same year he spent a month in Dorset and Devon obtaining beech for another large contract. He was in Buckler's Hard during November and December, 1768, and in January, 1769, during which time he informed the Navy Board that, due to the wet roads, he would have to await the dry season of summer before he could deliver more supplies. Then in February, 1769, he went to Ireland in search of additional timber, leaving his nephew, Anthony, in charge at Buckler's Hard. He was back in Buckler's Hard for the summer of 1769, during which time he supervised several further timber shipments to Portsmouth dockyard.

The trade was not without problems. Due to a lack of communication between the Navy Board and the Commissioners of Portsmouth, on one occasion a delivery was refused at the dockyard as no authorisation had been received. Adams had to write to the Navy Board reminding them to inform Portsmouth about the contract.[6] On another occasion, Adams had timber at Poole, but was unable to hire a ship to transport it to Portsmouth. Again, a vessel en route for Plymouth was damaged in a gale, and had to remain in Brixham for a month for repairs.[7]

In 1771 Adams the timber merchant became a master shipbuilder once more. The Navy's sorry state was revealed by a crisis in relations with Spain in that year, when the opposition gave voice to Fleet deficiencies. This led to an increase in naval expenditure when the Earl of Sandwich, though hampered by Lord North, tried to improve the state of the Navy. Adams, with his yards at Deptford and Buckler's Hard was in a strong position. On 15 February, 1771 he wrote from Deptford to the Navy Board, *Having heard that your Honours intend Building some 74-gun Ships by contract, I beg leave to treat with your Honours for building one of them in our yard at the Lower Well Dock Deptford . . .*[8] Three days later Adams signed a contract to build the 74-gun *Hector* at Deptford, and on 20 February he obtained a further contract to build the 32-gun *Ambuscade* there, together with a third assignment to repair and rebuild the 32-gun *Brune*, a captured French ship, also at Deptford.[9] This considerable building programme was for the firm of Adams and Barnard, for which Adams would receive only one-third of the profits. Adams also obtained contracts to build three small ships in his own right, the *Thetis*, 32-gun, and *Greyhound* and *Triton*, both 28-gun, at Buckler's Hard.

His ambition was to build larger ships at Buckler's Hard. Previously, the Navy Board had deemed the site to be unsuitable, but in 1771 Sir John Henslow, who became Surveyor in 1784 but was then Quarterman to the Navy Board, examined the site, and made recommendations which were acceptable to the Board. He proposed that four slipways should be built, two at the extreme east, or downstream of the shipyard, to be 140ft long, and suitable for the construction of 28-gun ships. A third slipway, 150ft long, for the building of 32-gun ships, was to be laid down opposite the houses on the eastern side of the village. The fourth, 165ft long, for the building of 64s, was to be laid down further upstream, and angled towards the bend in the river in order to allow additional sea-room for launching. The remains of this launchway can still be seen immediately downstream of the jetty. Henslow also proposed that a dock should be built between the smaller and the larger slipways.

Henry Adams began the major task of the construction of a proper shipyard at Buckler's Hard immediately. In his own words, *But in the year 1771, When the Navy Board desir'd I would build another 64-gun ship, I had an Idea; that on laying out some Money, I could make Bucklers hard capable of building a 64- or 74- gun ship, Which Idea I communicated to the Navy Board; and desir'd they would send some Officers to Survey the Ground and River; which they comply'd with, and on my pointing out to them what might be done, both on the Ground for Launching and in the River, they gave a favourable report of both; and I was then admitt'd to Build a 64-gun Ship here; I then sett about digging and making Launches down to low water mark, and filling up the Spaces between them with Earth; all of which I piled and plank'd, as I likewise did some hundred feet of Wharfing in the front of the River, and buried several hundred pounds worth of Timber for Groundways, to support the Ships while Building . . .*[10] Adams later claimed that the whole operation cost him £3,000, although in an earlier letter he had stated that it cost him £2,000. Whichever was correct, it was a vast capital outlay at that time. Before the year was out, Adams began work on the 64-gun *Vigilant*, the first ship-of-the-line to be built at Buckler's Hard, under the supervision of Robert Carleton, appointed by the Navy Board as Overseer.

His energy has to be admired. In his 59th year he had negotiated an intensive building contract for Grove Street, Deptford where, although Barnard was to supervise the work, Adams had to supply the timber. At the same time, new launchways were built at

Buckler's Hard, where four ships were being built concurrently. Also, he had some contracts to supply timber to Portsmouth dockyard unfulfilled. In August, 1771 he wrote to the Navy Board that he would be unable to deliver timber to Portsmouth on time due to a shortage of labour; he had only ten pairs of sawyers working on the four ships at Buckler's Hard, instead of the 20 pairs he needed, so that it was not possible to direct them to other tasks.[11]

In September, 1771 he bought two cutters, *Prince George* and *Hunter*, from Portsmouth dockyard for £120 the pair, presumably to facilitate the movement of materials. Communications between London and Portsmouth were still inadequate, for when Adams sent the money to the Naval Treasurer, it was returned as the latter did not know the cutters were to be sold! In January, 1772, Adams was in Herefordshire — a regular haunt of his — buying great quantities of timber to be transported down the Severn, and loaded into ships at Chepstow.

● In the 1770s Henry Adams was anxious to enlarge the shipyard at Buckler's Hard, but the Navy Board were sceptical about the merits of the site. In 1771 Sir John Henslow, then Quarterman to the Navy, surveyed the site and reported that four launchways could be laid down. At its height, there were eventually five launchways at Buckler's Hard

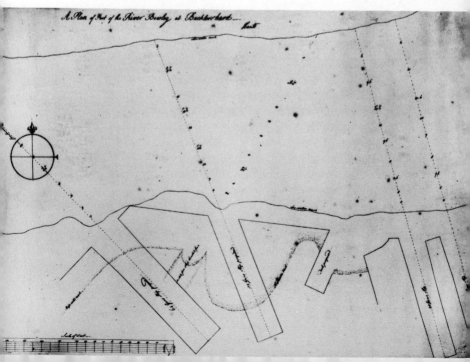

Despite bad weather during the winter, by the spring of 1772, work was going well on the four Buckler's Hard ships. The three small frigates were launched at Buckler's Hard in 1773: *Greyhound* on 20 July; *Triton* on 1 October; and *Thetis* on 2 November. By then, Robert Carleton had been replaced as Overseer by James Dann, who remained at Buckler's Hard until 1779. In 1774 Dann married Ann Adams, daughter of the late Anthony and niece of Henry, at Beaulieu Church, so that builder and overseer now had a family relationship. It was Dann who wrote to the Navy Board asking for 'a perfect Bill' for *Greyhound* on 20 July.[12] Despite this, the Board made deductions from the final payment for both *Greyhound* and *Triton* on the grounds of work not completed to the store rooms, cabins, and shot racks. Adams received £6,614 for the hull of *Greyhound,* £6,585 for that of *Triton,* and £7,602 for the *Thetis,* together with additional payments for other fittings. As *Ambuscade* was launched at Deptford in the same year, his cash flow was considerable.

With the launching of the three smaller ships, Adams could concentrate his labour force on the *Vigilant.* A ship of that size would have towered over the houses at Buckler's Hard and been the focal point of local interest. *Vigilant* was launched on 6 October, 1774, three weeks late. Adams claimed that an abnormally wet August had delayed caulking and painting. The first ship-of-the-line to be built at Buckler's Hard was given, literally, a royal welcome, as the launching was attended by the Duke of Gloucester, who spent much of his time at Lyndhurst as his wife was not received at George III's Court. The *Hampshire Chronicle* described the event, *On Thursday last was launched by Messrs Adams at Bucklers-hard, a fine ship of 65 (sic) guns, called the Vigilant, at which the Royal Highnesses the Duke and Duchess of Gloucester, with a great number of gentlemen and ladies were present. His Royal Highness was launched in her and had an exceeding fine launch; She is allowed to be as fine a Ship as any of her class in the Navy'.*[13] Five days after the launching, *Vigilant* was towed to Portsmouth, where she arrived on the same day; the Duke of Gloucester and several of his male friends were on board for the ship's first journey.

Vessels of the size of *Vigilant,* 160ft long overall, could not be launched by the limited labour force of a rural shipyard. In such cases, Portsmouth dockyard supplied the bilgeways, spurs, stopping and bolts, a moveable prefabricated 'launching kit'. A master-rigger would be sent from Portsmouth two or three days beforehand, to be followed by as many as a hundred riggers for the launching. The dockyard working-party then had to tow the rather unwieldy ship by a fleet of rowboats. The arrival of *Vigilant* at Portsmouth in 24 hours was unusual; more often the tow took two or three days.

Adams received £22,026 11s 7d for the *Vigilant* hull,[14] as much as for the three small frigates together. The bigger the venture, the greater the profit; so it must be assumed that Adams' desire to build ships-of-the-line was not for prestige only. With the *Vigilant* gone, no further work was on hand at Buckler's Hard. Nor could much work be obtained in the building and repair of merchant ships, due to the remoteness of the site. Luckily, the Grove Street yard at Deptford remained full of work. The 74-gun *Hector* and the 50-gun *Experiment* were launched there in 1774, followed by a 14-gun sloop the *Hound* in 1776. In addition, work on merchant ships could be obtained on the Thames. With this other business interest, Adams did not have to rely entirely on the trade of timber merchant to bridge the gap between naval contracts.

The expansion of the Buckler's Hard shipyard was not matched by great enlargement of the village. One new house was built in 1768, and two others may have been added in the late 1760's or 1770's. This is not surprising as shipbuilding in the rural areas did not usually lead to the development of permanent housing. Much of the labour force was itinerant and temporary, very much as sub-contractors are today. Many of the local labour force lived, not in Buckler's Hard, but at Beaulieu Rails, near East Boldre. However, the hamlet was growing at a time when some villages were declining. By 1776 there had been changes in tenancies, including that of the Ship inn, where John Hewett was succeeded first by the Misses Street and then, not later than 1767, by Thomas Floyd. Buckler's Hard was a village with a shipyard, but it was not inhabited exclusively by shipwrights and other craftsmen. A well was sunk at Henry Adams' house in 1767, and a pump installed four years later; new tiles were put on the Master Builder's House and the three adjoining houses, together with repairs to the tenements under the mould loft.[15] Otherwise there was no housing boom.

While shipbuilding expanded at Buckler's Hard, the ironworks at Sowley declined. Abel Walter took over the tenancy from 1759 to 1762, and William Ford from 1763 to 1770. By then, the furnace was no longer in use, and even the forge ceased to operate until 1789, when it was put into use again by Charles Pocock, in company with Henry Adams. Sowley's decline accorded with the national trend: local hammer ponds were being replaced by larger ironworks near or in large towns, close either to iron and coal, or to potential customers. In Hampshire Henry Cort established an ironworks at Fontley, near Fareham, well placed for work for Portsmouth dockyard, and Henry Adams was a customer and a friend of Cort.

So by 1776, Henry Adams had built a proper shipyard at Buckler's Hard, with a launchway capable of building ships-of-the-line. The years of greatest fame lay still ahead.

References

[1] PRO Adm 95/12 and Bill Book 112
[2] PRO 30/8/153
[3] Prerogative Court of Canterbury: Will 324 Taverner
[4] Dews' *History of Deptford* (1884) pp 270-271; A J Holland *Ships of British Oak* (Newton Abbot 1972) p 96
[5] PRO Adm/NB 106/1162
[6] PRO Adm/NB 106/1175
[7] PRO Adm/NB 106/1185
[8] PRO Adm/NB 106/1194
[9] PRO Adm/NB 106/1207; 106/1263
[10] PRO 30/8/153; Adm/NB 106/1207
[11] PRO Adm/NB 106/1194
[12] PRO Adm/NB 106/1218
[13] *Hampshire Chronicle* 10 October 1774
[14] PRO Adm 95/84 and Bill Book 116
[15] Beaulieu Muniments: Audit Memoranda

● These drawings, owned by the Maritime Museum at Buckler's Hard, show designs for the figureheads of *Greyhound, Vigilant, Brilliant* and *Triton*. All four ships were built by Henry Adams at Buckler's Hard between 1773 and 1779. The drawings were probably done by a wood carver from Owlesbury, for Adams' approval

7 High Noon: (1776~1792)

THE OUTBREAK OF WAR IN 1776, beginning as a war of independence by the 13 American colonies, and developing into yet another struggle with France and Spain meant that naval shipbuilding in the merchants' yards began again. Henry Adams and Buckler's Hard were to play a full part in the war effort, but during this period other Hampshire shipbuilders rose to prominence, notably Thomas Raymond in Northam, Southampton, Robert Fabian at Cowes and Eling, John Nowlan and Thomas Calhoun on the Hamble, and George Parsons at Bursledon. Adams was acquainted with all his fellow entrepreneurs, and did not regard them as rivals. Indeed, in the matter of contracts, the Hampshire shipbuilders usually tendered the same terms, indicative of prior consultation. However, Raymond, Fabian, Calhoun and Nowland all became bankrupt, while Parsons and Adams remained solvent. In terms of fame, Adams and Parsons also outshine their rivals, for both were the builders of ships which played a part in the life of Nelson — Adams as the builder of *Agamemnon* and Parsons as the builder of the *Elephant*. Nelson lost his right eye whilst commanding the former, and applied his telescope to that eye on the deck of the latter.

At the outset of the war, Barnard and Adams obtained a contract to build the 24-gun *Pelican* at Deptford, while Adams began the 44-gun *Romulus* at Buckler's Hard. The *Romulus* was launched on 17 December 1777, by which time Adams was engaged in the rebuilding of a French prize, *Pacifique*, renamed the *Pacific* and later sunk as a breakwater at Harwich in 1781. Then there followed a period of intense activity at both Deptford and Buckler's Hard. In 1778 work began at Grove Street on the 24-gun *Pandora*, launched in 1779, on the 32-gun *Orpheus*, launched in 1780, and on the 64-gun *Africa*, launched in 1781; these ships were followed by the 64-gun *Scipio*, begun in 1779, and the 32-gun *Andromache*, begun in 1780.

At Buckler's Hard, Adams was busy enough. He launched two fire ships in 1778, followed in 1779 by *Sibyl* (later renamed *Garland*), a 28-gun sixth-rate, launched on 2 January, the *Brilliant*, another 28-gun ship, launched on 13 July, and *Hannibal*, a 50-gun fourth-rate, launched on 24 December. All three vessels were built under the supervision of George Polyblank, James Dann's successor as Naval Overseer at Buckler's Hard. With a one-third share of the profits at Deptford, and a monopoly interest at Buckler's Hard, Henry Adams must have made a fair profit. However, he claimed that he made a loss of £500 on *Brilliant*, for which he was paid £8,067, and a loss of £1,000 on *Hannibal*.[1] This claim, however, may have been a piece of special pleading as he was contesting a mulct of £150 on *Brilliant* for late completion. He stated that he could not get a sufficient labour force, so that *Brilliant* stood ten months in frame, and that the cost of materials had risen since the contract had been signed. Adams concluded in his letter to the Navy Board as follows, *Before I took these ships to build, I had built Eleven sail for his Majesty's Service, and always compleated them as soon as any person, and have done the utmost in my power to get these compleated. But I could not purchase men . . .*[1] The difficulties experienced by Adams were not unusual; during wartime skilled workers were in short supply, needed both by dockyards and civilian shipbuilders. The yards, often by impressment, increased their work force in time of war; certainly merchant builders near London were better placed to attract men than those in the rural areas like Adams. But, by 1781 Adams was complaining that he had men idle.

Athough Adams professed to have made a loss, he was quick enough to accept a further contract, beginning work in 1779 on the most famous ship built at Buckler's Hard — the 64-gun *Agamemnon*, Nelson's 'favourite ship'. Her gun-deck measured 160ft, keel length 131ft 8in, extreme breadth 44ft 4in, draught 19ft, burthen 1376 tons. As she was launched without masts, stores and fittings, her draught then was considerably less than 19ft. *Agamemnon* entered the water on 10 April, 1781, a blustery day when the rain fell in torrents, so that 'only a few persons were present.'[2] The riggers then took four days to tow the hull to Portsmouth dockyard. Adams received £28,579 for his work.

In 1780, while *Agamemnon* was being built, Adams had three launchways idle. During the summer of that year he met Robert Fabian in London, having already been in communication with Thomas Raymond. On 20 July Adams wrote to the Navy Board, *Having at this time several Ships unimployed a large Quantity of Timber both in a rough and converted State by me and ten pairs of sawyers almost out of imploy — I pray leave to offer my service to Build at Buckler's Hard a 74-gun ship and 32-gun frigate.*[3]

Adams was building a 64-gun ship, but he was still hankering after one of the new ships-of-the-line, which had 74-guns on two decks, and which became the utility vessels of the late 18th century. However, Adams had to wait for another nine years before that ambition was realised. The Navy Board gave him a contract to build the *Gladiator*, 44-guns, a sister ship to *Mediator*, given to Thomas Raymond at Northam, Southampton. *Gladiator* was launched on 20 January, at a cost of £14,771 including masts and yards, but by the time she was fitted out the war had come to an end. Meanwhile, Adams had embarked on a brave enterprise. With empty launchways and an under-employed labour force, he began to build a 32-gun man-of-war as a speculation in 1782. Normally the shipbuilder received an initial payment on the signing of a contract, and further instalments as the work progressed; now Adams would have to use up to £10,000 of his own capital, with the risk that the ship would be unwanted when completed. In this case, the gamble succeeded; the *Heroine*, launched in August, 1783, was bought by the Navy Board for £10,274. Adams was able to take this risk as he had obtained a contract to build another 64-gun ship at Buckler's Hard. It was advantageous to any builder to construct a small ship concurrently with a larger, as timber too small for the latter could be used on the former, while the labour force needed the second project in order to ensure continuity of work. The 64-gun ship, *Indefatigable*, was launched in July, 1784, at the beginning of the ten years of peace which followed the end of the war of American Independence.

Adams was able to speculate on the building of *Heroine* as his other interests were thriving. At Deptford, the 24-gun *Pandora* was launched on 17 May, 1779, the 32-gun *Orpheus* on 3 June, 1780, the 32-gun *Andromache* on 3 November, 1780, the 64-gun *Africa* on 11 April, 1781, the 64-gun *Scipio* on 22 October, 1782, and a 74, *Carnatic*, in January, 1783.[4] Additionally, throughout 1781 and 1782, Adams was supplying timber to Portsmouth and Plymouth, in which business his nephew Anthony, together with John Ayles, played a prominent part. Most of the timber for these contracts was obtained from Devon and Cornwall.[5]

These ventures enabled Henry Adams to survive the ten years from 1783 to the outbreak of the French Revolutionary Wars in 1793. Three men-of-war were built at Grove Street, Deptford during those years — the 32-gun *Solebay,* launched in 1785, and three 74-gun ships, *Majestic* and *Zealous,* launched in 1785, and *Orion,* launched in 1789. Adams supplied much of the timber for those contracts, while still honouring contracts for the royal dockyards. By then Henry Adams was more than 70 years old and left most of the 'field-work' to his nephew. This involved Anthony in a great deal of travel. For example, in the year 1786, he was in Ringwood at the end of February, in Exeter in May, in Portsmouth in August, in Exeter again in October, and in Barnstaple at the beginning of December, an itinerary typical of a timber merchant's life.

● Design for the figurehead of *Heroine,* 32 guns, launched at Buckler's Hard in 1783. Figureheads were originally intended to appease the gods of the sea. Pliny the Elder (born c 43 AD) wrote: "A storm may be lulled by a woman uncovering her body at sea". Elaborate figureheads and stern carvings reached a peak in Stuart times. During the 18th century, a cost-conscious Admiralty, anxious also to preserve timber tried to discourage elaborate figureheads, but shipbuilders clung to the old traditions. Figureheads were designed and carved by specialists, and not by the shipwrights

Although Anthony Adams was the active partner in the timber merchant business, Henry Adams was consulted, along with other civilian shipbuilders, about the vexed problem of the preservation of timber, and in the 1780's he took part in an experiment at the request of the Navy Board. The motive force was Thomas Nicholls, of Redbridge, Purveyor of the New Forest. As Purveyor, Nicholls had the practical task of organising the felling and carting of timber from the New Forest to the dockyards, and he wrote two important pamphlets, *Observations on the Propagation and Management of Oak Trees* in 1791, and *Methods Proposed for Decreasing the Consumption of Timber in the Navy,* published in 1793. Nicholls gained the support of Thomas Mitchell, Deputy Surveyor to the Navy Board, who asked Adams to strip the bark from two oaks, two elms, two beeches and two ash trees while they were still growing. All the trees were in the manor of Beaulieu, and the bark stripping was done by Adams in 1784; in the following Spring, all the trees were still alive, but in 1786 the oaks appeared to be dead, whilst the other three species were still living. In 1788, all were felled, and found to be unsuitable for shipbuilding. Nicholls, with the help of Adams, was able to prove that those who advocated bark stripping were mistaken. On 22 June, 1791, Adams wrote to the Navy Board a report on the experiment, in a letter signed also by John Ancell, the Overseer at Buckler's Hard.[6] Nicholls visited Adams in 1791, and asked him many questions about timber. Adams was quite definite: he preferred to have timber in the rough, with the bark still on.[7]

Henry Adams also built three men-of-war at Buckler's Hard during the ten years of peace. The 44-gun *Sheerness* was launched on 16 July, 1787, by which time Adams had begun work on a 74-gun ship. In the previous year he had attended the Navy Board in company with George Parsons of Bursledon and Thomas Raymond of Southampton: all three Hampshire builders were given a contract for a 74, Parsons for the *Elephant,* Raymond the *Saturn,* and Adams the *Illustrious,* the first 74 to be built at Buckler's Hard.

It is probable that *Illustrious* was built on the launchway laid down for the 64s, on which *Agamemnon* had been built. With an overall length of 168ft, she was only eight feet longer than Nelson's ship. As early as 1782 Adams suggested building a 74 in a field behind his garden,[8] in his earnest attempts to persuade the Admiralty that he had the space so to do. But there is no evidence to suggest that *Illustrious* in fact was built there.

She was launched on 7 July 1789, after a week's delay in the vain hope that King George III and Queen Charlotte, who were staying at Lyndhurst, would visit the site. Adams made preparations for a royal launching, and fitted a cannon on board. However, though the royal pair visited Beaulieu, they did not go to Buckler's Hard. Undeterred by this Adams had a 21-gun salute fired in honour of the King whilst the ship was still on the launchway. The inhabitants of Beaulieu, however, were given a taste of royal colour. The *Salisbury and Winchester Journal* described the visit graphically, *On Monday last their Majesties with the Princesses and their suite paid a royal visit to Beaulieu, the seat of His Grace, the Duke of Montagu. The King came hither on horseback attended by the Gentlemen, and the Queen and other Ladies in coaches. The latter were conducted to the Mansion House by Mr Warner, Steward of the Manor, and all his Lordship's tenants, who, with 60 men dressed in white bearing colours and white wands preceded the Royal carriage, as did six running footmen, dressed also in white with scarlet livery caps and a flag. The Royal Standard of England was hoisted as they passed, and they were saluted by 21 guns from the Illustrious, now building in Mr Adams' yard at Buckler's Hard.*[9]

Illustrious was embellished with beautiful carvings on stem and stern, the original drawings for which, together with a model, can be seen in the Maritime Museum at Buckler's Hard.

- **Designs for the bow and stern of** *Illustrious,* **74 guns, launched at Buckler's Hard in 1789. This original drawing is in the Maritime Museum, Buckler's Hard**

In addition to the three men-of-war, Henry Adams built two East Indiamen, begun in 1786, and completed in 1789, and a small mooring lighter of 119 tons for the navy. In 1787 the 110-ton merchant brig *Dawkins* was launched at Buckler's Hard and sold for £901 14s 9d, with all the masts, yards, rigging, boats, oars, anchors, tackle and furniture. At the beginning of 1790, Adams had no work in hand, so he decided to build another ship as a speculation, as he had previously successfully done with *Heroine*. In this case, the risk was less, as Britain's relations with Spain were strained over Nootka Sound and the fleet was mobilised. Work on the ship was still in the preliminary stages when the Admiralty signed a contract to buy the ship on 4 June 1790, for the sum of £12,250. Eventually, a further £218 11s was paid for extra work done.[10] Such was Henry Adams' standing with the Admiralty, in his 77th year, the doyen of the shipbuilders, that he was accorded the honour of naming the vessel. He chose an appropriate title — the *Beaulieu*. She was launched on 4 May 1791 by Sir Harry Burrard, an influential landowner from Lymington. Afterwards, Adams entertained 80 guests, including John Ancell, the Navy Board overseer, in the wooden banqueting hall which Adams had built on the west side of his house. The guests danced until three o'clock next morning, and consumed vast quantities of liquor.

In retrospect, the launching of the *Beaulieu* was the beginning of the end for Henry Adams. Although he was to live until 1805, his remaining years were to bring many sorrows and misfortunes. But in 1791, after nearly 50 years of shipbuilding at Buckler's Hard, Adams could have been well satisfied.

Adams' business at Buckler's Hard would have ended in 1785, had Temple Luttrell had his way. Temple Luttrell was the son of an Irish peer, Lord Carhampton, and the brother of Colonel Henry Laws Luttrell, Wilkes' opponent. Temple Luttrell was the builder and the owner of Eaglehurst, a bizarre residence between Cadland and Calshot. He was the originator of several impractical schemes. In one, he wrote to Pitt the Younger suggesting that a royal dockyard should be established at Buckler's Hard. His idea was that the dockyard should be where the timber was, in order to obviate the difficulties of taking the materials to the dockyard.[11] Luttrell continued, *Great advantage wou'd accrue if Ships and Vessels of War were built on the King's account at, or near the Heart of the New Forest And this may be done . . . by purchasing for the Crown the Slips,*

Magazines etc. of Buckler's Hard . . . belonging to the Adams's, and by them holden on lease from the Montagu family. I shou'd think it an important benefit to the State to buy the whole Manor of Beaulieu, together with the Lands of Gilbury, belonging to Mr Mitford; but especially the Former. Both these estates are richly productive of Oak, Beech, Elm, Fir . . . and tho' the Agamemnon and others lately built at Buckler's Hard . . . are found very defective in their ironwork . . . yet no man of war, from a King's Yard, can show finer Frames of Timber. By possessing this property, you wou'd carry the Royal Demesne from the confines of Wiltshire quite down to the sea, taking in Both Shores of the Beaulieu River, from Beaulieu Town down to Leap.

Luttrell continued by stating how the money for the purchase of the Estate should be raised, by selling the northern part of the New Forest from Ringwood to Downton, where there were no trees. In a footnote he suggested peremptory compulsory purchase, *Lord Beaulieu and Duke of Montagu. An Act of Parliam^t easily gets over the obstruction of Settlements on Private Families, where the public weal is concerned, by granting full Indemnification.*

Luttrell's scheme also envisaged the building of a large prison between Buckler's Hard and Beaulieu, the convicts to act as a labour force, under a detachment of marines. His ideas found no support, and there was no real threat to the Manor of Beaulieu, or to Buckler's Hard.

● **Luttrell suggested that Buckler's Hard should become a major dockyard, with the compulsory purchase of part of the Manor of Beaulieu**

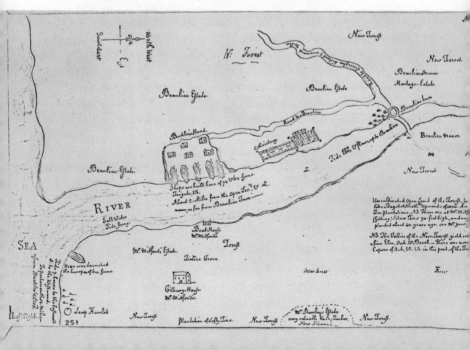

Adams had more immediate problems when his landlord proposed to raise his rent in 1780. This led him into a dispute with the Manor of Beaulieu which had its origin in changes which had taken place since 1765. In that year William Warner, the steward, had died, and his son and successor, John Warner, was unable to keep for Henry Adams, his brother-in-law, the favoured and privileged position which he had hitherto enjoyed. The succession of Henry Hoyle Oddie as the chief administrator in London of all the Buccleuch estates further weakened John Warner's freedom of action. Oddie was concerned more with profits than with people and the economic climate of 1780 differed from that of the 1750's, when Adams was persuaded to stay in Beaulieu.

In 1780 Adams was still paying only £5 15s a year for the shipyard, with an additional £5 for the Ship Builder's House, and £1 6s 8d for the four houses which he had built for his workmen. Oddie was perhaps nettled by Adams' refusal to take more timber, in addition to the 134 trees at St Leonard's which he bought for £209 5s. Oddie accused Adams of having, in the past, taken oak, elm and beech from the Manor without paying for it, including 40 trees cut down in Hill Top Copse in 1769. Also, according to Oddie, Adams had cut down part of Clobb Copse in order to make room for the east timberyard, near the shipyard, had used the timber without paying for it, and had added land to the shipyard, without paying an additional rent. Oddie informed Warner that Adams' rent should be increased to £30 a year.

Warner did his best to obey his superior's owners. He ascertained that Thomas Raymond, shipbuilder of Northam, Southampton, was paying £30 a year and informed Adams of the new rental. This suggestion brought a vigorous response from Henry Adams: he pointed out that he had built up the shipyard, at a personal cost of £3,000; that, although he had done over £100,000 worth of business with the government since 1771, he was not better off as he had spent his profits on the premises; that his family lived frugally; that he had built four houses for his workmen and many improvements including £50 on road repairs. He compared his tenancy with other Hampshire shipbuilders. At Northam, Raymond paid £20 a year (*sic*), but he could get timber cheaper than Adams could, and he could build more ships at any one time; at Bursledon, Parsons paid £15 a year for a better site than Adams had, and he could also get cheap timber; at Cowes, Fabian paid £30 a year, but this included several houses, at a yard where merchant shipbuilding could also be done.[12] He, Adams, had a weekly wages bill of £80, and he would find himself hard pressed to find the proposed rental of £30 a year. Apparently, relations between Adams and the Manor of Beaulieu were already strained due to the valuation of some timber. Adams protested that he was 'as Innocent as a child just born', and was in London when the valuation was carried out. He ended with a quaint postcript, 'In the whole time I have been here I never fired a gun on the Estate. Nor never would employ any persons that I had a suspicion were Poachers'. The matter was concluded with a compromise, whereby Adams was to pay £21 a year for the Shipyard and the tenements, plus £5 for his house.

The raising of the rent to a reasonable one as far as the landlord was concerned was done during wartime. Adams' problem was that in peacetime very little shipbuilding or repair was available. In 1789 a survey of the Manor of Beaulieu was carried out by Joseph Amsburg, and he recommended that the annual rental of £21 was too high in peacetime.[13] But this recommendation was not heeded: Adams' rent remained as before.

By 1790 the village of Buckler's Hard comprised some 19 houses. The Master Builder's House, occupied by Henry Adams, had been improved by the addition of a wooden banqueting room. Adams had built stables and he had laid out a garden stretching towards the river, and erected a fence round it. He also rented some 26 acres of ground near the village. Adams no longer leased the shop; by 1789, at the latest, this was being run by the Wort family. Wort's shop was housed in the building which is now part of the Maritime Museum, outside which is the inscription 'Jos Wort 1774'. The date probably means a rebuilding, as the house was there long before that date. It is possible that James Wort took over the premises in 1774, but the inscription of 'Jos' for 'Joseph' must remain obscure. Joseph Wort did not take on the lease until 1804, and he remained there until 1819. The Beaulieu rentals show James Wort as the lessee between 1781 and 1804 and at some time between 1791 and 1804 the shop was converted into the 'New Inn', so that the small hamlet had two ale-houses during the Napoleonic Wars. One of the houses was still occupied by a Salt Officer, but the presence of a government official there did not prevent friction between locals and customs officials. Attempts by the government to tighten control led to a petition from the inhabitants of Beaulieu and the neighbourhood to the Commissioner of Customs against a requirement that the export of sheep to Portsmouth required a customs seal. Then, in 1778, the Commissioner of Excise closed the excise 'Office' at the Montagu Arms in Beaulieu, and centralised transactions for the area at Southampton. A petition sent to the Commissioner by the people of Beaulieu had no effect.[14]

The ownership of Beaulieu was still in the names of two landlords: the Earl of Beaulieu, second husband of Isabella, 'John the Planter's' daughter, and the Duke of Montagu. The latter died in 1790, and his moiety passed to the Duke of Buccleuch, who became the sole owner in 1802.

In 1789 the forge, but not the furnace, was again set up at Sowley. The new tenant was Charles Pocock, who had a manufactory in Reading. He was assisted by Henry Adams in the revival of the ironworks, Adams supplying timber and other materials. The two families became firm friends, and were later related through marriage. But the revival of Sowley was but an Indian summer: its industrial life was to survive during the French wars, but became a victim of the peace which followed Waterloo in 1815.

References

[1] PRO Adm NB 106/1241
[2] *Hampshire Chronicle* 10 April 1781
[3] PRO Adm NB 106/1255
[4] PRO Adm NB 106/1263
[5] PRO Adm NB 106/1269
[6] *A Collection of Papers on Naval Architecture* (London 1800) from the European Magazine, pp 91 and 120
[7] *ibid* p 133
[8] Beaulieu Muniments S/89
[9] *Salisbury and Winchester Journal* 4 July 1789
[10] PRO Bill Book 120
[11] PRO 30/8/153 ERD/7122
[12] PRO 30/8/153 and Beaulieu Muniments S/89
[13] Beaulieu Muniments EII/SR8
[14] Beaulieu Muniments 16 & 18

● This model of *Illustrious* was made by A W ('Pat') Curtis. Pat Curtis became the Custodian of the Maritime Museum at Buckler's Hard at its opening in 1963, and rapidly established a reputation as one of the leading model-makers in Britain. The stern and bow carving was done by Gerald Wingrove

8 From Indian summer to bleak mid-winter

IN 1793 BRITAIN was once more at war against France, in a struggle usually known as the Revolutionary War and which lasted until 1802. Then, after a brief period of peace until 1803, the Napoleonic War began, which ended with the defeat of Napoleon at Waterloo in 1815. During these wars, the Royal Navy achieved several spectacular victories, and naval officers such as Nelson, Collingwood and Jervis became national heroes. It was a period of patriotism and hardship, of technical change in agriculture and industry, and of inflation. They were dynamic years, in which the business entrepreneur needed to be both foresighted and fortunate. These wars were the last period of greatness of the builders of wooden ships, and the Adams family of Buckler's Hard were no exception. They were to have two golden decades, followed by a dramatic fall.

In 1793, Henry Adams was 80 years of age, but still actively pursuing his lifelong career. He had survived as a businessman at Buckler's Hard by a diversity of interests. The sale of timber had seen him through the lean years, whilst the Deptford Yard had brought him profits additional to those from Buckler's Hard. Unfortunately for Henry Adams, his connection with Deptford came to an end on Christmas Day, 1793, when the lease expired and the partnership of Adams, Barnard and Company was dissolved with some acrimony.

In June, 1792, Henry Adams sued his partners in the Chancery Court for monies owed to him.[1] According to Adams, in 1763 he was invited by William Dudman and William Barnard to enter into a partnership with them in order to obtain a 30-year lease of Grove Street, Deptford. Adams advanced money, at 5% interest, and supplied, during the first nine years of the partnership, large quantities of timber and other materials worth £8,374 12s whilst his two partners were unable to contribute their share. In 1772 William Dudman died, and Adams went to Deptford to ask for Dudman's debts to be paid to him from the estate. Barnard, acting as Dudman's executor, said that the latter's cash book was lost; according to Adams, Barnard had hidden it to obscure the debts. Then Barnard, without consulting Adams, allowed Dudman's son John to live in the dwelling-house in the yard, and to enter the firm as a partner in place of his father. In 1779, William Barnard and John Dudman took over the lease of another shipyard, immediately adjacent to the Grove Street Yard. This new yard was known as the Lower Yard, rented for 21 years from Thomas West for £4,500, in the name of Barnard and Dudman only. Adams' contention was that Barnard had used £1,600 from the tripartite firm to secure the lease, and had used timber destined for that firm for the new firm. Further, Adams claimed that some naval contracts were diverted from the old firm in the Upper Yard to the Lower Yard. On 10 February, 1792, Barnard wrote curtly to Adams informing him that the Upper Yard partnership would be terminated on 1 March, just over two weeks later. This caused Adams to instigate legal proceedings against his former partners.

The lawsuit was a lengthy one. After the long vacation, Barnard's answer was heard in October, 1792. According to Barnard, the partnership of 1763 was on an ad hoc ship-by-ship basis, and that it could be dissolved without notice by any of the partners. His contention was that Adams had promised to quit Buckler's Hard, and move to Deptford to help run the business. Adams, however, had taken little interest in the affairs of the Upper Yard, and had left his two partners to run the business. The two partners had continued to see to things, frequently asking Adams to help them. Then, in 1779, with the Upper Yard full of work, Barnard and Dudman obtained the lease of the Lower Yard so that more contracts could be obtained. Although £1,600 was taken from the books of Adams, Barnard and Co for the purchase of the lease, this was debited against Barnard only, so that it was, in effect, his own money. Moreover, Adams took no interest at all in the new venture, and little in the old. Indeed, the first complaint made by Adams was in 1789, when he accused Barnard of using timber sent from Buckler's Hard to build a ship for Sir Benjamin Hammett in the Lower Yard. The Lower Yard was run by Barnard only, whilst John Dudman looked after the firm of Adams, Barnard and Co at the Upper Yard. Any timber from the latter was paid for by Barnard, who built ships at the Lower Yard only when the Upper Yard was full. Henry Adams was well aware of all financial transactions, and in 1784 the firm's accounts had been audited. In 1785 Barnard was appointed as the 'only shipwright to His Majesty's Customs in the Port of London'. This monopoly led to his taking out a 51-year lease on the Lower Yard, and extending the property. Adams' claims for moneys owed him were quite wrong. At William Dudman's death, Adams was owed £2,180 4s 10d, and this he was paid from Dudman's estate. Since then, Adams had advanced £1,586 towards the expenses of Grove Street, and had sent timber, knees, and plank worth £362 5s 9d. During the same period, Adams had received 50% of the profits of the Yard, considerably in excess of the money he had put into it. Henry Adams had been 'an inactive partner', while Barnard should be paid an allowance 'for his diligence and attendance' to the business.

Henry Adams lost the case, and the end of his business interests there meant that he and his family were entirely dependent thereafter on the success of Buckler's Hard. The firm of Barnard and Co was to continue to thrive throughout the first half of the 19th century, whilst that of Adams at Buckler's Hard was to wither away. The second generation of Adams' should have emulated their father by migrating, if they wished to survive as shipbuilders.

But, in 1793 Henry Adams was still very much alive, and the shipbuilding business at Buckler's Hard still had an Indian summer to come. From that year until his death in 1805, Henry Adams left the day-to-day running of his business to his sons, though he remained in financial control and played a full part in general administration. The working of the shipyard and of the timber business devolved on Balthazar and Edward Adams. Balty married Anne Maria de Burgh, the illegitimate daughter of Lord Clanricarde at Beaulieu on 7 March, 1793, and on 24 October, 1799 Edward married Mary Welsh of Southampton. The two brothers had been trained as working shipwrights under their father, and contracts signed after 1793 were in the name of 'B and E Adams'. The third brother, Henry, after graduating from Wadham College, Oxford, took holy orders, and became 'perpetual curate' at Beaulieu in 1790. As perpetual curate, he performed all the duties of parish priest for the pluralist, Hand, until 1834, when on Hand's death, Henry became vicar of Beaulieu — just five years before his own death. Henry married Susannah Green in 1795. The youngest son, John, who suffered periodic bouts of epilepsy, became a lawyer and transacted much of the legal business for the firm. It was John Adams who visited Barnard at Deptford in 1791, on the eve of the dissolution of the partnership. John Adams also visited Portsmouth frequently in order to conduct business with Navy Board officials.

Henry Adams' four sons were used to a less frugal life than their father. They led an active and expensive social life, in the manner of lesser gentry. They frequented the theatre in London and in Lymington, the Assembly in Southampton, and the Dog's Nose Club in East Street in that town: Balty and his wife owned a house in Bugle Street, Southampton. In 1791 Edward Adams built himself a yacht, which he used for fishing and pleasure. Henry Adams' three daughters also had expensive tastes. Whilst Lucy married Charles Pocock, of Sowley, in 1795, Mary and Elizabeth remained unmarried. So long as Henry Adams remained alive, the family finances remained reasonably secure. In 1791 he invested £1,800 in a share of the Sowley Iron Works, run by the Pococks. In the same year, on the advice of John, he advanced £4,000 to the purchaser of an estate in Hendon at 4½% interest.

Meanwhile, shipbuilding was continuing at Buckler's Hard. In 1793 the rebuilding of the *Santa Margarita*, a 38-gun fifth-rate captured from the Spanish in 1779, was completed. Work on this ship had begun in 1791, after an inspection by Marshall, the Deputy Surveyor to the Navy Board. In March, 1793, B and E Adams signed a contract for the 32-gun *Cerberus*, launched in the following year. Also in 1794, John Ancill was succeeded as Navy Board overseer at Buckler's Hard by James Williams, who remained in that post until 1799.

With the launch of *Cerberus* in 1794, B and E Adams had no naval work at the shipyard. Henry Adams, then aged 81, rode to London on horseback, sought an interview with Admiralty officials, and returned with a contract for a 50-ton mooring lighter, launched in 1795. However, the yard was engaged in some merchant building at that time. In 1795 the *Columbus*, a West Indiaman was completed, and in 1796 the *Princess Mary*, an East Indiaman. During the next four years, B and E Adams built the *Heart of Oak*, a coaster; the *Endeavour*, a timber hoy; two small privateers *Hard* and *Neptune*, and the *Active*, a timber hoy completed in 1800. In addition, they built the 18-gun *Bittern* for the Navy, launched in 1796.

In 1795 B and E Adams were invited, together with 12 other firms from other parts of England, to tender for the building of 74s. All refused the terms offered, but in 1797 the Admiralty increased the price to £20 a ton, and the Adams' brothers undertook to build a ship-of-the-line. For the next three years, Buckler's Hard was the scene of great activity. A modest building programme of merchant vessels was augmented by naval shipbuilding. Work began on the 74, with smaller rates on the other launchways. The 38-gun *Boadicea* was launched in April 1797 and the 16-gun *Snake* in December 1797.

In September, 1799, the 24-gun storeship *Abundance* was launched as a speculation, and immediately bought by the Admiralty for £9,758. Then in May, 1800, the 74-gun *Spencer* was launched, at a contract price of £38,021 1s 3d. The *Portsmouth Telegraph*, dated 19 May, 1800, commented, *On Saturday one of the finest ships of two decks in the Royal Navy, was launched from Mr Adams' dock, at Buckler's Hard. But, as Earl Spencer did not come, as was expected, to name her, she was christened* The Spencer *by Sir Charles Saxton, a Commissioner of the Navy, and Resident at Portsmouth. She went off extremely well, and, although the weather was unfavourable, a great company was assembled on the occasion. Mr Adams provided a costly and elegant collation for his friends.*

B and E Adams then signed a contract for another 74, as part of a programme of building shared with others. This ship, the *Swiftsure*, was launched in 1804, and the period of her building was a difficult one for shipbuilders. The Adams brothers were to make a loss on *Swiftsure*, through circumstances outside their control. The war economy, coupled with changes in industrial technique, led to inflation, and those engaged in long-term enterprises, such as a ship, costed in 1800, and completed in 1804, were the main sufferers. Shortages of bread and other basic foodstuffs hit the poor, and added to inflation. In addition, political instability caused some anxiety. William Pitt the Younger's administration gave way to Addington's in February, 1801. Addington's period of power included the signing of the Peace of Amiens with France on 25 March, 1802. Although Britain declared war on France once more on 17 May, 1803, during the 14 months of peace the First Lord of the Admiralty, Earl St Vincent, cut expenditure to the delight of taxpayers, but not shipbuilders. Although Pitt returned to power in 1804, Addington had instituted the practice of an annual survey of government accounts, giving parliament some control over expenditure. Thereafter, government contracts for shipbuilding were to prove less profitable.

However, in 1800, those problems were in the future. B and E Adams had plenty of work, although there were shortages of timber and skilled labour which had to be obtained at higher prices. Overtime had to be worked also in order to meet contract dates, entailing the payment of double, sometimes triple rates, and thus adding further to the final cost. As B and E Adams needed some short-term contracts in order to get a quick return of profit, they built three small merchant coasters, all launched between 1800 and 1803. In addition, the 36-gun *L'Aigle* was launched on 23 September, 1801, 16 months late, which resulted in a fine of £1,000 from the £14,322 price.[2] In 1802, they produced three gun brigs, the *Starling* on 4 April, the *Snipe* on 2 May, and the *Vixen* on 10 June. The first two were completed early, and B and E Adams were rewarded by a premium of £276, but *Vixen* was one month late and earned a deduction of £150. The contract price of each of the three 16-gun ships was £3,319. In 1803 B and E Adams completed the *Hope*, a merchant ketch of 166 tons, and on 6 June, 1803, the *Euryalus*, a 36-gun naval frigate, entered the water 17 months late. For this late launching a fine of £1,000 was deducted from the price of £15,568 16s. On 24 July, 1804, the 74-gun *Swiftsure* was launched, an occasion of great rejoicing in Buckler's Hard. Between 3,000 and 4,000 people attended the launching, some arriving on foot and others in 135 carriages which filled the tiny village. The Adams brothers entertained 110 guests at the celebration dinner, held in the wooden banqueting hall, an extension on the western side of the Master Builder's house, whilst Charles Hemans, the landlord of the Ship Inn, drew five hogsheads (2,100 pints) of beer for the multitude. But beneath this gaiety, the shipbuilders had some cause for concern. They were paid £21 10s a ton for the ship, or a total of £35,787 17s 9d, from which a mulct of £500 was taken as the completion was ten months late. B and E Adams informed the Admiralty that they had made a loss on the venture, but this may have been a stratagem in an attempt to get better terms for their next venture.

Messrs Adams had already signed a further contract for another 74. This contract, signed in January, 1804, was negotiated by John Adams, the shipbuilders' lawyer brother. The price was to be £25 10s a ton, and was one of nine such contracts, the other eight all going to Thames builders. This contract was to be the ruin of the firm. The Admiralty's first price of £24 10s a ton was refused, and John Adams asked for £36, which he later reduced to £34. But the Admiralty would not move beyond £25 10s, and they insisted on a severe penal clause.[3] Although the Admiralty had increased the payment, it barely covered inflation. Moreover, the shortage of timber was exacerbated by stockpiling in the royal dockyards. Work began on the new 74, due for completion under the contract in three and a half years. But the vessel, named the *Victorious*, was not launched until October, 1808, nearly two years later, and the Admiralty applied the penal fine of £3,000. During that time, the Adams brothers built other small naval vessels. The 12-gun *Growler*, begun in August, 1803, was launched on 10 August 1804, on time. But two other 12-gun brigs, due for completion at the same time, were late. The *Fervent* was launched on 15 December, 1804, and the *Dexterous* on 2 February, 1805, B and E Adams suffering a £300 fine on each. The place of building of the *Dexterous* is uncertain. She is shown as built by Adams at Eling in one authority,[4] but this is unlikely. The site at Buckler's Hard had the capacity to build the three small ships simultaneously with the larger 74 and to build one of them at a different centre would have been uneconomical. Moreover, another builder, Robert Adams, no relation of the Buckler's Hard family, was using Eling at that time. The *Dexterous* was not built by Robert Adams, but by B and E Adams, as other Admiralty records clearly show,[5] so that the Eling location is doubtless a clerk's error. B and E Adams launched the 18-gun brig-sloop *Columbine* on 16 July, 1806, within the contract time. On 23 April, 1807, the 38-gun *Hussar* was launched, 17 months late, and incurred a fine of £1,000, reduced to £500 by extenuating circumstances. By the time the *Hussar* entered the water, B and E Adams were still building the 74-gun *Victorious*, by then one year overdue, and they had begun work on yet another 74, the *Hannibal*. The contract for the *Hannibal* was signed in January, 1805, after much wrangling with the Admiralty, settled only when the price was raised to £36 per ton.[6] Again, the Adams' contract was in line with those given to other merchant builders, including both Barnard and Dudman, old Henry Adams' former associates. The *Hannibal*, the fourth naval ship to be so named, was launched in May, 1810, one month early, so no fine was incurred.[7]

Although B and E Adams had incurred some fines for lateness in launching, their record was comparable with that of other merchant builders. Unfortunately, their reputation was impugned in the House of Commons by Mr Jeffrey, MP for Poole, who complained that the contract for the *Victorous* should not have been given to B and E Adams as there was 'so little dependence on her being finished according to . . . contract, that the keel of the . . . ship is not yet laid down.'[8] But Jeffrey, speaking in the House in 1805, was engaged in the political intrigues of the time aimed at discrediting the administration of Earl St Vincent as First Lord of the Admiralty. Politicians are not the best of historical sources, and have been known to bend the truth. Jeffrey's biased pronounce-ment led to a fierce reply by Messrs Adams, who complained of 'this libellous statement'. They prepared a list of the ships built at Buckler's Hard from 1789, which, however, is not altogether accurate.[9] Further, they pronounced that the Admiralty's faith in them was unimpaired, as further orders had been placed with them.

This unsolicited publicity in the House of Commons did little harm to the firm, but real troubles were looming large. Balthazar and Edward Adams were experiencing difficulties in the financing of the business: inflation, a shortgage of skilled manpower, the cessation of an income from Deptford, and, above all, the shortage of timber, resulting in a rise in price, all had an effect. Also, the Adams brothers had problems over Admiralty payments which were in the form of bills, usually redeemed by the builders to the discount houses at much less than their face value. In 1802 B and E Adams sued their London broker, Bayley, for failure to pay up.[10] Further, whilst Henry Adams had had little competition in the buying of timber from the Manor of Beaulieu where he had the support of his relatives, the Warners, as stewards of the Manor, his two sons found changed circumstances. Timber from the manor of Beaulieu was in demand, and, for some obscure reason, Hoyle Oddie, the commissioner or 'financial adviser' to the Duke of Buccleuch, was hostile to the Adams brothers. As early as 1802, Oddie wrote to the Duke that, *As Mr Adams has not been punctual with his payments, that alone might be a sufficient reason for not selling so great a Quantity to him.*[11] Three years later, Edward Adams visited Oddie in London, asking for time to fulfil payments for timber obtained from Beaulieu, as the Government had been tardy in paying him. All was not well with the shipbuilding business. In 1805, Warner, the steward of the Manor of Beaulieu, inherited a fortune from an uncle in Suffolk, and it was assumed that he would leave Beaulieu. Balthazar Adams applied for the stewardship, *I do not think him properly qualified*, wrote Oddie, *the difficulties we have had . . . in obtaining his payments for Timber form a very material objection, though he is I believe a well disposed man.* [12] In 1806, the Adams brothers were involved in legal proceedings brought by one of their creditors, which involved them in further expense. Then they began negotiations with the Admiralty for a reduction in the fines incurred for the naval ships which wranglings were not settled until 1811, when the courts found in favour of the Admiralty.

By then, there were no large naval contracts to be had, and Oddie in effect detonated the bankruptcy of the Adams brothers. On 30 July, 1810, he wrote that they, *have not yet brought their concern into such order as to enable them to pay with punctuality. They are very liberal, good natured, and I believe honest men. But it is unprofitable for me to say that their Bond is to be relied on.* Oddie informed the Duke that the Adamses owed £835 5s 4d, of which £162 10s was for rent, including £21 for the shipyard, and a further £662 15s 4d for timber. Faced with a lack of shipbuilding, Balthazar Adams then decided to attempt to extricate himself from financial difficulties by offering to buy a considerable quantity of timber from the manor of Beaulieu to be paid for in instalments. He hoped to sell the complete lot to John Larkins, a government contractor.

• *Agamemnon,* **leaving Portsmouth Harbour 1781. By Nelson's time, Portsmouth had become the most important British naval base. This bitten etching, by Harold Wyllie, is in the Maritime Museum, Buckler's Hard**

On 30 November, 1810, he wrote to the Duke of Buccleuch offering to buy £50,000 of timber . . . *having no prospect of anything to do as a Shipbuilder (Government having declined to contract for Ships at present) I am the more anxious to employ myself as a Timber Merchant, and to do that as near home as possible.*[13] Oddie was quick to advise the Duke to have nothing to do with this proposition. He reiterated the debts still unpaid, together with a further £859 10s 0d for timber bought by Adams in the Spring: that Adams had no shipbuilding and no prospects of a contract; and that the timber should be sold in lots at auction. Further, as Balthazar Adams had suggested that the timber should be valued by Thomas Hellyer, tenant of Swinesley's Farm and later steward of the Manor, Oddie gave this warning . . . *He (Hellyer) was originally introduced by Mr Adams. I have no Suspicion of Mr Adams' integrity. But a person valuing timber for such a purpose has much in his power.* Balthazar Adams was still hopeful. He was still in communication with Larkins, a major supplier of timber to the royal dockyards; he saw himself as the middleman, with the Manor of Beaulieu as the supplier, and Larkins as the buyer. However, Oddie sold the timber direct to John Larkins at £13 15s a load. Thus, Adams' last attempt to save the firm had failed. On 18 February, 1811, Oddie instructed solicitors to begin proceedings against Messrs Adams. *I am very sorry for Messrs Adams,* Oddie wrote, *who, after all, I believe to be well meaning people. But I fear their affairs have been so managed as will make it difficult for them to go on.* John Larkins, who had on previous occasions acted as surety for the Adams brothers withdrew his support; bankruptcy followed. They were sued in the Chancery Court by two other creditors, Edward Toomer, a Southampton ironmonger, and Christopher Westbrook, brewer and maltster of Beaulieu. The firm of B and E Adams was dissolved, although the two brothers were to build small ships separately in the future.

Bankruptcy in those days was a common occurrence, and did not mean penury, but the prolific days of shipbuilding at Buckler's Hard were at an end.

What had gone wrong? The cause was due only in part to the conduct of the business by the Adams' brothers. Their father, Henry Adams, had survived because he was active in a long period of almost continuous naval expansion; he had an interest in the Grove Street Yard, Deptford; he had a thriving timber business with a virtual monopoly of Beaulieu estate timber; he had business acumen and a prodigious capacity for work; he was unable to build a large ship for several decades due to Admiralty doubts over the site, and, therefore, was unable to overstretch his resources. Balthazar and Edward Adams began their work at a time of high inflation, when timber prices soared, and when the Manor of Beaulieu had other eager buyers. Warner, the steward, was unable to shelter them from Oddie. Further, the Adams' brothers attempted to build ships beyond the capacity of the site; smaller ships over a shorter time span would have been safer during a period of inflation. The two brothers lived a much more varied social life than did their father, lacking his frugality. But shipbuilding at Buckler's Hard on a grand scale would have ended due to circumstances beyond the control of the Adamses. From 1811 there were no large building contracts to be had from the Admiralty. The Napoleonic Wars were over in 1815, and the reduction of timber duties in 1822 led to its importation to the detriment of native suppliers. The bankruptcy of 1811 was symptom rather than cause.

Fortunately, old Henry Adams did not live to see the downfall of the firm which he had created. Although he had left the running of the business to his two sons from 1793, he continued an active life almost to the end of his days in 1805. He played a part in the affairs of the local community. For example, when, in 1799, the Lymington Agricultural Society was founded at the behest of the newly created Board of Agriculture, Henry Adams was an original subscriber and a founder member. In addition to regular visits to the Pococks at Sowley, or to Southampton, when he was more than 90 years of age he travelled to Ipswich with his wife to visit friends, and went to London in the same year. A year before his death, he had a tooth extracted! Although no longer directing shipyard operations, he had a semi-circular room built at the Master Builder's House, now known as the 'Adams Room' from which he spied on the work in progress, using a telescope to aid his failing eyesight. When he saw something of which he disapproved, his servants hoisted a number pennant and rang a bell, known as the Summons Bell. Each workman had his own number, and the man thus summoned had to come to the house, climb up a rope-ladder to the window, where he was told by the old master shipwright how to do the job properly. At his death, Henry Adams was able to leave his family ably provided for. Balthazar and Edward had the shipyard; Henry was a clergyman; John was a lawyer. His sons and his widow inherited investments and property. while his two unmarried daughters Mary Ann and Elizabeth received £2,000 each.

Henry Adams was buried at Beaulieu Church[14] on 3 November, 1805, later to be joined by his widow and others of his family. His obituary in a local newspaper read, *On Friday 26th (October) died, at the advanced age of 92, Henry Adams, Esq, of Buckler's Hard . . . universally respected and beloved by all who knew him, and sincerely lamented by his surviving relatives, to whom his memory will be ever dear. It pleased God to bless him with the full enjoyment of his intellectual faculties to the day of his death. He was a man of most amiable disposition; mild, open, and affable in his deportment, humane, friendly, and social in his intercourse with the world. During a long life, the strictest principle of rectitude governed all his actions, and he supported the real character of a good member of society with uniform fidelity. He was a good and pious christian, a tender and affectionate husband, a kind and indulgent father, and a sincere and faithful friend.*[15]

The man who had courageously migrated from Deptford, was laid to rest a short distance from the Beaulieu river which he had grown to love.

References

[1] PRO Chancery Proceedings C12/1401/4
[2] PRO Adm 49/102
[3] PRO Adm 30/8/246 Part I
[4] J J Colledge *Ships of the Royal Navy* Vol I, (Newton Abbot 1969) p 162
[5] PRO Adm 49/102
[6] NMM, Greenwich, Adm letters 31/1/1805
[7] PRO Adm 95/102
[8] Key to the Papers presented to the House of Commons, 1806
[9] Beaulieu Muniments Miscellaneous 21(b)
[10] *The English Reports* vol 31 (Chancery II, Vesey Junior, vols 4-6)
[11] Boughton House: letter dated 22/11/1802
[12] *Ibid:* 29/4/1805
[13] *Ibid:* 30/11/1810
[14] PCC Crickell 1520/158
[15] *Hampshire Telegraph* 2/12/1805

9 The end of the Adamses

THE DISSOLUTION OF THE PARTNERSHIP of Balthazar and Edward Adams in 1811 was not the end of shipbuilding at Buckler's Hard, nor of the family's connection with the business. Anthony Adams leased Clobb and Great Purnell farms, and made a living from agriculture. The Reverend Henry Adams leased a house in Beaulieu, and took services in Beaulieu Church as well as preaching sermons in the surrounding villages. Old Henry Adams' widow continued to live in the Master Builder's House, together with John, the lawyer, and the two unmarried daughters. Balthazar Adams leased and lived at Curtle Farm; Edward Adams leased Salternshill Farm.

The shipyard was divided into two establishments; Balty rented most of the west side, and Edward the east. Balty took over the slip used for building the 74s, together with two smaller launchways.[1] He occupied the ground floor of the mould loft, two forges, the blacksmith's shop, the west half of the coalyard, the shed for grinding stone, the west half of the trenail house, the west furnace for boiling pitch, the west half of the kiln for steaming plank, the north half of the sawhouse and sawpits, and part of the East Timber Yard. Edward Adams took over the lease of two launchways and the upper floor of the mould house.

Balthazar paid £195 a year in rent for all his tenancies, of which £50 was for the shipyard: and Edward paid £85 a year for his, of which £75 was for the yard. The two brothers were still relatively well-to-do, contributing to the poor of Beaulieu, and to other charities. They were to attempt to make a living from farming, with some sporadic shipbuilding enterprise. In 1812 Edward Adams completed the *Lady Hannah Ellis*, a West Indiaman of 400 tons, followed by two 20-gun naval brigs, the *Medina* and the *Carron*, launched on 13 August, 1813 and 9 November, 1813 respectively. Meanwhile Balthazar completed two vessels, the 18-gun *Tay*, launched on 26 November, 1813, and the 24-gun *Towey*, on 6 May, 1814. (The latter is shown in some navy lists, in error, as the *Fowey*). In 1815 Edward Adams completed a merchant brig, the 125-ton *Neptune*. This was the end of naval building by the Adamses at Buckler's Hard. The war had ended, there were no more shipbuilding contracts to be had. The attempt by the Adams' brothers to resuscitate shipbuilding for the Crown was short-lived, and as the price of farm produce was to slump, their secondary living was to become precarious.

In addition, a death saddened the Adams family. In December, 1814, John Adams was in Shropshire obtaining timber. Journeying home, John joined the timber ship *Sulterton* at Chepstow; she was wrecked on Berrow Sands, near Bridgewater, and John was drowned. The news reached Buckler's Hard on 19 December — Edward travelled to Bridgewater and returned with the body on Christmas Eve. Elizabeth Adams recorded in her diary for Christmas Day, *a most dismal Christmas Day for us — Henry Pocock dined with us.* Also in 1814, Anthony Adams, old Henry's nephew, died. He was then leasing Clobb Farm, where his widow remained until 1820.

The years immediately after the end of the war, in 1815, were to see further deterioration in the fortunes of the Adamses. Their three main interests, shipbuilding, farming and the timber trade were all, within a few years, to enter a period of depression. By 1819 Balty Adams, again in serious financial straits, gave up the lease of Curtle Farm and his half of the shipyard. So bad was his plight that his uncle, John Warner, the former steward, gave him £25 a year from his own pension. But Balty's penury was shortlived; he died in 1821.

When Balty gave up his half of the yard, the steward of the Manor, Thomas Hellyer, was gloomy about the future. He reported that the four cottages which Balthazar Adams had surrendered were in a bad state of repair. One cottage, not worth repairing, was demolished in order to use the materials for the repair of others for which Hellyer felt he could find new tenants. The shipyard, however, was a different matter; he would be unable to find another tenant.

Meanwhile, Edward Adams was attempting to keep going,

both as farmer at Salternshill and shipbuilder. Edward had moved into the Master Builder's House, by 1813 at the latest.

By 1822 old Henry's widow and the two daughters, Mary Anne and Elizabeth, had moved to Beaulieu, to live in Warner's House, in the middle of the village. The mother died in 1827 in which year Elizabeth was a teacher at the Beaulieu girl's school, in the western part of the Poor House, where she received £40 as her annual salary.

In February, 1819, Edward Adams bought £460 worth of oak timber at an auction in Beaulieu, at which Mark Richards, a Hythe shipbuilder, bought £446 worth, and Charles Mortimer Wheeler of Redbridge bought £778 worth. This may possibly have been connected with the building of a sloop and a brig. But he still owed £414 of the purchase price in August, 1820, and only settled the account in January, 1821 after many written requests, and a visit from Hellyer, who then went to Edward's bankers in Southampton. Edward was not the only one in trouble in 1820. Hellyer reported to Oddie, the Buccleuch's financial manager, that there was the 'greatest distress among the Poor', and that there were so many men without employment. Several of the tenant farmers were also in arrears in rent.

Edward Adams survived this crisis and in 1822 was allowed a considerable reduction on the £20 rent for half the shipyard as there was no shipbuilding work done. But, in the previous year, William Good began to build a revenue cutter, the *Repulse*, at Buckler's Hard. The nature of his occupancy of part of the yard is obscure, as he does not appear on the rentals. Good had moved from Bridport to Hythe soon after the end of the Napoleonic Wars. At Bridport, Good, with his partner Bools, had built five gun-brigs for the navy between 1808 and 1813 before becoming bankrupt. In 1821 orders were placed for the building of revenue cutters, as a result of the reorganisation of the Customs service. The *Repulse* was launched at Buckler's Hard on 14 November 1822, and Good then took over the site at Hythe recently vacated by Mark Richards. Good also started a bank in Hythe, but both businesses failed in 1824, when he was declared a bankrupt with debts of £19,000.

But that was in the future. The launch of *Repulse*, the revenue cutter, at Buckler's Hard brought some semblance of life to the village. A few weeks after the launching, on Christmas Eve, 1822, Elizabeth Adams recorded that she and her brother Edward and William Good were entertained to supper on the revenue cutter by the commander, Captain Williams.

At the end of 1826 steward Hellyer was informing the owners of the Manor of deep distress in Beaulieu, where there were nearly 100 men on relief. He attributed the cause to the failure of the crops and to the fact that there was *in the Shipbuilding business nothing doing*. If Edward Adams' Account Book is reliable (see page 106) the *Arab* should have been near completion. It is possible, but unlikely, that Thomas Hellyer was painting too gloomy a picture in order to obtain agreement for his taking on labour to do odd jobs on the Estate. As shipbuilding was long term, there was a need to obtain a new contract when the current project was far from complete.

Thomas Hellyer died in 1827, aged only 40. He was the steward in a most difficult period, and he did his best for Edward Adams, and for the other leaseholders. Hellyer was a farmer with some knowledge of the timber trade, but no expertise in shipbuilding.

He was replaced by Thomas Cheyney who in November 1827 wrote to Oddie that there was *no shipbuilding going forward at Buckler's Hard*, and that there were 75 men without work in Beaulieu. Even so, this did not spell the end of Edward's shipbuilding at Buckler's Hard. He stayed in business until 1838, by which time he was aged 71. Between 1827 and 1838 his work was sporadic, with no building between 1831 and 1836. Certainly he should be given credit for remaining in shipbuilding as long as he did. The 1820s and the early 1830s have been described as the most severe depression that Britain has ever suffered — worse than the so-called Hungry Forties. Perhaps Edward prevented Buckler's Hard from becoming a 'deserted village' during that period; later, from about 1850 onwards, agriculture saw better days and was to provide work for the next generation. At least there were still shipwrights resident in Buckler's Hard between 1827 and 1841, including Charles Glastonbury, who later became foreman (see page 202), Edward Burlace, Charles and John West, Benjamin Fielder, John and Henry Scaines, Thomas Payne, John Puss, and Thomas Westhrop. Edward's work was not on the scale of his illustrious father's, or even of his own younger days. As early as 1814 his sister Elizabeth had noted wistfully that only ten guests were entertained at a launching party at the Master Builder's House, where 20 years earlier there were more than 100.

Edward kept the business alive by diversification, and by small-scale jobs which grander shipbuilders of the previous century might have scorned. He repaired the revenue cutters, based on the newly established coastguard stations at Lepe and Pitt's Deep. It was Edward Adams who erected gates, fences, posts and stiles round the cottages at Lepe. He even built a flat punt for Thomas Cheyney, the steward.

Edward's shipbuilding enterprises after 1815 can be gleaned from conflicting sources. First, the National Maritime Museum at Greenwich has the Longstaff Collection of drawings and plans. These plans were sold in 1930 by the widow of Edward Adams' grandson, Henry, who had died in Hull in 1927, to Longstaff, who later gave them to Greenwich. However, these plans contain some material on ships built at Poole by Richard Pinney, who married Edward Adams' daughter. Second, Portsmouth City Library owns what should be an incontrovertible source, *Account Book of Edward Adams 1824-1841 of vessels built and repaired at Adams' shipyard by Edward Adams,* which needs to be treated with some caution, however, as the time scale of the accounts starts in 1816, and was probably not the work of Edward himself. His son, Henry, became a draughtsman at the Pinney yard in Poole, and the book contains details of several ships which were built there, and not at Buckler's Hard. Third, the *Lloyds' Registers* of the period are not always impeccable sources for the place of building, ie Southampton is shown for several sites in the Solent region.

- **This model of** *Neilson* **was made by Pat Curtis, at the Maritime Museum**

The list from the account book is summarised below, with the Lloyd's building place shown in the right hand column. It is probable that the year 1838 saw the end of Edward Adams' activities at Buckler's Hard.

1816	*William Bryan* West Indiaman, 290 tons	Southampton
1817	*Otter* Schooner, 74 tons	
1818	*Thalia* brig	Southampton
1818	*Mary* brig	
1819	*Betsey* sloop or smack, 32 tons	
1821	*Sir Charles McCarthy* brig, 188 tons	Southampton
1824	*Friendship* schooner, 118 tons	Southampton
	Neilson brig, 232 tons	Southampton
1825	Repaired – Lepe preventitive boat, cutter. Built a punt for Hurst coastguards, fences for Lepe Coastguard station, repaired Pitts Deep preventitive boat and three tenders	
	Henry barque, 259 tons	Buckler's Hard
1826	*Australia* barque, 373 tons	Buckler's Hard
	Dwarf Navy Board cutter, 51 tons	
1827	*Arab*	
	Lady of the Lake revenue cutter (repaired)	
	A flat punt for Thomas Cheyney	
1828	Small boat for his son George Anthony Adams 3 tons	
1829	*Sincerity* lengthened by 8ft, 100 tons	
1830	*Trial* sloop, 30 tons	
	Idas yacht, 26 tons	
1835	*Teazer* lengthened yacht, 20 tons	
1836	*Emerald* barque, 216 tons	Poole
1837	*Spheroid* (masts and spars only) brig	
	Gertrude revenue tender	
1838	Coasting vessel for the Ordnance Survey, 82 tons	
	New Express barque, 278 tons	Poole
1838	*Chilmark* brig, 209 tons	Poole
	Coquette yacht, 12 tons	
	New Kingston cutter	
1839	*Hebe* schooner, 173 tons	Poole
	William Woolley brig, 209 tons	Poole
1840	*Canopus* barque, 321 tons	Poole
1841	*Camaieu* barque, 393 tons	Poole

The price of these ships varied, according to size, from £11 per ton for the larger, to £9 10s a ton for the smaller vessels. The size of the contracts can be estimated roughly as ranging from about £400 for *Betsey*, to £4,000 for the *Australia*. The brig *Neilson*, a two-masted vessel launched in 1824 had, according to one authority 'a good turn of speed'[2]. In 1827 she left Deal in Kent, on 15 September, and reached Trinidad 44 days later on 29 October. In addition to cargo, *Neilson* accommodated six passengers. Her dimensions were, 89ft 4ins keel length; 24ft 1¾ins breadth; 16ft 2ins depth in hold.

This work schedule over two decades, shows Edward Adams making a living as a shipbuilder by supplementing the occasional building of a barque with what may be described as 'odd jobs'. Despite these efforts, the yard was silent from 1830 to 1835. Edward Adams was now more farmer than active shipbuilder.

The yard's decline was due to no lack of skill, labour, or facilities. Shipbuilding had moved to the towns, as a result of technical changes brought about by the steam and iron of the Industrial Revolution. Shipbuilders at Hythe, Ryde, Bursledon, Eling and Redbridge, all near Beaulieu, suffered similarly. Moreover, from 1815 to 1854 Britain fought no major war, 40 years of peace without parallel in the previous two centuries. Even Henry could not have survived without the incidence of war. These changes were noticed by contemporaries. A journal, written in 1831, says . . . *Buckler's Hard, where ships used to be built for the Royal Navy and where in my younger days I well remember having attended the launch of the* Active *Frigate . . . I made . . . a sketch showing the upright Poles or Sticks by which the vessels were supported while building; there were three sets of these supporters, so that three large ships might be built at one time . . . Now all is quiet as the grave, no sound of axes or hammers, no shouts of active men, the business is decayed and the men engaged in it, I suppose, employed elsewhere.*[3]

In fact, the *Active* was launched at Northam, Southampton, and not in Buckler's Hard and there was only one launchway for a 74 at Buckler's Hard. But the writer was aware that the village had 'missed a heart beat' while much of Britain was pulsating with the Industrial Revolution.

The late 1840's saw the end of the Adams' era at Buckler's Hard. By 1845 the west and the east timber yards had become pasture land for cattle, and in 1847 Edward Adams, now 80, gave up the lease of the shipyard but remained in the Master Builder's house. His eldest son, Henry (1800-1863), a shipwright at Buckler's Hard, had moved to Hamworthy, Poole as draughtsman in the yard of Richard Pinney, a shipbuilder there. This Henry was appointed Lloyd's Surveyor in 1845, Cork in 1847 and Hull in 1850. Edward's daughter, Anne Maria, had married Richard Pinney (1804-1853), while his youngest son George Anthony (1805-1877) had married Elizabeth Pinney.

Edward died in 1849, aged 82, at his son George's house in Poole; his widow, Mary, stayed in Buckler's Hard until 1852, when she died. Balthazar's sons had long left the Beaulieu area; the younger son, Henry Balthazar joined the army, and served as a major overseas. The one remaining link of the Adams' family were his two unmarried sisters, Mary Anne and Elizabeth, who still lived in Warner's House. Although throughout the 19th century there were Adamses living in the locality, they were not descendants of the master builder. They were the family of an Edward Adams, a farm labourer who came to Buckler's Hard in the 1840's. However, before 1914, William Montagu Adams, a Portsmouth dentist, descended from old Henry, rented a cottage as a 'holiday home'.

The link with Buckler's Hard has been forged by two of Henry's descendants. First, R Bingham Adams spent most of his spare time in a long and varied life piecing together the story of his famous forebear. He wrote many articles and innumerable letters in local newspapers, and collected valuable historical documents. Many of the draughts of Buckler's Hard ships were given by him to the National Maritime Museum in 1948, where they remain. At the end of his life he lived with his daughter, Mrs Tree, at Waterlooville, and Portsmouth City Library became the recipient of other valuable items. Secondly, Cecil Ellis, a descendant of George Anthony Adams, old Henry's grandson, had preserved many family papers, some of which he generously presented to the Maritime Museum at Buckler's Hard when it opened in 1963.

Thus, the year 1847 marked the end of the 'Adams' period of Buckler's Hard; they had remained in the industry for a longer period than had any other Hampshire shipbuilder.

References

[1] BM Survey of 1813
[2] D R McGregor, *Fast Sailing Ships*
[3] British Library Addn Ms 33722

10 The building of the Ships

FROM 1740 TO 1815 shipbuilding for the Crown was the staple industry of Buckler's Hard. The needs of the Royal Navy was the main reason for the development, though not the origin, of the village. Similar developments took place in other parts of Hampshire, for wooden naval vessels were built at Cowes, at Hythe, Eling and Redbridge, in Southampton on the river Itchen, and at Hamble, Bursledon and Warsash on the Hamble river. This proliferation of shipbuilding in Hampshire stemmed largely from the expansion of the royal dockyard at Portsmouth, as Navy Board officials wanted contracts to be placed where regular visitations and inspections could be easily effected. The industry in Hampshire was more concentrated and more prolific than in any other county, excluding London's riverside; and more naval vessels were built at Buckler's Hard than in any other Hampshire centre (53 between 1740 and 1820, with a further three at Lepe, compared with 47 at Southampton and 46 on the Hamble river). The Hampshire civilian builders were responsible for about 11% of all naval building during that period; Buckler's Hard alone built about three percent of the ships entering royal service. The village therefore, was no insignificant outpost, but the most important of all the rural centres of naval shipbuilding. As most of Buckler's Hard houses still stand, further archaeological exploration is needed to supplement and expand the documentary evidence of the site in the 18th century. In 1980, a preliminary resistivity probe was carried out by the Department of Environment; the next decade should see an organised investigation in progress. But, as shipyard buildings were usually wooden and temporary, archaeological exploration may yield no drama.

A picture of the yard can be reconstructed from the limited evidence available. In 1800 there were more houses than at present (see chapter 15). The wide street leading to the village ran almost at right angles from the road to Beaulieu; today, the southern end of this road is blocked in order to preserve the vista, and visitors now enter the village by modern access routes. On the left-hand side was a large open space, the west timber yard, used for the storage and working of large timbers. The east timber yard stood by the water's edge, downstream of the village street, near an unloading jetty, and was used for timber imported by water from other parts of England or from Europe. There were five launchways, one large and four small, sited at intervals between the line of the village street and the east timber yard. All except one has been largely obliterated by modern developments, notably the use of the river by the Royal Navy during the two world wars of the present century, when some of the riverside was concreted. In 1962 the author supervised an archaeological investigation of the launchway immediately downstream of the present jetty, the work being carried out by the Southampton Sub-Aqua Club and students from King Edward VI School, Southampton. Under-water diving revealed nothing of note, but a series of spade excavations at low tide uncovered an elm launchway, running from above to just below the water-line, and about 18in below the surface. The elm was in a delicate state of preservation, so the mud was replaced carefully to prevent further deterioration. At the end of the next inlet downstream, there are large timber balks which may once have been part of a launchway. But for the remainder, concrete and levelling have made archaeological investigation difficult.

There were two forges and a blacksmith's shop, the site of the latter being established by the author in 1962. It stood inland of the east timber yard, to the east of the village. Excavation revealed considerable amounts of clinker and iron pieces. The building, made of wood, probably rested on brick piers. There is no evidence of a sail-loft at Buckler's Hard but if there was one, it would have been near the forges, as their heat helped to keep the loft dry. The wooden, two-storey, mould-loft also stood near the forges. Earlier in the 18th century, the upper floor of the present numbers 82 and 83 in the western terrace of the village probably comprised the first mould loft. The restoration of these houses in 1980 revealed that dividing walls had been added after the original construction.

Documentary evidence shows that the upper storey was made into tenements by Henry Adams, and a separate mould-loft built on the site. There was a coalyard, probably near the east timber yard, for coal had to be brought by sea. There was also a shed for grinding stone, a furnace for boiling pitch, and a kiln for steaming plank. Probably such steaming took place on the ground floor of number 82 early in the 18th century, and that the kiln there was later converted into a baker's oven (which was uncovered during the cottage's restoration in 1980). There was also a saw-house near the east timber yard, where men could work under cover, together with at least two saw-pits. There were additional saw-pits in the west timber yard. There was a shed for storing treenails, probably near the east timber yard. Although most shipyard sites had a counting house, or 'finance office', where wages were calculated and paid, it is probable that at Buckler's Hard the Master Builder's House was so used. Payment to casual labour was done at the Ship inn.

On this site a labour force of some 30 men including apprentices built men-of-war. The master shipbuilder may or may not have done manual work in the yard according to his circumstances. Herring, Darley and Moody Janverin were working shipwrights, but for Henry Adams and his sons the organisational and administrative pressures were such that they had little time to devote to the daily labour in the yard. The shipbuilder, the capitalist employer, had to negotiate a contract with the Navy Board usually entailing spending several days in London. The Board gave the shipbuilder the 'draughts', the detailed drawings of the ship to be built. These drawings were then scaled up by the shipbuilder, who usually drew the lines in the mould-loft himself. Also the shipbuilder had to ensure timber for the contract. Indeed, it was usual for the Admiralty to insist that the builder was possessed of enough seasoned timber before the contract was finalised. Adams, therefore, like other shipbuilders, had to keep up his stocks, travelling miles in search of the right timber.

Oak, preferably the *quercus robus,* was needed in considerable quantities. Oak is the only large tree in which the branches spread out almost horizontally, and the length of the lower branches are as far from the trunk as the extremities of the roots. Stem and stern posts were hewn out of the solid parts of the trunk, so that the shipbuilder usually sought trees with a circumference of at least ten feet. The frames were built in sections, known as futtocks, while the knees, or 'angle-brackets' which fastened deck-head to hull, were made from the junction of the small branches with the trunk, so that the grain ran true in both directions. The calculation of the amount of timber in each tree needed experience and expertise. Although the circumference of the base of the trunk could be measured, using a 'needle' or 'sword', ie a piece of slender curved iron with a hook on each end, to which was fastened a piece of string, height and circumference at the topmost usable part of the tree had to be estimated. The mean of the two circumferences then calculated was divided by four (the quarter-girth), which was then multiplied by itself and the height to give an approximation on the cubic content of the tree. If the circumference at the base measured 10 feet, and at the top 2 feet, the mean circumference was 6 feet. One quarter of this was 1.5 feet; if the tree was 100 feet high, the cubic content was 1.5 x 1.5 x 100ft = 225 cubic ft. The unit used was called a 'load, or 40 cubic ft, about one ton in weight, the amount that could be transported in one horse cart unit. Thus, the tree above would have between four and five loads. Henry Adams used 2,000 loads in *Agamemnon*'s construction, the equivalent of 40 acres of centry-old oaks.

Adams, like most shipbuilders, preferred to buy standing trees and spent January and February selecting the timber he required. However, he had a near monopoly of the Beaulieu oaks, and acted as timber merchant in his own right. Oak was usually felled in the winter, in the mistaken belief that it lasted better if thrown then. The 'unusable' timber, the 'lop and top' were cut off at the felling site, as were the twiggy boughs which were sold for firewood.

Adams insisted that the bark should be left on, although some timber-merchants stripped it off to sell to the tanners. The tree trunk was then hauled to the timber carriage by horses pulling a chain attached to the butt end, known as 'tushing'. Then a rope was fastened to the trunk, which was rolled up on skids, by means of wooden levers, on the the the cart, butt-end foremost. When the trunk was chained and spiked, horse teams began the long haul to the shipyard. Carting, an expensive operation, had to be done in the summer months, when the ground was firm. Where possible, shipbuilders sought compass timber near water transport, so that the vagaries of the weather were less critical.

In addition to much oak, Adams needed elm for keel and keelson, beech for the 'walls' of the ship, comprising some 14% of the whole, planking varying from one and a half inch to four inch thick, and, occasionally, fir for masts and spars. Most of the elm and beech were brought in from neighbouring counties; mast and spar timber had to be imported, mainly from the Baltic. Adams also had to buy or make tens of thousands of treenails, varying from one to three foot long, which were used as fasteners. They had to be the same species of wood as that being fastened, to minimise rot. Some were made on site by his workforce, some bought in from Owslebury, near Winchester.

• Carting timber. This was done by horses, in tandem. Haulage by land could only be done in fine weather, and was more expensive than transport by water. In the north of England canals were built to facilitate the carriage of heavy goods. In the south of England, there were many navigable rivers. New Forest timber for Portsmouth dockyard was carted to Redbridge, and thence by sea

Adams had to acquire copper bolts, not made on site; iron for anchors, bolts, rudder pintles, and nails so he was an important client of the Sowley ironworks. He needed steel for tools, jute and hemp for caulking and paint, tar, and oil. Until the end of the 18th century, the tar was usually heated in copper pots; then cast iron containers came into use. As paint was expensive, shipbuilders used tar, oil and whitewash where possible. However iron oxide paint was applied to the ship's bottom; where paint was required on the upper parts, blue, red, green and yellow ochre were preferred to white which was even more expensive, and usually dried yellow. Adams could obtain rope from the rope walk at Beaulieu, between the Mill and Carpenter's Dock, run by Westbrook who moved to Hatchet Mill in 1816.

As well as materials, Adams had to acquire a work force. Although during the 1690s there were problems caused by the royal dockyards and the civilian shipbuilders competing for the same skilled labour, with shipwrights in particular being impressed into royal service so that the civilian builders needed to apply for exemption for their own men, there is no evidence to suggest that Adams had difficulty in recruiting a labour force. There is no extant wages book for Buckler's Hard in the 18th century, but it is safe to assume that the men there were paid much the same as in other parts of England. In general, civilian shipbuilders offered a higher rate than the royal dockyards. In the 1690's Hampshire shipbuilders were paying their shipwrights 3s (15p) a day, 3s 6d (17½p) in the 1740's, and 5s (25p) a day in 1800. This was lower than the rates paid by shipbuilders on the Thames, as a 'London weighting allowance' operated even then. The civilian worker spent exceptionally long hours in the summer, and was paid by results, or on a piece-work basis. He was usually paid fortnightly, whereas the dockyard worker was paid twice a year, always three months in arrears. But the dockyard worker had some advantages over the employee in the civilian yard: free medical attention, a lodging allowance, greater chances of promotion, permanent guaranteed employment on light work when frail with age, and a pension on retirement.

The master shipwright in the royal yards had the prerequisite of receiving the wages of the apprentices whom they were supposed to train. In both the royal dockyards and the civilian yards, the men expected to be able to take away 'chips', or small pieces of wood which were, in theory, waste. Many complaints were made against the dockyard workers: that they spent the last hour of every working day sawing up wood to create such chips. In 1776 the commissioner of Portsmouth dockyard, who obviously knew *Macbeth,* wrote to the Navy Board, *A Birnam wood is carried out of the dockyard once or twice every day to accommodate the habitation of every individual artificer and mechanic.*[2] In the civilian yard, such as Buckler's Hard, the vigilant employer could control what was taken, although pilfering was relatively easy in an unfenced, unenclosed site. In some of the Buckler's Hard houses, pillars intended to help to prop up a ship's deckhead were used for newel posts, and it is possible that furniture was made from chips. This prerequisite was abolished in the royal dockyards in 1801, when the men were given twopence halfpenny a week in lieu. By so doing, the royal dockyards adopted what was already common practice in the civilian yards, where the men were usually given twopence a week in lieu of chips.

An adze in use

Adams needed shipwrights, the most skilled men in the trade. They used a special tool, known as an adze, with which to fashion the timbers. The adze was used by a rhythmic between-the-legs movement; the shipwright put his right heel on the work with his toes raised to protect his shin. The adze had a poll peg on the back which was used for driving in broken nails.

The wright used augers to bore holes in the timber, usually a choice of ten sizes ranging from one half to two inch. He employed a hacksaw for ironwork, and a hatchet for deep wood cuts. With these primitive tools the shipwright constructed the keel, frames, stern and stem-posts and all the main parts of the hull.

The ship's carpenter was employed on the more delicate features of the ship such as carvings, figureheads, and rounded pieces. Michael Silver, who was employed as the ship's carpenter during the building of *Agamemnon*, died in 1778, before the ship was completed, and he is buried in Beaulieu churchyard. While little is known of the dress of the shipyard worker, it is probable that the little square hat of the Carpenter in Tenniel's illustrations for *Alice in Wonderland* was traditional.[3]

Sawyers worked in pairs, and as many as six pairs were needed in the early stages of the building of a ship. In England sawing was always done with the wood horizontal, unlike Dutch sawyers who used trestles with an uneven height, the timber angled. At Buckler's Hard there were at least three types of sawing appointments: a saw-house, under cover, where work could be continued in bad weather or even after dark in the winter: a trestle, on which the timber was placed well above ground level: and a saw-pit, in which the timber was at ground level and the bottom sawyer stood in an artificial rectangular hole in the ground. The advantage of the above ground level trestle was that the sawdust could be cleared easily, but the disadvantage was that the timber had to be lifted on the trestle. Sawyers used three main types of saw: the whipstaff, for sawing lengthways, the crosscut which needed two men, and the singlehanded saw. During sawing, the top-sawyer, the skilled man paid more than the bottom sawyer, was responsible for marking the cutting lines, and guiding the saw. The bottom sawyer's task was to pull the saw down sharply, thus providing the brute force in the operation. Bottom-sawyers had a reputation for ill-temper and pugnacity. The constant showering of sawdust, which covered his head, choked his lungs, and smarted his eyes led to a thirst, which could be assuaged during an hour's idleness whilst the top-sawyer sharpened the saw. After an hour in the Ship inn, the bottom-sawyer was ready to take on all-comers.

Caulkers were employed to fill in the seams; oakum picked from old rope was rolled or spun between the palm of the hand and the knee into long strands. These strands were then driven into the seams with a caulking iron, hammered in with a wooden mallet, and then hardened down with a 'making iron'. Then the seams were sealed with pitch, a process known as 'paying'.

The remainder of the labour force comprised a blacksmith and his apprentice, at least one carter, and several general labourers. The labourers, hired on a temporary basis, had to seek work elsewhere during some of the winter months.

The building of a ship at Buckler's Hard took from one to three years according to its size. When Henry Adams had signed the contract, obtained the timber and the labour force, work began in earnest. At the outset, a Navy Board overseer arrived at Buckler's Hard to supervise the building. He was a skilled shipwright, seconded from one of the royal dockyards, for the duration of the contract, and paid by the Navy Board. He helped the master builder to interpret the line drawings, which were then drawn out in chalk in the mould-loft; wooden patterns, usually of ash, were then cut out and passed to the shipwrights. It is probable that, like other merchant builders, Adams used a model, built to the scale of 1:48 as a visual aid for himself and his men. Extant documents show clearly, however, that Henry Adams and his sons had a sufficient knowledge of mathematics and draughtsmanship to work from the Navy Board drawings, unlike some of his contemporaries who worked from a model only.

There would have been constant activity in the village while the ship was building. Timber came by road from Beaulieu into the west timber yard, iron from Sowley, and stores from Lymington. Timber, coal and other goods were transported up the Beaulieu river from various parts of England. Quantities of ale and food were needed for the workforce, and again this had to be brought into the village.

Ships at Buckler's Hard were built on launchways, above the high water mark, sloping towards the river at a declivity of 1 in 12. In the royal dockyards, some ships were built in docks with the advantage that the workmen were sheltered from the wind, and heavy pieces of timber could be lowered on to the construction. At

Buckler's Hard, this was not possible. The men had little shelter from the biting north wind, so workmanship must have suffered during the winter months. Derricks were needed to lower the large pieces into position, a delicate and dangerous operation. Keel blocks, large rectangular pieces of elm about five ft high, were placed on the launchways five ft apart so that men could work underneath. Large poles were placed round the launchway to serve as 'scaffolding'. Above the construction, wooden derricks were positioned. Meanwhile, the shipwrights made a false keel of either beech or oak; this was the equivalent of a car's bumpers — if the vessel grounded, the false keel would be ripped off or damaged, but not the main keel. Then the keel, of elm, was made in sections of about 25ft, and laid on the keel blocks. These sections were joined by scarf joints made in the vertical plane, the joints then lined with tarred flannel and strengthened with iron bolts. Both keel and false keel were held on the blocks by treenails, driven in aslant to prevent sideways motion. Then the stem and stern posts were fitted, followed by the frames, built in sections known as futtocks in order to obtain the right curvature. These frames were locked to the keel by means of a keelson, usually made of oak, and joined with horizontal scarf joints. Next the deck beams were put in, running at right angles to the frames, and fastened to them by lodging and hanging knees. With this completed, the ship was said to be 'in frame'. At Buckler's Hard there is no evidence to suggest that ships were allowed to stand in frame in order to allow the wood to season. The contract had to be completed to time; usually there was a war on and the timber employed had been acquired two or three years before the contract was begun. Work was continuous; planking was put to frame, the walls of the ships filled in with beech 'thickstuff', decks built, and the hull completed. In most Buckler's Hard contracts, the builder was required to put in no more than a minimum of deck-fittings; the ship was finished at Portsmouth dockyard. However, in a few contracts Adams was required to supply masts and spars. In those cases, men would probably have made the masts and spars near the east timber yard, from imported fir or pine. This was a highly skilled job, as the centre of the tree had to be the centre of the mast. The tree trunk was first squared, then 'eighted', then 'sixteenthed', before being planed with hollow planes.

Treenails were usually made by the same method. Mast fitting was difficult at Buckler's Hard whatever the ship's size, due to the

118

height of derrick required.

When completion was near, the overseer had to report to the Navy Board that the work had been carried out satisfactorily, and it was usual for another official to work the project. Then Adams had to arrange for a launching party to be sent from Portsmouth dockyard, as some 200 riggers were needed — a labour force beyond the resources of the civilian shipyard. The launch was supervised by a master rigger from Portsmouth dockyard, who came to Buckler's Hard two or three days before the launching, and stayed with Adams at the Master Builder's House.

The launching apparatus was always referred to as Bulgways or Bildgeways by Henry Adams in his correspondence,[4] but a more appropriate term would be the modern word 'cradle', which comprised bilgeways, or long pieces of timber, at least five-eighths the length of the ship, to support her during the launch, and spurs, or timber props.

● **A saw pit in Herefordshire, c 1930. The bottom sawyer needed to keep his hat on as some protection from saw-dust.**
(Courtesy of the Museum of English Rural Life, Reading)

For several days before the launching, men were employed in building rails or tramways, known as slideways, from the building blocks under the stern of the ship, leading into the water. This work had to be done at low tide, so that at high water most of the slideways were covered. At Buckler's Hard, slideways had to be built for each launching, as the rails were wooden, usually elm, and they would have rotted if left in the water until the next launching two or three years later. Then the weight of the ship was gradually transferred from the blocks on which it was built to the bilgeways. This was done by strong men with mauls driving wooden edges under the keel starting at the stern. The bilgeways were then inserted between the keel and the building blocks. This was a long process and the men holding the bilgeways in position had, by necessity, to stand in water and mud in the early stages. Launchings were usually planned to take place one hour before high water, but men were at work long before that. At the preceding low water, which may have been during the night, the sliding ways were greased with melted tallow and soap. As the tide rose the stern of the ship and the afterpart of the cradle were released from the building blocks under the stern, and the latter removed. Later, the other blocks were taken away until only those under the bows remained. Then, the last props were knocked out and, with luck, the ship would slide into the water by gravitational force, steadied by the cradle and the slideways. The smaller the ship, the greater was the angle of declivity into the water, so that the launching of a big ship was not necessarily more spectacular. Drag chains and ropes weighted with heavy timber were used to brake the speed of the ship as it ran down the greased launchways. When the ship entered the water, the stern acted as a further brake; when she came to rest in mid-stream men on the deck threw ropes to riggers awaiting them in small boats.

Sometimes, at Buckler's Hard a bottle of wine was broken on the bows of the vessel before the launching, and the ship named. At other times, a short christening ceremony took place after launch. Whenever possible Henry Adams arranged for some dignitary to name the vessel; some of them wanted the excitement of being aboard during the actual launch.

It was a delicate and skilled operation, with the inevitable occasional accident. Once, an Adams' ship was damaged, on another occasion, during Edward Adams' time, a workman was killed when the ship moved too soon after the blocks

● Shipwright's tools

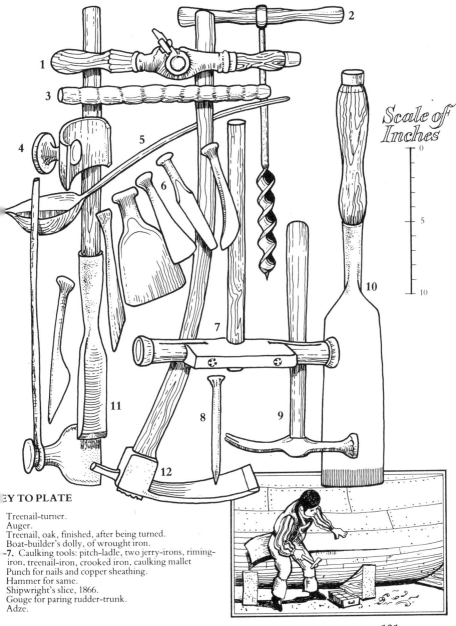

Scale of Inches

0

5

10

1
3
4
5
6
2
7
8
9
10
11
12

121

were removed. But, on the whole, the Buckler's Hard record was as good as any.

When the ship was attached to the small boats, she was towed to Fiddlers Reach, where she remained for the night. Next morning, weather and tide permitting, began the long and strenuous tow, by men in rowing boats, down the Beaulieu river, into the Solent, and beyond to Portsmouth. There, masts, rigging and fittings such as bilge-pumps and anchors, and armament were made and positioned. Fitting out, as it was called, often took a further six months. Although only the hull of the ship was normally built at Buckler's Hard, the village can rightly claim maternity rights.

At the completion of the launching, assuming no damage and the work done to contract, the overseer signed a document certifying a 'perfect bill' so that the builder could claim money outstanding from the Admiralty. On the evening of the launch, Henry Adams would entertain important guests, sometimes as many as 200 people in the wooden banqueting hall built as an extension to the Master Builder's House. Then, on the first Saturday evening after the launch, the workmen who had built the ship were entertained at either the Ship or New inn. In other words, the celebration took place during leisure hours, and not during the firm's time!

By that time, hopefully, work had begun on the next contract. If not, the launch, culmination of two year's endeavour, was not an occasion for unmitigated joy.

References

[1] A J Holland *Ships of British Oak* pp 55-62; J M Haas *Methods of Payment in Royal Dockyards,* in *Maritime History* Vol V No 2 Winter 1977

[2] N M M Greenwich *Extracts from the archives of Portsmouth Dockyard 1761-1782,* letter Gambier to N B dated 12/9/1776

[3] J E Horsley *Tools of the Maritime Trades* p 157

[4] PRO Adm/NB 106/1246

11 The Ships

A FEW MERCHANT SHIPS were built at Buckler's Hard, but their careers and, in some cases, their identity remain obscure. By contrast, the men-of-war are well known. Of the 33 British ships which took part in Trafalgar, three were built at Buckler's Hard; a fourth, *Spencer,* was detached from the fleet a few days before the battle. Eleven of the 33 were built in merchants' yards of which only three built more than one ship: Dudman of Deptford and Randall of Rotherhithe, who built two each, a remarkable testimony to the importance of Buckler's Hard.

The classification of naval ships into rates was changed from time to time during the 18th century. Until 1792, first-rates were called 100-gun ships, (110 after 1792); second-rates 90, then 98; third-rates had 80 to 74 guns; fourth-rates 60 to 44; fifth-rates 40 to 32; and sixth-rates 28 to 20. But naval vessels did not necessarily have the exact number of guns to match the rating. For example, a so-called 44-gun ship might have had 46 or 48 guns, even 42. The gun-rating was a formula used by the Admiralty in order to determine the size of the crew. The largest vessels built at Buckler's Hard were 74s or third-rates; most however were fifth- or sixth-rates, together with some small sloops and brigs mainly engaged in routine patrols and convoy duty.

Throughout the 18th century the enemy was France, usually in alliance with Spain. The acquisition of Canada, several West Indian islands, and parts of India by Britain meant that the Royal Navy had to safeguard the passage of goods and men between the mother country and her overseas territories, and to enforce a blockade of the French fleet in Brest. The Mediterranean was also an arena of conflict, and Britain acquired bases at Gibraltar,

Minorca and later Malta in order to counteract the French fleet at Toulon. Thus ships built at Buckler's Hard were to be found on duty in home waters, off the coast of France, in the Mediterranean, across the Atlantic, and, occasionally, in the Indian Ocean. After capture by the enemy some took part in actions under the French flag. This happened to the first Beaulieu river naval vessel, the *Salisbury*, launched by Herring in 1698. The ship saw service in the War of the Spanish Succession during the reign of Queen Anne. In 1702 she was part of a force under Sir John Munden, sent to Corunna to intercept a French convoy en route to the West Indies. In 1703 under the command of Sir Richard Cotten, she was attacked and captured by the French, after a two-hour battle in which 17 of her crew were killed and 34 wounded. Recaptured from the French in 1708, she was renamed the *Preston* in 1716, rebuilt in 1742, and ended her days as a hulk at Trincomalee in 1748.

The next phase of naval building at Buckler's Hard was during the Wars of the Austrian Succession (1742-1748) and the Seven Years' War (1756-1763). The *Surprize*, launched in 1745 by Wyatt and Major, under the command of Captain Antrobus, captured the French *Vieux* in 1759 during the British blockade of Dunkirk. She was in the Mediterranean in 1760, and was broken up in 1770. The *Scorpion*, launched in 1746, was one of the ships which took Wolfe's soldiers up the St Lawrence to capture Quebec in 1759. Two years later, under Captain Hallum, she captured the French ship *Boscawen*. *Scorpion* foundered in the Irish Sea in September 1762. The *Woolwich*, launched in 1749, took part in an unsuccessful attempt to capture Martinique ten years later, under the command of Captain Peter Parker, and then in the capture of Guadeloupe in the same year. In 1760 she was on duty in the North Sea, under Captain Daniel Deering, before going to the African coast. In 1762 she was again in the West Indies, and took part in the capture of Martinique. She was sold in 1763. The *Mermaid*, the first of Henry Adams' ships, saw service on the West Indies station, and was wrecked off the Bahamas in 1760, with the loss of her entire crew of 160 men, including Captain Hockman. The *Kennington*, launched in 1756, was in the Mediterranean under Captain Robert Barber during the Seven Years' War. The *Levant* was in the West Indies, under Captain Tucker, and even the *Lion* transport made one voyage to Jamaica. The remaining two ships built at Buckler's Hard during the Seven Years' War, the *Coventry* and the *Thames*, saw longer service. Both ships were together in the English Channel in 1758, when a French privateer was captured. *Coventry* subsequently took four other prizes between 1760 and 1762. In the War of American Independence she was captured by the French in the Bay of Bengal in 1783. The *Thames* had a long and remarkable career. In 1759 she was in action off Brest, and remained in home waters for the rest of the Seven Years' War. She saw service during the War of American Independence, and was still active at the outbreak of the Revolutionary Wars in 1793. In October 1793 en route to Gibraltar, under the command of Captain James Cotes, she was intercepted by five French ships, and taken into Brest as a prize. For the next three years she served in the French Navy, as *Tamise* and on 7 June 1796 fought a fierce action off Waterford with *Santa Margarita*. Thus, a British ship built at Buckler's Hard flying French colours fought against a Spanish ship rebuilt at Buckler's Hard flying British colours! The latter won the fight, and the *Thames* returned to the Royal Navy. In 1799 the *Thames* was in Lisbon, and in the following year was on convoy duty in the English Channel. She was broken up in 1803, after an active life of 45 years.

The first ships built at Buckler's Hard saw honourable service all over the globe as did those built later in the 18th century. The *Vigilant*, a 64-gun vessel and the largest built at Buckler's Hard when launched in 1774, was in action off Ushant in 1778 as part of Keppel's fleet, helped capture St Lucia, and two years later she was in action off Martinique as part of Rodney's force. She became a prison ship in Portsmouth Harbour in 1799. The *Sibyl*, a 28-gun frigate launched in 1779, was renamed the *Garland* in 1795, and became the subject of a West Indian folk song,

> *You go on board the flagship,*
> *Dey ask you for to dine;*
> *Dey give you lots of salt horse,*
> *But not a drop of wine.*

> *You go on board the* Garland,
> *Dey ask for you to dine;*
> *Dey give you plenty roast beef,*
> *And lots of rosy wine.*

> *Oh, de happy, happy* Garland,
> *With lots of rosy wine.*

The *Garland* was wrecked off Madagascar in 1798. Was it that rosy wine? The highlight of the 64-gun *Indefatigable*, launched in 1784 was a spectacular action with the French 74 *Droits de l'Homme*, in which the latter ran ashore and was wrecked. The *Indefatigable*, commanded by Sir Edward Pellew, had her masts badly splintered and four feet of water in her hold. A picture of this action hangs in the Maritime Museum at Buckler's Hard.

The first 74-gun ship built at Buckler's Hard, the *Illustrious*, launched in 1789 was wrecked near Avenza, in the Mediterranean, in 1795. Her commander, Thomas Frederick, spent two weeks trying to refloat the vessel; stores, guns, and iron ballast were removed, but the ship remained stuck, whereupon Admiral Hotham ordered Frederick to set fire to her.[1]

Several Buckler's Hard ships were in home waters during the naval mutinies of 1797. *Europe* was at Plymouth, and for a time she was controlled by the delegates. *Indefatigable* was at sea under the command of the formidable Sir Edward Pellew who took part in the trials of mutineers of single ship risings which occurred in the summer of 1797. One of Pellew's victims, a mutineer from *Hermione*, was hanged on *Gladiator*, a Buckler's Hard ship.

Three Buckler's Hard ships were in the North Sea fleet. *Brilliant* at one time was controlled by the delegates to blockade the Thames off Sheerness, thus preventing merchant ships sailing up river to London. Not all her crew were in favour of the mutiny, for four were punished for deriding the delegates. She was returned to the Admiralty on 14 June, when Lord Keith went on board and took off 14 of her crew. Later, 13 were pardoned, and one was hanged.

Agamemnon, after her adventures with Nelson in the Mediterranean, was due to rendezvous with Duncan's ships, off Yarmouth, when the men refused to answer the call of the bosun's mate after dinner. The officers were taken by surprise and 4th Lieutenant Brenton reported thus to Captain Fancourt, '*we went forward on the lower deck, and found the men had made a barricade of hammocks from one side of the ship to the other, just before the fore hatchway, and had left an embrasure on each side, through which they had pointed two 24-pounders; these they had loaded, and threatened to fire in case of resistance of the part of the officers. The captain spoke to them, but, being treated with much contempt, returned to the quarter-deck. A few minutes after a number of the people came up; some seized the wheel, while others rounded the weather braces and wore the ship, passing under the stern of the* Venerable. *The admiral made our signal to come to the*

126

wind on the larboard tack, the same as he was on himself. We answered with what was then called the signal of inability, being a flag half white and red over half blue and yellow, both horizontally divided. When the sails were trimmed on the starboard tack, and the course had been shaped by the delegates for Yarmouth roads, the captain went to his dinner with the officers, whom he had, according to the usual custom, previously invited, leaving me in charge of the deck, though without the smallest authority, if such an anomaly can be conceived. About half-past three, Axle, the master-at-arms, came to me, and openly, in the presence of others, said, "Mr Brenton, you have given the ship away; the best part of the men and all the marines are in your favour." I replied that I could not act by myself; that the captain had decided, and I feared there was no remedy. I, however, went into the cabin, and in a very clear and distinct manner told Captain Fancourt what the master-at-arms had said, and added my firm conviction that he was right, advising immediate measures to retake the ship, and join the admiral. His answer I shall never forget. "Mr Brenton, if we call out the marines some of the men will be shot, and I could not bear to see them lying in convulsions on the deck; no, no, a little patience, and we shall all hail unanimity again." I quitted the cabin and walked the deck until my watch was out, too much irritated to say a word more.

● *Agamemnon* engaging four French frigates and a brig near Sardinia, October 1793, whilst under the command of Horatio Nelson. The original watercolour is by Nicholas Pocock, 1810, and is in the National Maritime Museum, Greenwich

'On the following morning we reached Yarmouth roads, and joined three other ships, each having a red flag flying at her foretop-gallant-mast-head; the Agamemnon hoisted one also, which was called by the delegates the flag of defiance. During the whole of this time the officers kept charge of their watches, the seamen obeying them in any order for the safety of the ship, but no farther. A meeting of the delegates was immediately called, at which it was decided that the Agamemnon and Ardent, of 64 guns, and the Leopard and Isis, of 50 guns, would go to the Nore, to augment the number of ships at that anchorage in a state little short of open rebellion, but not with any view of assisting them or being assisted by the enemies of their country; and it is certain that, had these put to sea, we should have immediately gone in pursuit of them with the same zeal and loyalty as at the beginning of the war.'

Agamemnon then sailed to the Nore, to join the other 'red flag' ships, but the majority of her crew and the marines were not in favour of the mutiny. They were made to conform by 12 committee-men and, while anchored at the Nore, the guns of three other warships were trained on her, to ensure that she did not 'blackleg'. When the mutiny collapsed, she slipped her anchor and sailed into Sheerness to surrender and was sent to Gravesend. In the subsequent proceedings, all 13 who were tried were pardoned. However, like the *Brilliant* and the rest of the fleet, *Agamemnon* was brought from Gravesend to Sheerness, so that all the men were witness to the hangings of those from other ships.

The *Beaulieu*, a 36-gun frigate launched in 1790 had as her first commander the Earl of Northesk. In 1797, her crew took part in the aftermath of Mutiny of the Nore. An officer described one incident as follows,

Beaulieu in the Downs
June 26th 1797

My dear Father

In consequence of order as it was supposed being restored on board the Beaulieu — rejoined according to order from the Admiralty the 24th inst a Captain Fayerman now commands the ship — I had not been on board above five hours when they mutinously demanded the release of two men from Irons who had been confined for improper conduct — with this improper demand I absolutely refused to comply — the Captain being on shore I immediately assembled the officers who readily agreed with me that should they persist — force should be used — about nine at night they assembled and were proceeding to liberate their friends. I immediately armed the

128

officers and as many marines as from situation could join. I expostulated with them on the impropriety of their conduct and exorted them to go quietly to bed and that I was determin'd to put the Fiend to death that attempted to approach near the Prisoners. They mouthed contempt — one ran with a Cutlass in his hand rushed forward and was instantly shot through the Neck by the Purser and through the body by me — this checked them for a moment when they made a second attempt and had so far succeeded as to run one of the sentinels through and seize some cutlasses. We fired again when two drop't — they fled to the Forecastle and pointed the Guns aft but before they could get them primed we attacked them so close that they fled all but one Villain who told us to shoot and be damned. I put a ball through his shoulder which quieted him — on our return to the Quarter Deck one of them who is now in Irons, hid himself behind a gun and aimed a blow at me with a Cutlass which brought me down but luckily a piece of wood turned the cutlass and the flat of it only struck me across the belly — so that I am only a little blue without being lame. At half-past ten they were intirely subdued and 13 of the Principals put in Irons. Thirteen were wounded on both sides, four of the Mutineers desperately so — the first who had the two balls lodged in him only died this morning — the others cannot live long — but above all I am concerned for the poor Sentinel who cannot live — The Officers all behaved nobly as did the Marines

Remember me to all and believe me

Yours J Burn

(addressed to Alex^r Burn, Bonnington, North Berwick)[2]

Despite this frightening episode, the men of the *Beaulieu,* under the command of Francis Fayerman, later in that year took part in Admiral Duncan's victory at Camperdown, off the river Texel. The ship was broken up in 1809.

Most famous of the Buckler's Hard ships was the *Agamemnon,* affectionately known to her crew as 'Eggs and Bacon'. Built by Henry Adams and launched on 10 April, 1781, she was a 64-gun ship with a keel length of 131ft 8in, a gun-deck 160ft long, extreme breadth 44ft 4in, draught 19ft, burthen 1376 tons. In her construction some 2,000 trees were used, and she cost about £24,000. The classification '64 guns' meant that the *Agamemnon* had 32 guns on either broadside; in addition, she carried eight small shot guns known as carronades. Her crew numbered about 450 men. Three weeks before her launch, Benjamin Caldwell had been appointed as her commander, and he remained in her for one year. The *Agamemnon* was commissioned on 28 March, the day Thomas

Hardy was appointed to her as an officer. She arrived at Portsmouth Harbour under tow on the evening of 16 April,[3] whereupon shipwrights and other skilled craftsmen began the fitting-out process. The lower masts and the bowsprits were fitted on 20 April; on 23 April the ship was docked for the bottom of the hull to be coppered, as a protection against the sea-worm, *teredo navalis*, which wreaked havoc on ships in tropical waters. On Thursday 3 May she was provisioned and four days later left the dock and tied up at a jetty. On Thursday 17 May the officers' stores were put on board; on 4 June the shingle ballast was placed in the hold. The rest of June saw both the dockyard workmen and a skeleton crew busy; the former finishing the fitments, the latter engaged in splicing ropes, washing and scraping decks, and setting up the rigging. On 4 July 200 seamen from HMS *Nonsuch* were seconded temporarily to help in readying the ship for sea. Two days later the guns were taken on board and on the following Monday, 9 July, the *Agamemnon* sailed out of Portsmouth Harbour to begin her long and illustrious career. She remained at anchor in Spithead until 16 August, during which five weeks she received her full complement of men who scraped and painted the sides of the ship. On 11 August, the crew received their bounty, at that time £3 for able seamen, and £2 for landmen. On Thursday 16 August, the *Agamemnon* moved to St Helen's Roads, and on 19 August she sailed, in company with HMS *Prothic* to the south of the Isle of Wight. They cruised off Land's End for five days before returning eastwards to Torbay where they joined a fleet of 21 ships of the line under Admiral Darby and Admiral Sir John Ross. On 13 September the fleet sailed to a new anchorage off Berry Head, and then the whole force beat up and down the Channel for more than three weeks. *Agamemnon* then returned to Spithead for alteration and repair. Dockyard labour was rowed out to the anchorage, where a considerable amount of caulking was done, especially on the second deck. The ship sailed on Sunday 2 December to join a fleet under Kempenfelt, who was later lost in the *Royal George*. Off Ushant, *Agamemnon* took part in her first action. Supplies for De Grasse, the French Admiral in the West Indies, were being sent in a large merchant convoy, escorted by 12 ships-of-the-line. Kempenfelt's fleet captured 15 French merchant ships after a fierce short encounter.

On 30 December, *Agamemnon* was back at anchor off Spithead where she remained until 6 February 1782. Then, with 12 ships-of-the-line and a convoy of merchant ships, *Agamemnon* sailed to the West Indies, and reached Barbados on 19 March, just in time to take part in the one great naval victory of the War of American Independence, the Battle of the Saints. She was part of Rodney's fleet which defeated De Grasse in a running sea fight which lasted from 9 to 12 April. *Agamemnon* remained on the West Indies station until the war ended in 1783. Then she returned home, her crew paid off, and the ship lay idle, out of commission at Chatham for ten years.

In 1793, when the war against France began, *Agamemnon* was put back into commission under a new commander, Horatio Nelson, who after years of idleness, was delighted to be on active service once more. Many of the crew came from Norfolk, Nelson's home county, for he reckoned Norfolk men were worth 'two of other men'.[4] Nelson was later to write, *I not only like the ship, but I think I am well appointed in officers, and we are manned exceedingly well.* In an earlier letter he had written, *My ship is without exception the finest 64 in the service and has the character of sailing remarkably well.* Nelson's tribute to *Agamemnon* might be explained as the fondness of the true seaman, who will always consider his ship to be the best. But long after Nelson had left her, a report in 1802 said, *Very good Road* (ie rides at anchor well); *10½ knots before the wind and rolls deep; Steers easy, more dependent on Staying than in Wearing; In a gale, easily brought to her bearings and sails 7 knots; Best sailing draft of water when victualled — afore 20ft and abaft 22ft.*[5]

● **Battle Plan of Trafalgar, 1805.** *Agamemnon* and *Euryalus* are shown in the weather column under Nelson, whilst *Swiftsure* is in the column commanded by Collingwood. There was another *Swiftsure,* built at Deptford and captured by the French in 1801, fighting in the enemy fleet

Clearly the men of Buckler's Hard had done a good job. Nelson was always to refer to *Agamemnon* as his 'favourite ship'. *Agamemnon* left Chatham on 24 April, and arrived at Spithead on 29 April. After a shake-down cruise, she left Spithead on 11 May, on what was to prove a momentous period of service. She spent three weeks on convoy duty in the Channel approaches then sailed for Gibraltar arriving on 24 June. From there, *Agamemnon* joined Hood's fleet in the siege of Toulon. Then Nelson's ship was sent to Naples, arriving there on 12 September. During the four days spent there, Nelson entertained aboard his ship the King of Naples, the Bishop of Winchester and Sir William and Lady Hamilton — his first meeting with the famous Emma. The rest of the winter was spent in the western Mediterranean. On 23 October, *Agamemnon* fought the French frigate *Melpomene* off Sardinia, but otherwise the ship was engaged in diplomatic missions, including one to Tunis. At the end of 1793, the ship was in Leghorn.

On 3 January 1794, *Agamemnon* left Leghorn and took part in the long siege which ended in the capture of Corsica in May. Then she proceeded to Calvi where on 12 July Nelson landed with some of his men to capture it. A French shell threw up sand, splinters and stones which cost Nelson the sight of his right eye. *I got a little hurt this morning,* he wrote to Hood, *not much as you may judge from my writing.* For the remainder of 1794 and the first three months of 1795, the ship was on routine cruising and convoy duty, based on Leghorn. On 13 March, as part of Admiral Hotham's force, she was on action off Genoa, against 15 French ships which were trying to recapture Corsica. In the battle two French ships-of-the-line were captured. *Agamemnon* was the first into action, and alone put the 100-gun *Ça Ira* out of control at a cost of having her sails torn to pieces, and 13 crew members wounded. In July, *Agamemnon* took part in the indecisive battle of Hyeres, again under Hotham, and then returned to Genoa for repairs to masts, yards and rigging.

In the following January *Agamemnon* joined Sir John Jervis' fleet, and spent three months standing off Toulon. At the beginning of March, a north-east gale damaged *Agamemnon*'s stern, carried away her starboard quarter-gallery, and broke her main top-mast. Once more, she had to return to Genoa for repairs. At the end of May, she saw action off Italy again, where she captured supplies en route for Napoleon's victorious armies. The British position in the Mediterranean became untenable and Jervis was ordered to withdraw his ships. *Agamemnon* was by then in poor shape — 'a tub floating on water' was Nelson's description when he reluctantly transferred his flag to the *Captain,* while Captain J S Smith took *Agamemnon* back to England for repairs.

After a Chatham refit, *Agamemnon* joined the North Sea fleet. Four years later in 1801 she was at Copenhagen for Nelson's great victory which prevented the Danish fleet from joining the French. But as *Agamemnon* ran aground early in the action, she had no active role in the battle.

Under the command of Sir Edward Berry, *Agamemnon* took part in the Battle of Trafalgar in 1805, together with the 36-gun *Euryalus* (Sir Henry Blackwood), and *Swiftsure* (William Rutherford), launched at Buckler's Hard in 1804. On 20 October 1805, the day before the battle, *Agamemnon* narrowly escaped capture whilst towing a French merchantman prize. *Agamemnon* played a full part in the action in the weather column, and ten of her crew were killed or wounded. The ship was hit near the stern, so that her pumps had to be kept going throughout the battle. The *Swiftsure* fought in the lee column, and sank the French ship *Achille. Swiftsure* lost 17 of her crew, killed or wounded, and suffered damage to masts and rigging. The *Euryalus* became known as 'Nelson's watch dog' for it was she who, off Cadiz harbour, first detected Villeneuve's preparations for putting to sea. During the battle, *Euryalus* acted as the signal ship for Collingwood when his ship, the *Royal Sovereign,* lost her masts. The dispatch of the news of Nelson's death, sent to England by Collingwood, was also written in *Euryalus.*

• **Model of** *Euryalus*

Agamemnon was sent to the West Indies in 1806; in 1807 she was in action off Copenhagen; then, after taking part in the siege in Lisbon, she sailed for South America on 13 March 1808. She grounded on 16 June 1809 at the entrance to the river Plate where her bottom was pierced by her own anchor.

The *Swiftsure* served in the Mediterranean, and then was in the West Indies at the end of the war. In 1816 she became a hulk in Portsmouth harbour, and was used as a gunnery target for a short time in 1845.

The *Euryalus* saw action in the Baltic and in the Mediterranean, and finished the war in North America. She was in the West Indies from 1818 to 1821, and then in the Mediterranean until 1825, when she was paid off at Chatham. *Euryalus* was renamed as *Africa* and was used as a convict ship, first at Chatham from 1826 to 1844, and then in Gibraltar from 1845 to 1859.

The careers of the Buckler's Hard ships matched their builders'; after the first decade of the 19th century the great days were at an end.

Was their construction worthwhile? Expenditure of so large a proportion of the gross national product, the use of precious timber and rare skill on these ships, drained the country's resources, and retarded the rise in the standard of living of the British people. But the ships played a vital part in Britain's mastery of the seas, and helped to establish her trade, thus affording prosperity and employment. Buckler's Hard was no framer of national policy: it simply played an important part in the implementation of London-made decisions.

References

[1] *Journal of Thomas Frederick*, February 1793 - March 1795
[2] Scottish Record Office GD 51/2/1053/2
[3] NMM Greenwich *Log of Agamemnon*
[4] Carola Oman *Nelson* (London 1947) pp 115-185; R H Mackenzie *The Trafalgar Roll* (London 1913); Oliver Warner *Nelson's Battles* (Newton Abbot 1965)
[5] NMM Greenwich *Observations of the Qualities of HMS Agamemnon*, 29 April 1802

12 Rural Retreat

DURING THE SECOND HALF of the 19th century, Buckler's Hard became a comparative backwater, as the new industries gravitated towards towns. The Industrial Revolution ushered in an age when larger work units required larger workforces, thus causing the decline of rural crafts. Wooden shipbuilding sites in the country fell into disuse, as new and larger shipyards opened in towns. Hampshire shipbuilding concentrated on Southampton and Cowes, at the expense of the Beaulieu and Hamble rivers, of Hythe and Eling and Redbridge.

The year 1850 is a watershed in British social history; the population was in a state of equipoise, half living in towns, half in the countryside. Thereafter, the number of townsmen grew.

At the death of Edward Adams in 1849, Buckler's Hard comprised 36 dwelling units, of which one only was unoccupied. By then the village had already begun to shrink, as three houses had been demolished in 1840. Near the road to Beaulieu there were seven houses of which none now remains. In 1845 those seven houses were inhabited by the families of men engaged in agriculture. Six families lived in Back Street, the 'disappeared' terrace further east; one of those houses had become the village shop, another was occupied by Martha Burlace, widow of a shipwright. All the inhabitants were dependent on shipbuilding and allied trades, or on farming, forestry and fishing; all were to find employment difficult during the second half of the 19th century. But the village was saved from extinction as it was part of a manorial estate in which a limited number of 'service' jobs were always necessary. So Buckler's Hard shrank, but survived.

These figures taken from the Enumerator's Census returns, show the drift away from the countryside then,

	1841	1851	1891	1901	1911	1921	1931
Beaulieu, including Buckler's Hard	1259	1177	864	833	986	1011	1201
Exbury, with Lepe	402	384	329	293	244	350	368

The population decline was arrested after the 1914-1918 war with the development of motor transport. Until then the whole of the region became a backwater, with horse, water-ferry, or shanks's pony the inhabitant's only transport.

● Lord Henry Scott (1832-1905), later First Baron Montagu of Beaulieu, was the grandfather of the present Lord Montagu

The owner of the Beaulieu river in 1850 was the present Lord Montagu's great-grandfather, Walter Francis, the fifth Duke of Buccleuch, who gave the Manor to his second son, Henry Scott, in 1867. During this period, the economy of the river was at a low ebb. In 1850 he financed a scheme for the emigration of some of the tenants of his estates, including Beaulieu, to South Africa, an idea consonant with national policy, in which the Empire was seen as a safety-valve, or as a land of opportunity for those who could not make a living in Britain. In conjunction with Lascelles, ancestor of the present Lord Harewood, the Duke of Buccleuch arranged for 40 of his tenants, comprising 13 adult males and their families, to join a larger party of settlers on the 500-ton vessel, the *Lady Bruce*. The ship left London on 16 February, 1850, and put into Portsmouth to collect the Duke's settlers and their stores. The colonists venturing from the Beaulieu river left Buckler's Hard in a barge, the *John Samuel*. They had their first excitement when the master of the barge, Collins, grounded his vessel on the Gilbury shore. Eventually, the settlers left Portsmouth on 25 February, 1850, and arrived in Natal on 8 May. The Duke supported his former tenants generously; he paid their passage, gave them an outfit allowance, provided ox-wagons from port to settlement, paid survey fees, and supplied tents, seeds and other useful items, and a sum of money to last them for one year. The settlers founded a colony known as Beaulieu, later changed to Richmond, probably after the Duke's house in Surrey. Richmond, South Africa, was visited by Edward, third Baron Montagu, in 1959, and he found several Beaulieu names in the churchyard there.[1] Among those who emigrated to South Africa on that voyage were Charles Bound, John Crouch with wife and four children, William Crouch with wife and three children, and James and Henry Westbrook.

The shipyard at Buckler's Hard died slowly. Edward Adams' widow and executors leased the yard until her death in 1852. After a 12-month void, William Scanes took over the lease of the shipyard in 1853, at a rental of £6 per annum, but continued as landlord of the New inn until 1857, when he moved to the Master Builder's House. That year he did not renew the shipyard lease but took it over again in 1858 at £12 per annum including the house. From 1858 to 1872 Scanes had a continuity of tenure of both house and shipyard for which he was paying £18 a year at the end. He was perhaps a descendant of the first Buckler's Hard watchman in the 1720s, but there were many different families of that name, spelt variously Scaines or Scanes. William Scanes married Elizabeth Picket in 1823; in the 1851 census he was described as a licensed victualler, aged 48. He had no children, and his household comprised, in addition to himself and his wife, his father-in-law, Thomas Picket, his nephew, Walter Snook, and two servants. He did not build or repair craft, for he was no trained shipwright, but there were other Scanes' who were. Richard Scanes was a shipwright under Henry Adams in 1755, whilst a John Scanes served Edward Adams in 1813. His son Henry moved to the Isle of Dogs when Buckler's Hard declined. In 1870 a George Scanes, described as a shipwright of Poplar, Middlesex, married a Beaulieu girl. The Scanes' migration was typical; shipwrights who had formerly plied their trade there sought work elsewhere. The Blaker brothers moved to Southampton; Charles Glastonbury worked, perhaps at Deptford, until he retired to Buckler's Hard. In 1851 his wife lived in Buckler's Hard, and had five lodgers, four fishermen and one sailmaker. Glastonbury had married Frances Williams in 1811, and eventually became Edward Adams' foreman. It is possible that, at an advanced age, he also ran the yard for Scanes, but the work would have been only the maintenance and repair of small craft. He was remembered by locals as always wearing a top hat. But Glastonbury's son George, also a trained shipwright, was working in Stepney as early as 1844, when he married a Beaulieu girl. Another former Buckler's Hard shipwright, Benjamin Fielder, also moved, as did the younger Wests, a long-established local family. In 1851 Joseph West, then aged 73, was the only Buckler's Hard resident who was a shipwright, for the younger Richard West, who had married Glastonbury's daughter Elizabeth in 1837, was another shipwright who had moved away. Thus the general picture is of the dispersal of the trained labour force, not only of shipwrights, but of sawyers also. From 1851 onwards Buckler's Hard was inhabited by labourers and the occasional fisherman or estate worker. As Clobb Farm nearby had no houses for farm workers, Buckler's Hard became a predominantly agricultural community.

Scanes died in 1872, whereupon blacksmith Frederick Buckle leased the Master Builder's House, the shipyard, and the east timber yard, by the river side, until 1883. Buckle was no shipbuilder so presumably he used the premises for other than its real purpose. When the new owner of the Manor, Lord Henry Scott, needed repairs done to his steamboat, they were carried out at White's yard at Cowes. The task certainly would have been done on the Beaulieu river had it been possible.

By the early 1890s the Reverend G N Godwin described Buckler's Hard as a 'deserted shipyard' in which only mounds remained where the forge and other workshops once stood, and where the sound of the adze was no longer to be heard.[2] The closure of the shipyard led inevitably to the decline of the blacksmith's shop, which shut its doors in 1885. The two inns, the New and the Ship, suffered the same fate; there were no thirsty shipwrights and sawyers, and grand launchings to consume hogsheads of ale. Moreover, the attack on the consumption of alcohol, led by the Victorian middle classes, who regarded drink as the curse of the labouring population, was having effect nationwide. Instead of ale, Buckler's Hard inhabitants could read edifying books, issued free from Gosling's shop. In 1886 a reading room was established at Buckler's Hard.

The end of shipbuilding at Buckler's Hard coincided with the beginning of a decline in agriculture. British farmers, who had anticipated ruin when the Corn Laws were repealed in 1846, had enjoyed a temporary reprieve in the 1850s. Then in about 1873, the so-called Great Depression began, to last for the remainder of the 19th century. This long-term downward trend depressed profits, interest rates, rents, and prices, and affected the landord, and the farming community more than the town artisan. The economy of the river, which had rested so long on the twin pillars of shipbuilding and agriculture, had to suffer a profound change.

Little could be done to stimulate other kinds of employment although the development of the coastguard service led to some building on the river. At the end of the Napoleonic wars, a coastguard station had been developed at Lepe, and another at Pitt's Deep, near Sowley. In 1850 Henry Pocock, the steward, agreed to build a boathouse 32ft long, 10ft broad, and 6ft high for the customs at Pitt's Deep. Six years later, the Admiralty mooted the idea of building a new coastguard station at Need's Ore Point, immediately upstream of Bull's Lake. It was customary for a coastguard vessel to be moored in the Solent, and the Admiralty wanted a sheltered mooring, access to fresh water, and houses for men. Captain Balfour wrote to the Duke of Buccleuch, and after prolonged negotiations, an agreement was signed.[3] The site was ideal. Much later John, 2nd Baron Montagu, established a nature reserve there; today it is a grade I National Nature Reserve, where the cry of the sea-birds drowns the noise of the waves.

Work in 1857 began on the coastguard cottages which were completed in 1860. Eight cottages were built of local brick at the Duke of Buccleuch's expense to specifications laid down by Admiralty. The lessee had asked for downstairs rooms to be 14ft long, with pantry and kitchen adjoining, and with two bedrooms in each unit. In addition, there was to be a washhouse and two communal privvies.[4] As boring for spring water was unsuccessful, it had to be brought by lighter from Portsmouth Dockyard, to be stored in two large reservoirs; in addition a large tank was provided to catch rain-water. The cottages at Need's Ore were occupied by coastguards in 1860, when the Admiralty took over a 21-year lease for them at £68 5s a year plus £2 10s for the reservoirs. The coastguard stations at Need's Ore, and at Lepe, were closed in 1922, but the cottages remain.

In 1867 Lord Henry Scott, later first Baron Montagu of Beaulieu, acquired Beaulieu and its river from his father. His accession inaugurated a new era, as he made Beaulieu his home and began a far-sighted policy of reorganisation and revival. Lord Henry was a Member of Parliament, and a man of ideas. Between 1867 and his death in 1905, the manor was developed into a paternal estate, and attempts were made to find employment for the villagers. By the time of his inheritance, another of the old riverside industries, salt-making, had ended. The salterns at Gins, which had been developed and extended during the eighteenth-century, and which brought in an annual rental of £20 a year, had ceased operation by the beginning of the 19th century, long before the abolition of the salt tax in 1825 put an end to other local salterns at Lymington and Fawley.

Brickmaking, however, was still going on. In 1790 a new brickyard had been established at Bailey's Hard, where so-called 'white' bricks were made. At first this brickyard was leased out to a private company, but in 1828 it was taken over by the manor of Beaulieu, and remained as part of the industrial activities of the estate until 1877. During the 1840's and 1850's a considerable quantity of Bailey's Hard bricks were used in the building of Southampton Docks, and in the construction of the Eye Hospital in Bedford Place, Southampton; other consignments were sent to Portsmouth, London and Newcastle. To facilitate the movement of clay from Coles Coppice, a tramway was laid in 1855, the line of which ran diagonally across the present road to Bailey's Hard. In

140

addition to bricks, the yard also made tiles, drain pipes, and flowerpots. By 1877 it was moribund, and the agent advertised for a tenant. In the following year W Beauchamp Marshall took over the brickyard at an annual rent of £50, in addition to £1 a year for the cottage and garden on the site. Marshall himself became the tenant of Whitehall, previously occupied by the curate, and thus became the first 'residential tenant' in the village of Beaulieu. Marshall continued to run the brickyard until 1890; the tramway from Seville's Wood to Bailey's Hard was still in use and he added a smaller brickmaking unit at Oxley's on the eastern side of the River. However, Marshall was unable to make the brickworks profitable. Despite the natural advantages of the site, the accessible fuel and raw materials, water transport, and a helpful landlord, there were problems. As the topsoil was not removed from around the claypits in Seville's Wood, the clay diggings were forever falling in; the clay in the main pit at the end of the tramway proved unsuitable, and other pits had to be used, with the material taken in carts to the brickyard; the yard was not closely supervised so that the work force was not efficient. There is a story that small casks of beer were smuggled into the yard, and consumed during working hours.

When Marshall gave up the lease of the brickworks in 1890 it was taken over by Elliott Brothers of Southampton. They surrendered the tenancy in 1903, and, at the death of Lord Henry in 1905, it was once again in the hands of the Estate.

This activity at Bailey's Hard was matched by another brickyard, at Lower Exbury, at the head of St Catherine's Creek. Camden's *Britannia* of 1806 refers to Mr Wood making bricks there, and it is probable that Exbury bricks were used in 1788 when Henry Holland made alterations to Broadlands House, Romsey. Bricks from Exbury yard were also sent to Southampton during the dock-building, and to London, by sea. The two brickworks added to the river traffic, as chalk was imported from Fareham and Littlehampton. The Exbury brickyard, however, was almost moribund by 1905.

Although there was no longer so great a demand, or indeed so proliferous a supply, of hard timber from the manor of Beaulieu, in the new age of iron and steel, some revenue was brought in by the sale of pit props. Some fir was sent to Poole in 1867, and in 1874 40,000 props went to the Tyne, costing more than £600. Posts and fencing wood were despatched to Portsmouth, Richmond, and Scotland. During this period three ships, *Amy, Invicta* and the *Two*

Brothers were busily engaged in this trade. In addition, bark for tanners was sent from Carpenter's Dock to Edinburgh, in the *Indian Queen,* the *Sylphide,* and the *Richard and Elizabeth*.

An attempt was made to bring in some revenue from the fish in the river and a plan for the breeding of oysters was conceived. There had always been small beds of oysters in the river near Need's Ore where marine conditions suited them. It had been the practice hitherto for oyster catching to be leased to an individual for a yearly payment. From the 1830's the river had been rented to Henry Abinett, formerly of Kent, and David Thomas Alston for £35 a year. Alston, a Gosport man, moved to Buckler's Hard in order to manage the business. He and Abinett had the sole right to catch fish on the river; they employed Thomas Martin, and then his son William, as foreman. By 1867 both partners had died, but Alston's widow still rented the 'river'.

In 1869 Henry Scott took over the river himself to breed fish and oysters for which purpose he consulted marine biologists and French breeders. Ten years later he had two large rectangular oyster beds lined with tiles dug out downstream of Buckler's Hard, near Clobb Copse with banks and sluices controlling the water flow and level. W W Batten, of Portswood, Southampton, was given the contract for the work, completed in a year, at a cost of £823 2s 4d.[5]

In 1880 Henry entered into a partnership with Major Alexander Boyle, of Cowes, who owned oyster beds in Newtown, Isle of Wight, and along the coast at Fishbourne. Their partnership, known as the Newtown and Beaulieu Oyster Fishery Company, leased the new beds at Clobb at a rental of £40 a year together with a consignment of oysters which at that time fetched between 22s and 35s a thousand. They could be sent by rail to London from either Beaulieu Road or Portsmouth stations. The association of the Montagus of Beaulieu with the Newton Company was to be revived by Edward, third Baron Montagu of Beaulieu; the Newtown Company paid £250 a year in rent in the 1970's.

In the 1880s Beaulieu oysters were considered a delicacy. Some were exhibited in the Oyster Competition at the Great International Fisheries Exhibition, held at the Royal Horticultural Gardens in Exhibition Road, London in 1883 for which the Newtown Company was awarded a medal, now on display in Palace House. But they gave more pleasure to the gourmets than to the accountants. Even in the 1890s, after considerable expenditure each year, Lord Henry's annual consignment averaged only some £200.

Both Lord Henry and Major Boyle were amateur businessmen, with insufficient knowledge of oyster breeding. The former, as an MP, had to spend many days away from Beaulieu, and, although he visited the oyster ponds on the Beaulieu River at least once a week when he was home, there was a need for daily supervision. Also, Henry Scott visited Arcachon in 1881, studied their breeding technique, and bought French oysters which did not thrive in the Solent. Major Boyle was a little more knowledgeable, and visited the Newton beds twice a week, but he still went to Monte Carlo, or shooting with Major Forster at Lepe. Since Lord Henry and Boyle did not always see eye to eye, they indulged in an acrimonious correspondence. In April 1881 Boyle, thoroughly put out by an 'execrably managed shoot' at Exbury, wrote scathingly about the new oyster beds on the Beaulieu River, *I thought a battery was being created from the appearance of the stuff taken out. The planking is three feet deep and depth about four feet. This is absurd, and only a collector of mud and sand and will require cleaning every week. One foot of water is ample over oysters.* At the end of 1881 the Company had sold £40 worth of oysters, after an outlay of £2,000.

• Henry, first Baron Montagu of Beaulieu, built the oyster beds below Buckler's Hard, and founded the Newtown Oyster Company. During the 1939-1945 war, a concrete floating dock and parts of Mulberry Harbour were built there

In 1882 Lord Henry and Boyle had a fierce disagreement about the workmen at Newtown, formerly Boyle's employees, whom Henry distrusted. He insisted that the foreman, Mursell, should be brought to trial for stealing copper from a barge. Mursell, according to Lord Henry, was a robber and a rogue, who was feathering the nests of all his relations in St. Helen's. Mursell was later acquitted after a trial at Winchester, due to lack of evidence, and Boyle's ambilavence, at a cost to the Company of a further £100. In 1883 the prospects were no better. Anticipating a meeting of the directors of the Company, Lord Henry wrote, *Not a pleasant prospect. No funds . . . and but few oysters to sell this year or next.* Later, the partnership with Boyle was dissolved. Beaulieu Oyster beds provided delicacies for the local well-to-do, including the reverend Powles, but little profit.

If the river failed to make profits, at least it was a source of pleasure to the owner, his family and friends. As road transport was still primitive, Lord Henry Scott used the river en route to the Isle of Wight, Portsmouth, Exbury and Lepe. He also sailed for pleasure, and was the owner of a succession of steam launches. In 1869 he bought *Zenobia*, built by White of Cowes; she was a 16-ton steam launch, 60ft long, with a bunker capacity of three tons of coal. Her 12 hp engines gave a maximum speed of 12½ knots. Henry sold this vessel in 1872 to the Prince of Wales, (the future King Edward VII) for £1,000, but the boat was handed over before payment, which was a long time coming. After he had used the boat for several weeks, the Prince complained that the boilers were defective. Henry, perhaps in desperation, agreed to have them repaired at a cost of £150 when he received the purchase money. Henry owned *Osprey* for travelling, and *Dabchick* and *Heron* for sailing. In 1884 he was elected to the Royal Yacht Squadron, by then a coveted social cachet in part engendered by the presence at Cowes Week of the Prince of Wales. In the 1890's he raced regularly with the Hythe Sailing Club, then run by the redoubtable Sir Robert Hobart, who lived at Langdown, and with the Calshot Castle Sailing Club.

The development of the steam pleasure yacht led to visits to Beaulieu by distinguished guests: the Princess of Wales, the future Queen Alexandra, came in a steam launch, accompanied by Napoleon's wife, Empress Eugenie, in 1871; Frederick William, Crown Prince of Germany in 1881, and Alfred Lord Tennyson, the Poet Laureate, who travelled from his home in the Isle of Wight two years later. In 1902, King Edward VII landed at Buckler's Hard and was taken for his first drive as King, a visit commemorated by a stone still to be seen near the present jetty.

The last decade of Henry's ownership saw the beginning of popular tourism in the Beaulieu river. His plans in the 1880s for a railway line to Lepe and the building of an embarkation port for Cowes had come to nothing, largely due to opposition from Southampton business interests. But his own river was one of natural scenic beauty, and he was receptive to approaches made to him in September 1893 by the Gosport Steam Launch Company. Mr Sutton visited Palace House with a proposition: that the owner of Beaulieu should provide landing facilities on the river to which the Company would bring excursionists, who would pay landing fees. In April 1894 Lord Henry took the directors to Buckler's Hard which all agreed would be the most suitable landing place. A pier was built there at a cost of £150; in addition labour had to be paid for collecting the landing fees. The Gosport Company ran excursions on Saturdays, bank holidays, and mid-week in the summer but Sunday trips were forbidden by Lord Henry. Operations began in June 1894; between then and October 1,115 adults and 84 children landed at Buckler's Hard. Tolls of two-pence per adults and a penny for each child produced an income of less than £10 against weekly labour charges of two pounds. In 1896 3,637 adults and 212 children paid £31 in pier tolls; in 1903 the total receipts were £24 8s 1d, and in 1907 £44 12s 7d. In 1896 the return fare from Gosport to Buckler's Hard was 1s 8d — then a sizeable proportion of the weekly wage of the working classes. Such excursions, therefore, were special treats, not to be undertaken often by the family man. In 1906 John, Lord Montagu, who was not inhibited by sabbatarian principles, allowed Sunday trips, essential in an age when Saturday morning work was the rule. Then, and later, the Gosport Company were able to run the occasional trip in the reverse direction, taking Beaulieu people to Southsea or to Cowes for the firework display which traditionally brought the Cowes yachting week to an end in early August. People on the western side of the Beaulieu river joined the vessel at Buckler's Hard whilst a boatman from Exbury rowed passengers from that side of the river across from Gilbury Hard, at a penny a head.

If the day trips from Gosport and Ryde were not great money-spinners, at least they enriched the lives of Buckler's Hard people by ending their sense of isolation. About 2,000 excursionists came each year, a meagre influx by modern standards, but even this modest number caused A G Renshaw, who married Major Forster's widow, to write the following lines at Lepe House — in 1894 — the first year of the excursions,

> . . . these days of ease and wealth
> Find thee frequented but for sport and health;
> Now, in the evening cool, or moontide hot,
> Here plies the rower and here sails the yacht.
> And sometimes come — I wish they'd keep away —
> Excursionists from Ryde, to spend the day.

Upkeep of the river was expensive, considering the small return. Of the 85 men employed by the Beaulieu estate in 1885, eight were involved with the river. One was the head fisherman, Richard Barkham, and another five were continuously employed in fighting the erosion of the river banks, and the consequent flooding of the water-meadows. Sea defence had always been a problem for farms bordering the river.

● During the early decades of the present century, excursions were organised by the Gosport steam ferry company. The steamers took passengers to Southsea and to the Isle of Wight. This photograph was taken by Edward Mudge, of Fawley in about 1930

Four years earlier the foreman of the gang was 64-year-old Thomas Cox, who was paid £41 12s 0d a year, and his four labourers a total of £166 8s a year, wages which compared favourably with those of unskilled labour elsewhere. The men also enjoyed fringe benefits: for example, their weekly rent for a cottage was a shilling a week, and their widows were given a pension of about eight shillings a week at a time when there was no state insurance. If the employees lived to old age, they also received a pension from the estate. The ravages of nature afforded employment to some who, in earlier times, would have been at work in the shipyard, for among the men who worked under Thomas Cox were George Rawlence and William Reynard, descendants of inhabitants of Buckler's Hard in the 1800's.

The problem of erosion was eased, but not solved, by a botanical evolutionary process. As early as 1840, the suggestion had been made that reeds should be imported from the sand-dunes of the Netherlands, where they helped to bind the banks. This proved unnecessary as, in about 1850, a plant now known as *Spartina Townsendii,* or rice grass, mysteriously appeared in the Southampton water. By 1870, it had spread from Poole to Chichester, and was proliferating in the Beaulieu river. This plant, which grows to its full height of between two and four feet, has a yellow-brown flower in the summer, after which the grass turns yellow in the spring. It had the effect of binding the mud banks, and helped to prevent erosion. Its sudden appearance sired many a local legend. One such was that parasite seeds had blown into the sea from a ship returning home from the far east, its alleged home. However, it was not imported, as there is no other such specie anywhere in the world. Lord Henry Scott Montagu was one of the first to recognise its value. He consulted botanical experts who judged that the specie probably evolved through the accidental hybridisation of other types of spartina, the *Spartina stricta* and the *Spartina alterniflora.* Modern experts have discovered, however, that from about 1892, a second new specie, which produced seeds and spread rapidly, also made its appearance. This has been called *Spartina Anglicana.* Lord Henry wrote articles about the new specie, and in 1898 he effected plantations on the river banks to aid its growth. For the next 40 years it became the object of attention of scientists and conservationists alike: modest sums were even paid by the Dutch and some English river owners, for a few tons of Beaulieu spartina grass.

Apart from these problems, Henry, first Baron Montagu, had also to deal with the Civil Service. When the Board of Admiralty transferred its rights over foreshores and coastlines to the newly-formed Board of Trade, that department promptly claimed all rights in the Beaulieu river. In 1872, Lord Montagu acted with speed and decision. Lawyers were briefed, King John's charter was invoked, and the threatened take-over was aborted. But although the Board's frontal attack had failed, officials still tried infiltration. When flotsam and jetsam was washed up on the river bank, coastguards at Need's Ore Point recovered it, and reported to the Receiver of Wrecks in Southampton, whose right to dispose of it Lord Henry Montagu successfully contested in 1890. The station officer at Need's Ore Point wrote to Lord Montagu as follows, *The general custom is that all wreckage etc drifting on shore is taken charge of by the coastguard (acting for the Board of Trade) and immediately reported to the Receiver of Wrecks at Southampton. I shall report in this instance to the Receiver of Wrecks that, acting upon your rights and privileges as Lord of the Manor you claim this cask if not owned.*[6]

Lord Montagu had detailed two of his river men to retrieve planks and casks ahead of the coastguards, thus bringing the matter into the open. The Receiver of Wrecks, however, did not yield gracefully. When a small vessel was wrecked, he attempted to charge Lord Montagu instead of the owners for its disposal. This ploy failed similarly. Lord Montagu pointed out that he had only to tow the wreck into the Solent, where it would no longer be his responsibility.

Ownership of the river, however prestigious, had brought Lord Montagu no financial relief. Despite all efforts, he had been unable to find a new and meaningful role for Buckler's Hard or for the river. The former was by then in a state of decay, and the latter source of pleasure but little profit.

References

[1] H E R Widnell, *The Beaulieu Record,* p 242; J Clark, *Natal Settler — Agent* p 235
[2] G N Godwin, *Buckler's Hard: a deserted Shipyard; Hampshire Notes and Queries* Vol V, 1890 p 92)
[3] Beaulieu Muniments: EIII/H3+EIII/LE88+95
[4] BM EIII/LE8
[5] BM EIII/FS3
[6] BM EIII/RV9

13 The Wind of Change

JOHN SUCCEEDED HIS FATHER in 1905 as the second Lord Montagu, inheriting a large estate with a relatively small income. He himself was concerned with national affairs, both in the House of Lords and in the world of motoring. He founded *The Car Illustrated*, which entailed his spending much time in London. He had to formulate a policy to make Beaulieu economically viable, which his agent, Gerard Morgan, had to implement.

Yachting was becoming increasingly popular, and the rich sought houses with sea or river frontages. Some superior houses were built, on 99-year leases, but not at Buckler's Hard.

John Montagu's love of cars and engineering have overshadowed his maritime interests. He was a good swimmer, keen fisherman, and ardent yachtsman. In 1877, aged 11, he went with his father on a cruise in HMS *Hawk* from Hythe to the Scillies. Four years later, as a boy of 15, he crept out of his bedroom window in Palace House at dawn, walked to Buckler's Hard, and satisfied an ambition by sailing round the Isle of Wight in a small dinghy. While an undergraduate at New College, Oxford, he stroked his college eight and rowed at Henley. He was an expert fisherman, both with rod and net, and was a lifelong member of the Fly Fisher's Club. Even in middle age, when he had to deliver a lecture in Lymington, he travelled by boat from Buckler's Hard to Pitt's Deep, and thence by road, returning by the same route.[1] In his younger days, John Montagu had a racing yacht, *Siola*, and later a 24-ton yawl motor yacht, *Ytene*, launched in 1910. The latter was requisitioned in 1915 for use by the Royal Naval Boat Reserve. In addition, Lord Montagu owned a 4-ton motor launch, *Wild Duck*, a 5-ton cutter, *Cygnet*, and the *Ping-Pong*. In 1922, he bought a 17-ton motor cruiser, built at Hampton-on-Thames, also given the name of *Cygnet*.

The development of the marine engine at the turn of the century led to a new kind of seafaring, and John Montagu became a pioneer in motor boat racing.

In 1903 he watched motor boat racing in South Wales, and returned determined to engage in the sport. He got in touch with his friend, Lionel de Rothschild, one of the family of merchant bankers, with a view to the joint purchase of a boat. In 1904 they bought *Napier II* from S F Edge, and won the channel motor race in her. In August, over lunch, the two men formulated plans to build a new boat, and work began on it in December. The new boat was not ready for the 1905 season, during which Montagu and de Rothschild continued to race *Napier II* with great success, culminating in a victory in an international boat race in September. In 1906 their new boat, *Yarrow-Napier* swept rivals aside. In addition to winning several races in England, including that for the Enchantress Cup, *Yarrow-Napier* represented Great Britain in the Alfred Harmsworth Trophy Race, held off Bordeaux, and covered the course of 30 nautical miles in one hour 32 minutes to win. Thereafter, he was too busy to continue motor boat racing, so Lionel de Rothschild bought his share in the boat, and renamed it *Flying Fish*. In 1907 de Rothschild won an international race in the Mediterranean, and then, like his friend, gave up competitive motor boat racing.

● *Yarrow-Napier II* **off Arcachon, near Bordeaux, September 1905, with John, 2nd Baron Montagu at the helm**

Lionel de Rothschild's migration to the Beaulieu River meant that there were four men of wealth in the region interested in sailing — himself, John Montagu, Harry Forster, and Sir Fisher Dilke. Harry Forster (1866-1936), who had married John Montagu's sister Rachel, had inherited the Manor of Exbury from his father, Major John Forster, who had bought it from the Mitfords in 1879. After a distinguished political career, H W Forster was raised to the peerage in 1919, as Baron Forster of Lepe, having forsaken the manor house at Exbury for a home at Lepe, overlooking the sea. The old Ship inn had been enlarged and beautified into a residence befitting one who loved the sea. He lost both his sons in the 1914-1918 war, and this led to his sale of Exbury to Lionel de Rothschild, a regular visitor to the Beaulieu river from 1905 onwards. In 1914 he leased Inchmery House from Forster, and bought the freehold two years later.[2] In May 1916 he bought Exbury House, then tenanted by Major Cyril Potter, from Forster, and then purchased the Manor of Exbury in March 1919. To the eastward of Dark Water, there was a large white house, now demolished, called Solent Cottage, which was the home of Sir Fisher Dilke; he also was a keen yachtsman. All four were members of the Royal Yacht Squadron.

• John, 2nd Baron Montagu of Beaulieu (1866-1929), father of the present Lord Montagu. John's motoring achievements are well known – but he was also a pioneer of motor-boat racing

Lord Forster built a small jetty off Gipsy Lane, whence he regularly sailed in his motor-launch *Miramar*, whilst Lionel de Rothschild constructed a pier at Gilbury for his motor yacht, *Rhodora*, appropriately named after his favourite botanical specie. The building of Gilbury Pier, begun in June 1925, led to a small ripple in the smooth relations between the two estates, as de Rothschild had neglected to ask permission. He was told that although 'Lord Montagu is delighted that the pier is being built', the river bed which it impinged upon belonged to the Manor of Beaulieu. A very reasonable charge of 2s 6d a year was levied to maintain manorial rights.

The incidence of Cowes Week led to royal visits to Buckler's Hard. In 1926 Lord and Lady Montagu lunched aboard *Victoria and Albert*, after which Queen Mary came across the Solent in *Cygnet*, and landed at Buckler's Hard, the first of her three visits. She came again in 1927 and 1928, accompanied this time by the Duke of Kent, and took tea at Buckler's Hard.

In 1936, seven years after the death of Lord John Montagu, his widow, Pearl, married the honourable Edward Pleydell-Bouverie, at that time Commander of *Victoria and Albert*. In 1937 the royal yacht anchored off Need's Ore, and Queen Elizabeth landed, with her two daughters, Elizabeth and Margaret. The royal party were able to relax on Park Shore away from the public gaze. On this occasion, Queen Elizabeth surprised the occupants of Need's Ore cottages by visiting them. The tradition of royal visitors, begun by Frederick, Prince of Wales in 1750, had continued for two centuries.

From 1905 onwards there was demand for moorings and other facilities from owners of pleasure craft who did not live in Beaulieu. Moreover, as the river was privately owned, it was within the legal rights of the Manor of Beaulieu to charge for entry to the river. Thus standard charges were published annually. A few moorings were put down in the river's upper tidal reaches and in 1911 Drummond of Cadland was allowed to put down moorings between Lepe and Inchmery. Lord de la Warr, conveniently placed as the tenant of Inchmery, with a good view of the river traffic, was given the responsibility for the general oversight of moorings. At Buckler's Hard Jim Thomas, who was Lord Montagu's boatman, lived in the by-then dilapidated Ship Builder's House, and became unofficial harbour master.

Excursions for day trippers to Buckler's Hard remained the

monopoly of the Gosport Steam Ferry Company. John, Lord Montagu, had lifted his father's sabbatarian restrictions so that Sunday tours could be run. Other boat owners, including R H Collard, based at Southampton, tried to organise trips to the Beaulieu river before 1914; all were warned off by the ever-vigilant agent, Gerard Morgan.

The pre-war increase in yachtsmen and excursionists at least had one beneficial effect on Buckler's Hard. Hitherto villagers had to walk to St Leonard's, a mile away, to the nearest letter box. In 1909 Morgan used the needs of the visitors to persuade the postmaster at Lymington to instal a letter box at Buckler's Hard.

● **Queen Mary leaving Beaulieu for Cowes, in Lord Montagu's motor-yacht** *Cygnet* **in August 1926**

Between 1918 and 1939 the number of people able to engage in pleasure sailing vastly increased, with a comparable proliferation of small craft. The development of the motor car and improvement in roads enabled sportsmen to reach their boats, to sail them for an afternoon's pleasure, and return home in the evening. The river, hitherto the venue for commercial craft, fishermen in row boats, and the occasional fowler with his blunderbuss in a punt, became an attraction for the amateur yachtsman.

Beaulieu moved with the times. The Beaulieu River Sailing Club was formed in 1931, with Pearl, Lady Montagu, in the chair.[3] In January 1932, the BRSC took a lease on Buckler's Hard quay for a peppercorn rent, and agreed to pay part of the repairs necessary to make it usable. There they remained until 1936. In 1936 pontoons presented by Sir Francis Dent were moved to Gins Farm, and the BRSC paid a moiety of the cost of the upkeep of the gravel road, assessed at £10. However, though Gins became the sailing centre, Buckler's Hard remained the Club's headquarters until the outbreak of war in 1939. In the late 1930s, the grass running down to the river was known as Squadron Lawn and was kept mown. There, on fine afternoons in the summer, many a happy occasion was attended by members and their families. In those days, the competitive spirit was not as great as in today's world. Among the suggestions for a race in the 1930s was one to start at Lepe in the morning, break for lunch at Buckler's Hard; then sail to Beaulieu, followed by a break for tea, and then a return to Buckler's Hard.

At first the BRSC used scows; then international sharpies until 1932 when it was decided to have a new class specially built to suit the Beaulieu river, designed and built by Elkins, of Lymington, at a cost of £49 each, called the 'Montagu sharpie'. These boats, sturdy yet fast, with a cover-combing forward, a deep keel, and simple sails, were ideal for the river in the days when there was little instruction on 'capsize-drills' and lifejackets were not always worn. In 1939 a modified version came into existence, with a mast 19ft above the deck, with sails made of Egyptian cotton by Tillings of Southampton. The sharpies were to be built either by Elkins, who had moved to Christchurch, or by the Rampart Boat Building Company. Unfortunately, this new design coincided with the outbreak of war. Many members of the BRSC were called up for the armed forces, and on 3 September 1939 the Admiralty decreed that no boats were to sail south of Need's Ore without a pilot. In 1940, the year of Hitler's projected invasion, all boats had to be

154

removed from the Beaulieu river. Some 48 boats belonging to club members were stored under shrubs in the gardens of Palace House, and were still serviceable five years later.

It was symptomatic of a new economic climate that after 1918 the owners of the Beaulieu river owned no commercial craft. The last such vessel was the *Henry Stevenson*, a 50-ton ketch, built at Topsham in 1872, and bought by John Montagu for £50 in 1910. Wrecked entering the Beaulieu river in 1916, she was not replaced.[4] During the 1914-1918 war Buckler's Hard once more became a shipbuilding village, as an emergency site for Fairmile motor boat building. When the war ended, this activity ended also.

By 1918, road transport had replaced water transport for the carrying of grain, so that the corn jetties, once used by the farmers, had decayed. Nor was there a chance of capitalising on the sale of timber, as imported timber came in large ships to the wharves of Eling and Southampton. Between 1922 and 1924 Beaulieu lost some 2,000 oaks, killed by the Oak Leaf Roller Moth, as serious a devastation as the Dutch Elm disease of the 1970s. The brickyard at Bailey's Hard was still in operation, with two kilns, making both red and white bricks and roofing tiles, but they did not pay and were closed in the early 1930s. This had some effect on Buckler's Hard, as the coal for the kilns normally came by river, and it was usual for the barges to unload some at Buckler's Hard en route. Henceforth, the villagers had to rely on coal merchants with motor lorries.

• Seine net fishing on the Beaulieu river, near the Rope Walk, opposite the cricket ground, c 1914

Oyster beds were still in existence in 1905, cared for by Thomas Smith who lived at Buckler's Hard. But there was no oyster breeding after 1906 (until the present Lord Montagu's time); the harvest was small and in some years non-existent; oysters were often bought from Warsash, and then retailed to local customers. Theoretically river fishing took place only under licence. Beaulieu tenants were able to acquire a permit to fish below the Brickworks for £1 a year. Shrimps and prawns could be got at low water from Beaulieu spit off Lepe. Seine net fishing, whereby one end of a long net was held on land whilst a rowing boat set out from the shore, with one man paying out the net until the beach was reached after a semi-circular course had been completed, was carried out in various places in the Beaulieu river, from Beaulieu to Lepe. But mainly this was done by part-time amateurs rather than full-time professionals. The catch from seine net fishing is inevitably varied in kind and quantity but the tradition continues today. In season the Beaulieu river is netted fortnightly at high tide below Beaulieu Bridge. Lord Montagu has first choice, then the rest of the catch is distributed among the fishermen and estate workers present. Although today's nets are made of man-made fibres, in the 1920's and 1930's some nets were made by the fishermen, a task requiring endless patience, as they were about 100 yards long.

Outside the Manor of Beaulieu tenants or owners of houses had to pay larger sums to fish. In 1908 Cyril Potter, tenant of Lepe House, was given permission to fish within a mile of it. In 1914 Lionel de Rothschild, the new tenant of Inchmery, was allowed to fish on Sundays and Mondays for £40 a year.

In 1922 the Admiralty lease on Need's Ore cottages expired. Two of the cottages had been vacated in 1911, and let by John, Lord Montagu. Now, the remaining houses were converted into homes; larders, bathrooms, and water-closets were added, and the water-supply improved. Let as holiday homes for the wealthy, a resident caretaker-cum-handyman was employed by the estate to look after them.

The demand for such homes had some effect on Buckler's Hard, where two of the houses there saw new types of tenants. In 1908 W Hendy was moved out of Bath Cottage, by then too small for his large family. He was replaced, not by another Estate employee, but by the wealthy Mrs Ponsford of Southampton, who used it as a weekend and holiday retreat. Also, before 1914, Norton House, at

156

the south end of West Terrace, was leased to Montagu Adams, a dentist from Portsmouth and a descendant of the great Henry Adams. When his lease was not renewed in 1921, this house was rebuilt.

In 1926 a major enterprise was begun at Buckler's Hard to convert Henry Adams' old house into an hotel. Jim Thomas, the 'harbour master', had died in 1925, and his successor, Frank Downer housed in East Terrace. Many ideas had been floated about the dilapidated Master Builder's future since 1905. By 1926 the village was beginning to attract yachtsmen, in small numbers by modern standards, and the occasional knowledgeable motorist, apart from locals who walked or cycled to Buckler's Hard on a Sunday afternoon. The steam ferry was also still running excursions from the pier, and there was a need for accommodation for the yachtsmen, and for the sale of snacks to the day tripper.

John Montagu's sense of history led to the house being given the name of 'The Master Builder's House', thus reviving the memories of Henry Adams, the shipbuilder. Paradoxically, the memorial tablet to Henry Adams, his wife and daughters, in Beaulieu Church was allowed to disintegrate, and was thrown away in 1931. Today, there is no memorial to him in the church.

In 1918 H E R Widnell had come as Lord Montagu's agent to Beaulieu where he was to remain for almost 60 years. Harry Widnell, a man of ability and charm, also had a sense of past and future; his was a formative influence on the development of Buckler's Hard. Before the plans for the alterations to the Master Builder's House were finalised, Harry Widnell was sent by Lord Montagu to look at the Lygon Arms in Broadway, a hotel admired by Montagu, and whose owner he knew well. The actual work on the Master Builder's was carried out by Beaulieu Estate labour using, where possible, local materials. Before the alterations, there was a hall immediately inside the front door, with one room on either side. The dividing walls were removed, so that the former passage and the two rooms became one large area. Oak beams, fashioned with an adze by Alan Raynes of Lymington, were inserted where the partition walls had stood. On the side of the house, a large and almost derelict kitchen was lengthened and oak bearers put in to make a new lounge with a splendid view of the river and connected to Henry Adams' look-out room, the 'crows nest' from which he kept surveillance on the shipyard, by a flight of stairs. The original log-burning fire on the western wall was

157

carefully repaired and restored. In addition, considerable alterations were made upstairs to accommodate guests.[5]

The first tenant of the Master Builder's House, as an hotel, was Lord Montagu's friend George Foster Pedley, who was to become the first secretary of the Beaulieu River Sailing Club. No alcoholic drinks were to be served as Lord Montagu thought that a licence would change the whole nature of the village, a decision in accord with contemporary thought. The 'dry' clause in the lease of the Master Builder's House was only removed when a new tenant, D Wyatt, obtained a licence, after World War Two, with the estate's full support.

A greater problem was that of water for the new hotel. There was no mains supply in Buckler's Hard; all relied on a well at the southern end of the village street, using a bucket on the end of a crooked stick. Expertise was necessary in filling the bucket and then in keeping it upright as it came up. A simple hand pump had been installed which could freeze in winter, and the buckets rusted. In the 1920s John, second Lord Montagu, wanted to instal running water in all the Buckler's Hard houses, a plan which met with unexpected resistance from the villagers who petitioned against it. Village children obtained a useful addition to their pocket-money by drawing water for the elderly. As a consequence, water on tap was not available until after 1945. The hotel's water supply was obtained by tapping a spring in Great Close Field which fed newly-installed roof tanks. This was supplemented by an overflow from the village well, which ran into another well below the passage floor to the north of the lounge — discovered during the alterations. The establishment of the Master Builder's House as hotel had a double significance. First, it provided a social centre, in particular for the Beaulieu River Sailing Club a few years later. Secondly, it was used as a minor repository for relics of the past. Lord Montagu sought models of Buckler's Hard ships, pictures of actions, and prints of naval commanders from private owners and from dealers. During his lifetime he collected what was to form, some 30 years after his death, the nucleus of the exhibits in the Maritime Museum at Buckler's Hard. Most of his collection was put in Palace House, but some items, including a list of men-of-war, found a place in the Master Builder's House, thus reminding visitors of the history of the village. Moreover, as early as 1910 he had written a monograph of the village.

The development of yachting also meant that the river owner

had to improve the seafarer's facilities, particularly those navigational. As early as 1913 Jim Thomas had been placed in the Master Builder's with the responsibilities, but not the title, of Harbourmaster. The river was boomed, long branches of trees being used as markers for the channel. In 1924 a fuel pump was installed on the jetty at Buckler's Hard. A limited number of moorings were laid, and in 1927 Frank Downer was appointed officially to the office of Harbourmaster, and the house nearest the river in the East Terrace extended to accommodate him.

During the 1920s a charge was levied of 1s 6d a night, or 7s 6d a week for anchorage, a reasonable reimbursement for the owner's great expense on upkeep. But, as in the days of motoring when car parking fees were first introduced, this led to some resentment. In 1927, one yachtsman, a Major Bellairs, refused to pay dues for boomage and landing, arguing that Lord Montagu had no right to levy such charges. Instead of direct attack, Lord Montagu went to the Board of Trade with his claim, and asked them to disprove it. The Board began a remarkable and meticulous enquiry, pursued by one of their antiquarians. The subsequent report, issued on 12 October 1928, historically of great interest as it contains copies of charters and documents dating from the early 13th century, found without reservation in favour of the Lord of the Manor. The inspector proved that, although the original charter for the foundation of the Abbey did not, *per se,* include the rights of the river, a subsequent grant included the waters within the region, and exemption from the jurisdiction of the New Forest. Moreover, John, second Duke of Montagu, had enquired into the rights of the Manor of Exbury prior to the foundation of Montagu Town, and the Board of Trade report contains many references to Exbury also. The following extract from the Report summarises the lengthy findings, *The Board of Trade are prepared to admit and hereby admit your claims as Lord of the Manor of Beaulieu (1) to the foreshore of the Solent from the old Coast Guard Station at Pitt's Deep on the west to the Eastern boundary of the Parish of Exbury at the point marked BC on the six-inch Ordnance Sheet M 12231/23 (Green No 15261); (2) to the foreshore and bed of the River Beaulieu on both sides as far as the tides flow; (3) to unclaimed wreck washed ashore within the limits mentioned in (1) and (2) above; and (4) to flotsam, jetsam and lagan (i e wreckage lying on the bed) within the entire area of the water of the River Beaulieu inter fauces (i e within the river passage) from the highest point to which ordinary tides flow as far as a point drawn across the river from the Coast Guard Station at Lepe on the East side thereof, ie at Need's Ore Point. Claims no (3) and (4) above are admitted subject to the provisions of the Merchant Shipping Act.*[6]

This official recognition of the transmission of the old manorial rights to the owners of Beaulieu was to be significant. Lord Montagu could control the river's destiny, and prevent undesirable developments. In 1927, a year before the Board of Trade ruling, the New Forest Rural Council had attempted to force him to lay down gravel in the main street at Buckler's Hard, and at one time threatened to tarmac it. Fortunately, the grass street was preserved. The ruling also meant that local inhabitants could be controlled. Edward Mudge, the Fawley photographer, who used a fowling point at Lower Exbury, had to pay ten shillings a year for the privilege.

However, the matter of manorial rights was complicated by the sale of parts of the foreshore and river bank on the Exbury side to two of his neighbours. In 1927 he sold a parcel of about 12 acres, including 500 yards of foreshore opposite Lepe House, running eastwards from Gipsy Lane, to his brother-in-law, Lord Forster, so that the latter could have some privacy. This was a family arrangement rather than a commercial transaction, for the purchase price was £50.[7] Lord Forster was given the mudlands down to low water mark. The need for Lord Forster to do this was caused by the increasing use of Lepe for swimming.

Also in 1927, Lord John Montagu sold to Lionel de Rothschild, the owner of the manor of Exbury, the banks of the river from Stone Point to Otterwood, excluding the parcel brought by Lord Forster. Before this sale, the boundary between Beaulieu and Exbury was the high water mark of ordinary tides. Under the sale, the new boundary became the low water mark. Harry Widnell had the novel task of arranging for stakes to be placed at intervals in the saltings, so that precise limits could be drawn.

This sale led to some complications in 1933 over the matter of car parking fees instituted by the Beaulieu trustees at Buckler's Hard that year, followed by Exbury Parish Council at Lepe. The manor of Beaulieu considered the matter — for although the land where the cars were parked at Lepe was not theirs, visitors who paddled or swam or walked below low water mark were on Beaulieu property. After a long discussion on whether or not Exbury should be asked to pay over a proportion of the fees, the matter was wisely dropped: the fact that the Exbury Estate now had the expense of maintaining the crumbling shore from Stone Point to the White House was a telling factor.

After the premature death of John Montagu in 1929, at the age of 62, the river was managed by trustees for his heir, Edward, third Baron Montagu of Beaulieu, then aged two-and-a-half. They still had problems over manorial rights. In 1930 members of the Cruising Association refused to pay dues. Counsel's opinion was sought, and the legal experts confirmed a high degree of probability that the estate had the right to charge for quays and boomage, whether by occupation or by ownership, but some caution was urged, especially as Schedule A, a tax now defunct, was involved. In 1931 agreement was made with the Cruising Association by private negotiation, under which they agreed to pay nominal fees. The gradual increase in the number of yachtsmen led to the appointment of an assistant habourmaster at Buckler's Hard, and the establishment of a small chandler's store. In the same year a new petrol pump was installed, together with better facilities for water.

• The Chapel at Buckler's Hard, which contains the memorial cross to Lady Poole's son, who was drowned in the Beaulieu river. The words were composed by Sir James Barrie, the author of 'Peter Pan', and by Winston Churchill – a notable combination

During 1933 a small field at Buckler's Hard was made into a car park, with space for 123 vehicles. Small posts were erected, with moveable chains. Motorists were charged sixpence, and the car park opened at Easter. By 10 May, £19 6s 6d had been collected, against £7 paid in wages. But as the car park had cost £270 to lay out, return on capital investment lay far ahead. During the first summer season 5,225 tickets were sold, producing £134 17s 5d at a cost of £71 in wages.

The trustees tried to maintain the rural simplicity of Buckler's Hard. When, in 1932, there was a request from the villagers for a public telephone kiosk, it was turned down as there were already two telephones there, one in the Master Builder's House and another in one of the cottages. Also in 1932, when H Compton of Cowes applied for a piece of land to start a small boatyard at Buckler's Hard, this was not approved. During 1938 two cottages at the south end of West Terrace were almost completely reconstructed, obliterating most of the original 18th century work.

By 1939 the trustees had preserved the rural nature of the river, during a period of economic and social change. Their wisdom, and their courage, were to be truly tested in the years immediately ahead.

References

[1] Beaulieu Muniments *A tribute by a Friend*
[2] Exbury Estate Office. Summary of conveyances
[3] Minutes of Beaulieu River Sailing Club
[4] BM Registration certificate
[5] BM *What I Remember* H E R Widnell
[6] Beaulieu Muniments
[7] BM John Montagu to Widnell, 21 April 1927

14 Spring Tides

AFTER WAR BEGAN in September, 1939, Beaulieu river saw no land or sea battles, and the few bombs which fell in or near the river were mostly unintentional, destined for Southampton, or the deliberate jettisoning of a deadly cargo by enemy aircraft returning home. A bomb fell near the river in September, 1940, a few incendiaries in October, 1940, and again in October, 1941. Then, there was a lull in aerial bombing until the Flying Bombs or VIs, in 1944. One fell near Keeping Farm on 22 July 1944, and another on 23 September 1944, which cracked the east wall of the Master Builder's House. But far more damage was done when a Halifax bomber crashed at Park Farm in December 1942. The beaches, at Warren and Park and at Lepe, did not suffer the indignity of barbed wire and concrete defences during the invasion danger of 1940; and, apart from one short period in 1940, the entrance to the river was not boomed.

Widnell, as agent for the trustees, had the difficult task of trying to preserve private property, with due regard to the emergencies of war. His employers, the owners of the estate and the river, were unavoidably absent in the early years of the war. Edward, third Baron Montagu, was still a child. He attended Ridley College, in Canada, from 1940 to 1942, before being sent to Eton. Captain Pleydell-Bouverie, commander of the royal yacht when war began, was appointed liaison officer to the French fleet at Toulon on 25 August, 1939, and early in 1940 became naval attaché in Paris. His wife, Pearl, joined him in France, and they were there during the traumatic days of the fall of France. On their return to England, Captain Pleydell-Bouverie was given command of HMS *Abdiel*, a mine-layer. Pearl returned to Palace House.

During the first winter of the war, the Beaulieu river remained relatively unaffected. Yachting for pleasure was still possible; mooring holders still paid their three guineas a year for the privilege, although many yachtsmen had joined the forces. Some yachts were laid up, and in January, 1940 a list of these craft was supplied to Portsmouth Dockyard. The fall of France, and the evacuation of the British troops from Dunkirk in June, 1940 saw the end of boating for pleasure. On Admiralty instructions, the river was immobilised, and all craft had to be removed or made unserviceable.

The shadows of war then crept rapidly over the river. By August, 1940 there were but nine immobilised craft left in the river. By September all the cottages at Need's Ore were empty, as were several of the houses near the river, including the House on the Shore. In October 1940 a log boom was put across the river below Exbury Point in case of German invasion. Despite Admiralty orders, some brave locals still contravened them. An Exbury man regularly moved across the mouth of the river from Brickyard Creek to catch shrimps and winkles on the south bank; on one occasion a fishing smack entered the river from Cowes.

● **The Master Builder's House Hotel, Buckler's Hard, once the home of Henry Adams**

During the first year of the war, the manor of Beaulieu could still exercise its right of ownership. In February 1940, when four large Admiralty mooring buoys were washed up on the foreshore, Widnell wrote to the Receiver of Wrecks in Southampton claiming them in accordance with the 'custom and rights' of the manor. He also wrote to the Admiral Supervisor at Portsmouth dockyard on the matter.[1] The Royal Navy acted differently from civil servants. No written reply was sent, but a naval lorry was despatched from Portsmouth, and returned there with the buoys. For once ancient medieval rights were over-ridden.

Gradually, the army and navy made further demands on the use of the river. In April 1942 it was requisitioned by the Admiralty at an annual rent of £50, a nominal sum which was intended to preserve the river's proprietorship for Beaulieu. On 13 April, 1942, Frank Downer, the harbourmaster since 1927, and his assistant were seconded to Admiralty. On 5 November, 1943, the Admiralty took over all premises at Buckler's Hard, as well as the brickyard at Bailey's Hard. Nissen huts, with concrete bases on which semi-circular corrugated iron 'uppers' were erected, accommodated Naval personnel at both. Buckler's Hard was used as a motor torpedo boat base, and the Master Builder's House requisitioned for additional living quarters. The Royal Navy laid down a concrete slipway, parts of which can still be seen at Buckler's Hard, installed a motorised winch, and erected a small crane on one of the quays. For the remainder of the war, Buckler's Hard was used for the repair and servicing of the motor torpedo boat flotilla which was based there. The long trip up the river must have seemed tedious to the young men who commanded these fast craft, and it is not surprising that the steward of the manor had to ask the Admiralty to observe the six-knot speed limit from Need's Ore Point.[2] This was of genuine concern, for the reclamation of land and the sea wall between Need's Ore and Gins was not built to withstand excessive wash.

For the first time since the 1690s (the Crimean War excepted), no men-of-war were built on the Beaulieu river during a war. However, the banks of the river saw some activity akin to shipbuilding, though not at Buckler's Hard. Husbands', then a recently founded shipyard at Marchwood, on the western side of Southampton Water, were engaged in building wooden mine-sweepers to counteract the German magnetic mines which lay on the sea bed, and were activated when a mass of metal, namely a ship, passed over them. Admiralty's counter was to produce a number of small wooden vessels, 105ft long, which towed long cables astern, at the end of which an electric current produced a magnetic field which set off the mine. Husbands' built six of these, at a time which coincided with intensive German incendiary bomb attacks. The site at Marchwood, around the old Ship inn, was conspicuously open. Admiralty requisitioned the brickyard at Bailey's Hard on 11 March 1941 at £75 a year; this historic site, where Herring had built *Salisbury* in 1698 was used by Husbands' to complete the fitting-out of these Marchwood-built minesweepers. Here was 'history in reverse', for in former times ships were built on the Beaulieu river, to be fitted out elsewhere. At Bailey's Hard, the minesweepers were well hidden by the riverside trees. Some of the labour force were drawn from the Beaulieu region, whilst other men lived in temporary huts near the old brickyards. Husbands' built sheerlegs at Bailey's Hard near the quay, the wooden bases of which can still be seen there today; they were cut down after the war. This fitting out at Bailey's Hard took place between 1941 and 1942, after which naval personnel replaced the civilian shipyard workers there.

Bailey's Hard was then used as a base for men engaged in mooring large numbers of dumb barges, intended for the carriage of men or stores at some time in the future when the invasion of Europe became a practicality. These barges were moored on both sides of the river, under and to the overhanging trees and thus screened from enemy reconaissance aircraft. The strength of the tide was such that some trees were uprooted from the river bank.

Towards the end of 1942 private moorings from Gilbury Pier to Gins were replaced by heavier ones, later used for LCTs (Landing Craft, Tanks). These were moored three or four abreast, to await their departure for the Normandy beaches in June 1944. Other landing craft were beached on the shore at Lepe. To provide accommodation for the base parties, Exbury House, owned by de Rothschild, and Lepe House, the home of Lady Forster, and Gilbury House were all requisitioned. Unfortunately Gilbury House, a beautiful thatched residence, was burned down while under naval occupation. The Montagu Arms Hotel was taken over for the WRNS, as part of HMS *Mastodon*, which was to play an important part in the preparation for D-Day. Several of the landing craft were used in the ill-fated raid on Dieppe in August 1942.

The most famous of the military personnel were the Special

Operation Executive — an independent British Secret Service, established in July 1940.[3] They were a select group of men and women who were trained in subversive warfare, and who were parachuted into Europe to co-ordinate sabotage against the German occupying troops. Many of the SOE were Europeans whose countries had been overrun by Germany. They had to be skilled in all the various activities to which an irregular, underground movement must resort; they needed to be brave, for capture in most cases meant death. The SOE were given preliminary training near Arisaig, in Western Scotland, on the 'road to the Isles'. A second area, where training could be done in comparative secrecy, was needed. In January, 1941, General Buckland, who lived in Beaulieu, requisitioned ten houses in the village, including his own, Curtle Mead, and the House in the Wood, which was the administrative headquarters; then more were taken over, including Inchmery House, the property of Lionel de Rothschild, near the mouth of the Beaulieu river. Each house was used for a different purpose; some developed by nationality, for underground work in France, or Belgium or the Netherlands.

Among the many famous personnel were Peter Churchill (his wife Odette), Hardy Amies, Paul Dehn, Sir John Wedgwood, Captain Ramsey, and the notorious Kim Philby. At Beaulieu, under Colonel Spooner and others, SOE personnel were trained in the cloak-and-dagger skills of survival behind enemy lines. They were given a special four-day course on how to identify contacts, by prepared conversation or other means; they were taught how to send coded messages in seemingly innocent letters or postcards, or how to look natural and ordinary when doing unnatural things. One of the instructors there was King George VI's gamekeeper from Sandringham, who taught students how to live off the land — a prime example of gamekeeper turned poacher. A memorial plaque to these brave patriots was erected by Lord Montagu in the cloister of Beaulieu Abbey and unveiled on 27 April, 1969 by Major-General Sir Colin Gubbins, a former SOE head. The words composed by Paul Dehn, a former instructor at Beaulieu, were well chosen, *Remember before God those men and women of the European Resistance Movement who were secretly trained in Beaulieu to fight their lonely battle against Hitler's Germany, and who, before entering Nazi-occupied territory here found some measure of the peace for which they fought.*

167

Another soldier who spent some days at Beaulieu, not in any way connected with SOE, was General Charles de Gaulle, who stayed at the Montagu Arms Hotel, accompanied by General Spears after the Dakar fiasco of September, 1940. Although supposed to be incognito, his tall figure was quickly recognised.

In 1942 building of an unusual kind began on the river at Clobb Copse, downstream of Buckler's Hard. Due to a shortage of steel Admiralty decided to experiment with the building of a concrete floating dock. The work was entrusted to Wates and Marley's who needed a secluded site. Beaulieu river was already well known to Charles Mitchell of Wates and to Owen Aisher of Marley's who had much to do with the construction of the floating dock. Owen Aisher's son now lives at Clobb Copse, so that the site, once used by Lord Henry Scott for his oyster beds, is in no danger of being forgotten.

● **The building of the experimental concrete dry dock No 33 in the Oyster Beds 1943-1944**

Work began on the preparation of the site in 1942 when it was cleared by Beaulieu woodmen; security fences were erected and the area declared 'top secret', although most of the local inhabitants well knew what was happening. The oyster beds were dug out and a concrete floor laid. Then concrete pedestals, about two feet six inches high, were placed vertically, on which the base of the dock was built. This method, reminiscent of the old wooden blocks of the shipbuilders, ensured that the dock would have water underneath it when launching day arrived. The construction site was sealed by the building of caisson gates, and was ready by 5 April 1943. A hundred men were employed in the building of the dry dock, most travelling daily from Southampton. The building dock was kept dry by steam pumps, which meant the carriage of coal by water to the site. From time to time, Ernest Crouch, then chief mechanic at Marvin's garage in Beaulieu, was called upon to effect repairs to the pumps. The concrete floating dock was launched, or rather floated off, on 25 March 1944. At the height of

the spring tide the caisson gates were blown off, water flooded in, and the huge dock floated off its pedestals. It was hauled into mid-river by winches strategically placed and then taken in tow by a tug, to Southampton. There was some anxiety that the dock would not clear the bar at the entrance to the Beaulieu river, but Frank Downer, the harbourmaster, correctly forecast that it would. On the day of the tow he preceded the dock in a rowing boat, and guided the project safely into the Solent. From Southampton, it was towed to Portland, given Admiralty number 33, and saw honourable service for the repair of destroyers of up to 1100 tons. It was used in Ceylon, then in North Africa, and is still operating in Norway.

● 'Beetles' for the 1944 Normandy landing were built at Clobb Copse, near the Oyster Beds

While the floating dock was building, the oyster bed site was also used for the construction of components for the Mulberry Harbours. Before the Allied invasion of Normandy, because of the seemingly impregnable German defences round the French Channel ports, two prefabricated harbours were built, one for the British landing and one for the American sector, to be towed across the Channel in sections in the wake of the first landings. Their building required a total labour force of 20,000 men, working on individual units in docks, harbours, and beach sites all over Britain. Beaulieu river was ideal for construction that had to be done in secrecy, and not exposed to German reconnaissance aircraft, so here a new site was excavated, immediately adjacent to the oyster beds, at right angles to the river, for the building of components for Mulberry B, intended for the British beaches at Arromanches. A large number of concrete barges, which were in effect hollow floats were built at Clobb Copse. Code-named Beetles, they were used to carry the steel bridge sections which held the pier roadway.[4] In addition, components for Minca wooden barges, manufactured at the Bay de Chaleur in Canada, were shipped across the Atlantic to Liverpool, and then transported by train to Beaulieu Road Station, and thence by road to Clobb's Copse for assembly. The Mincas were used for carrying troops and stores. Throughout the winter of 1943-1944 tugs towed away the completed Mincas and Beetles downstream. At Stone Point, near Lepe, Lovatt Ltd built concrete breakwaters (Phoenix) for Mulberry Harbour, employing at one time as many as 700 men. At Lepe, as there was no dock, the building took place on the beach, and were launched from a slipway. Today, the basins where they were built can still be seen, as can the winching bollards.

Prior to D-Day the field behind the Master Builder's House was used for the construction of dummy landing craft intended to confuse the enemy.[5] They were made of light steel tubular scaffolding, floated on oil drums, and covered with canvas. A funnel and superstructure was fixed on top. They were moored for a few days off Buckler's Hard in the hope that German reconnaissance planes would photograph them. Then they were dismantled, taken to East Anglia, and reassembled to convince the Germans that the landing would take place in Northern France. Both Beaulieu and Buckler's Hard were restricted areas, and a present resident, then a boy, recounts the dummy barge story as follows, *On some days the meadows near Bath Cottage were filled with trucks and tanks which mysteriously appeared and disappeared. Not quite so mysterious really, because they were actually dummies, inflated and deflated at will. Buckler's Hard village was closed to all except residents, but local children were impossible to contain, so nothing remained secret for long.* The security was also hard on the young Lord Montagu, who had to apply for a special pass to visit his parents in Palace House at the end of the Eton term.

Also before D-Day, experiments with guided missiles from Landing Craft (Rockets) were made on the river near Buckler's Hard — when the invasion of Normandy began in June 1944 the river was an important departure point for landing barges for men and stores. Significantly, Nevil Shute, in his *Requiem for a Wren*, uses Buckler's Hard, Inchmery, and Lepe as the scene of his romantic novel about Wren Janet Prentice and the Australian Commando Bill Duncan. As early as 3 June, the small craft sailed from Buckler's Hard and anchored off Lepe. There they were loaded with men and stores, and moored off shore. But bad weather caused a 24-hour postponement, and the men were ordered to throw away their half-consumed 48-hour ration packs, and draw fresh supplies. Local inhabitants collected the precious jetsam as a welcome addition to their rations.

When the Germans were driven out of France, Buckler's Hard was no longer near the front line, but the MTB base remained there during the last winter of war.

The end of the war in 1945 entailed no instant return to normalcy. Admiralty did not rerequisition the Beaulieu river until the spring of 1946, when followed considerable negotiations concerning compensation for the damage done to piers, farm property, and moorings. Exbury House remained in the hands of the Navy until 1951, as HMS *Hawke*, a training establishment for officer cadets and MTBs were sent to Buckler's Hard for repair at a private yard opened by James Wrann of Hythe.

When the war ended, Husbands' shipyard began negotiations for the exclusive use of the river, and the establishment of a shipyard at Buckler's Hard. Although the estate's trustees seriously considered this, the final decision was against. The former wanted a relatively small boatyard; Husbands' envisaged a larger enterprise.

The river's future was to lie in another direction. Edward, third Baron Montagu of Beaulieu, came of age in 1951, the year in which

172

his step-father, Edward Pleydell-Bouverie died. His task, as owner of the river, was to prove more difficult than that which had faced his father and grandfather before him. His inheritance, the manor of Beaulieu, was intact; no land had been sold; but leases were yielding a low income in an age of inflation; there was a backlog of maintenance and repair work which needed considerable financing. Moreover, the war had led to a social revolution with far-reaching consequences on estates such as Beaulieu. Governmental fiscal policy was aimed towards a redistribution of wealth, which inevitably entailed high taxation on unearned income. The state, by various statutes, took some control over land usage and building, so that any changes or development needed prior planning permission from either central or local government. The emphasis in the next few years was on the encouragement of industry and technological progress; later, inflation was to gather momentum. But a far deeper and more significant revolution had occurred. No longer could the lord of the manor act on his own; persuasion had to replace compulsion, new policies first explained then implemented slowly in accordance with the general will. The next ten years were to see the advent of the so-called 'affluent society', a rapid growth of population, and increased urbanisation. Edward Montagu was the proprietor of what was becoming a scarce commodity, land. Moreover, he owned a manor of great scenic beauty, and the town-dwelling Briton increasingly sought the solace and peace of the countryside. His property was within day-trip distance of 25 million people. Further, it was near Bournemouth, a popular holiday resort, and the New Forest, which attracted a considerable number of campers. Beaulieu and its river was a natural honey-pot for the tourist. In addition, the British Isles began to attract a considerable number of foreign visitors, many of whom were to come to Beaulieu. By 1951, the trends were apparent to the far-sighted; as the decade unfolded, they accelerated with unparallelled rapidity. People wanted to motor to the river, walk near it, sail on it, and swim in it. Each group of pleasure-seekers was inimical to the rest, quite apart from those who lived near the river; conflict was certain to arise. A policy to resolve these incompatible demands while still preserving the river's natural beauty demanded cool determination, a quality fortunately possessed by Edward Montagu. Professional management was needed too. Here, Brian Hubbard, who came to Beaulieu in 1953, was to play a major part in the development of the manor and of Montagu Ventures Ltd until his death in 1979. In 1952 Edward Montagu founded a collection of old cars at Beaulieu. The Abbey had been open to the public since 1905, so that the car collection, which eventually became the National Motor Museum, together with Palace House, gave the growing number of visitors a third attraction.

Developments on the river occurred later, as if a ripple, starting at Beaulieu, slowly carried downstream. A small boatyard, called Agamemnon, after Nelson's famous ship, was opened at Buckler's Hard in 1947, to serve as a repair base and store for yachtsmen. The old policy of a ban on houseboats, for which there was a great demand, was continued. About 150 moorings were laid in the river, of which 100 or so were hired by non-local yacht owners. Despite growing demand, moorings were limited, on the grounds that an overcrowded river was no asset to anyone. Those who witnessed the vast increase in the number of small craft in the Southampton Water, the Hamble river and Lymington, sympathised with this view. Yet some expansion had to be allowed, and this caused aggravation among a few members of the Beaulieu River Sailing Club, who could not sail the river as easily as they had pre-war. The BRSC used Buckler's Hard again from 1946 to 1956, when it moved to new headquarters at Need's Ore. In 1960 there was friction between them and water-skiers, another symptom of conflict of interest. BRSC built a new club house at Need's Ore in 1959, and in the following year the Royal Southampton Yacht Club was allowed to use Gin's as its sailing headquarters.[6] Buckler's Hard, therefore, was no longer a base for any of the organised sailing clubs. As the river at Buckler's Hard was unsuitable for swimmers, the village suffered no pressure in that respect (unlike Lepe, where facilities were improved by the creation of a Country Park by Hampshire County Council, on lease from the Cadland Estate).

But the problems of the social revolution were felt at Buckler's Hard. Motorists came in their thousands to a hamlet not designed as a visitor centre. Cars crammed into the village street, thus spoiling the beauty of the very scenery which the visitor had hoped to enjoy. Once there, he expected some form of entertainment or instruction, instead he found a small village of great interest to the cognescenti, but with little meaning for the casual untutored visitor.

So, in 1962 Edward Montagu decided to found a Maritime

Museum there. The old New inn, at the south end of the East Terrace, was chosen as a most appropriate available house for the new museum, and a wooden extension was made in Bristol, to run eastwards from the brick house. G B Bagnall, of Lymington, was appointed as the architect of the project. There was one amusing misunderstanding, when a council official misinterpreted a sign on the plan, which read 200, meaning car parking for 200 cars, as zoo, and objected rather strongly if irrelevantly to the idea of wild animals in Buckler's Hard. Work began on the adaptation of the building in April 1962. In the same month the author was asked to act as curator to the new museum, and in the following month he issued a memorandum which began by defining the Museum's purpose, *to serve as a memorial to those men of Buckler's Hard who built men-of-war in the period of England's maritime greatness: to give an additional interest to the many visitors: to collect and collate valuable material of local interest, and to preserve the same by giving them a permanent home.*

● **Earl Mountbatten of Burma, then Chief of Defence Staff, with Edward, 3rd Baron Montagu of Beaulieu, arriving at Buckler's Hard for the opening of the Maritime Museum, 1963**

An advisory board was formed, and met for the first time on 2 June, 1962. It comprised two necessary elements: organisational skill and historical scholarship. Lord Montagu, chairman, was supported by: Harry Widnell, by then the first archivist at Palace House; Colonel Edward Cadogan, the administrator at Palace House; and agent Brian Hubbard. 'Outside' members included Vice-Admiral Sir Ballin Robertshaw, a Beaulieu resident; Professor John Bromley, an eminent maritime historian from the University of Southampton; Maldwin Drummond, of Cadland, an enthusiast on all maritime affairs; John Ehrman, of Clobb Copse, the author of *The Navy in the War of William III,* and an expert in maritime history; and George Naish, of the National Maritime Museum, Greenwich. Later in the year, R C Anderson, the doyen of maritime historians, also joined the board.

Already a nucleus of exhibits for the new museum existed; the collection of models, prints and documents collected by John Montagu some 40 years earlier and accommodated in Palace House and the Master Builder's House. Established museums were good enough to help, especially the National Maritime, Greenwich, the Science, Kensington, and Southampton Museums. Other exhibits were given, loaned or sold by private individuals. During that summer of 1962, H M Government decided to disperse the collection held by the Royal United Services' Institution in the former banqueting hall in Whitehall, from which source Buckler's Hard Maritime Museum was able to buy several items of outstanding local importance, including Nelson's baby clothes, the recruiting poster for HMS *Beaulieu,* and the humorous prints of sailors. Sir Francis Chichester, one of the mooring holders in the river, gave many exhibits from his famous *Gipsy Moth* yachts. John Ehrman was particularly hepful, with his unique knowledge of documentary sources, and he presented the museum with a reproduction of the beautiful 1698 map of the river. C G Ellis, a descendant of Henry Adams, was also a benefactor, giving the museum many original Adams' documents. Unfortunately, figure-heads of ships, which 20 years earlier were plentiful, were by then in the hands of the already-established museums. An advertisement in the press brought an offer of a yacht's figure-head which, when renovated, was placed above the front door outside the Maritime Museum. After a few years it was brought inside before going to the Master Builder's House.

The museum was opened on the first Saturday of April, 1963 by

Earl Mountbatten of Burma who, with Lord Montagu, travelled from Bailey's Hard to Buckler's Hard in *Cygnet* which flew Mountbatten's flag as Chief of Defence Staff. As the party landed, a naval band played *Rule Britannia*; when the opening ceremony was completed, Lord Mountbatten was presented with a painting of HMS *Kelly*, the destroyer which, under his command, had so many adventures in the 1939-1945 war. When the museum opened, A W (Pat) Curtis, who had served in the Royal Navy, and was a man of great skill as a craftsman, was appointed its first custodian. He taught himself the art of model-making, and many of his models, Buckler's Hard ships to a man, are to be seen in the museum today.

• At the opening of the Maritime Museum at Buckler's Hard in 1963, Earl Mountbatten was given a painting of H M S *Kelly* by Lord Montagu. Noel Coward's film 'In Which We Serve' was based on Mountbatten's adventures in *Kelly*

In 1969 an information centre was built at the east end of the museum, which became the visitor's entrance instead of the old front door. This change helped to preserve the homogeneity of the village street's appearance. In August, 1968, Lord Montagu commissioned Gerald Wingrove, of High Wycombe, to make a scale model of the village. Initial research by the museum's curator and others used all available documentary evidence — which sometimes conflicted! Wingrove built the model on a ply base, with glass cloth and resin for contours, all overlaid with a coarse resin filler. The model (used on this book's dustjacket) showed Buckler's Hard on 3 July 1803, three days before the launch of *Euryalus*. In addition to shipbuilding, it depicts rotation of crops, diverse farm and timber-carts, various types of contemporary fencing, and typical gardens. In short, it was intended as an exhibit on social history of the time. Another spectacular exhibit was the figurehead of *Gladiator*, built according to an original Adams' drawing, and made by Jack Whitehead on the Isle of Wight.

From its opening in 1963, the Maritime Museum at Buckler's Hard has more than fulfilled its purpose. In addition to affording interest to tourists, (there were 166,000 in 1983) and preserving valuable local artefacts and documents, it has been used by thousands of schoolchildren for projects and has made a contribution to national maritime history, helping researchers, both at home and abroad.

● **Earl Mountbatten in the Maritime Museum, with the author A J Holland, Curator, April 1963**

In 1965 a new dining room extension to seat 90 people was made at the Master Builder's House, which blended well with the original, as old Beaulieu tiles were obtained from obsolete properties, and tiling was done without lead valleys, in accordance with 18th century building practice. This extension was opened by Sir Francis Chichester. After his circumnavigation in *Gipsy Moth IV* in 1966, which began and ended at Buckler's Hard, he was given a hero's welcome by Lord Montagu in a spectacular event which included a string orchestra playing Handel's *Music for the Royal Fireworks* accompanied by a pyrotechnic display, from a platform moored in the river. At that ceremony, Sir Francis was made a Freeman of the Beaulieu river.

During the 1960s it became apparent that the restoration of the village required considerable monetary outlay. The number of visitors had grown to some 250,000 a year, in addition to an increasing number of yachtsmen for which the small hamlet, with its cul-de-sac street and its limited catering and other facilities, was ill designed. Above all, the essential character of the village as a place in which to live was being eroded.

• Sir Francis Chichester, who set out from the Beaulieu river on all his record-breaking voyages, gave many of his nautical possessions to the Maritime Museum. Here Sir Francis is presenting his barometer to Edward, 3rd Baron Montagu

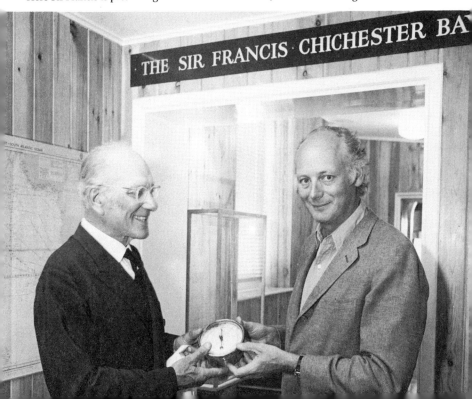

Edward Montagu, determined to conserve Buckler's Hard, modernised it without destroying its 18th century atmosphere. For example, television aerials were placed away from public gaze. In 1966, he commissioned Elizabeth Chesterton, of Leonard Manasseh and Co, who had successfully planned the development of King's Lynn, to prepare a study of the entire estate. Her proposals resulted in far-reaching changes to the Abbey and the Motor Museum, but Buckler's Hard was studied in depth also. The proposals embodied the separation of the different types of visitors, the motorist, the hotel guest, and the yachtsman. The plans, completed in 1966, were finally approved by Hampshire County Council in 1970, when Beaulieu and Buckler's Hard were designated as Conservation Areas.

In December, 1970, work began to put the Chesterton Plan into effect, and it was completed in 1972. The Agamemnon Boatyard, which first opened in 1947, had had a chequered career under three owners, and by 1971 was almost defunct. A new boatyard was built upstream thus removing it from the end of the village street; a new access road had to be built dipping downhill, through the beautiful woodland of Dungehill Copse. The boatyard had facilities for the repair and maintenance of sailing craft, and for chandler's stores. Moorings for yachts were also removed from the river at the end of the village street. At the same time, a new marina was built, entailing the dredging of 48,000 cubic yards of mud which was placed upstream to act as a sea defence, and to facilitate the reclamation of additional pasture land for Keeping's Farm. The marina, with berths for 76 craft, was built in a curve consonant with the river's bank, and was opened by Chay Blyth in 1971. Later the old Bath Cottage was converted into a club-house for yachtsmen. Thus, the sailing fraternity had their own access to the river, both by land and water, separating them from the day tripper.

Also in 1971, major changes had taken place in the access to Buckler's Hard for other visitors. A new road was made, westward of and parallel to the main street, leading directly to the rear of the Master Builder's House, for the use of visitors to the hotel. A car park was put there also, as well as an annexe, with 17 bedrooms, and a conference room, opened in 1972 by Robin Knox-Johnston.

For the visitors to the historic village, a new car park was laid out for coaches as well as cars, and an approach from the east of the main street. Motor vehicles, except for essential purposes and deliveries, were banned from entering the main village street. Short river cruises, in a motor-boat named *Swiftsure*, after one of Henry Adams' men-of-war, began in 1973 and enabled some visitors to enjoy the river scenery. A riverside walk, planned by the newly established Education Department, was laid out alongside part of the footpath from Buckler's Hard to Beaulieu, so that enthusiasts of all ages could enjoy that unspoilt stretch of the river.

By the early 1970s, Buckler's Hard had become an integral part of the tourist trade, albeit as a satellite or appendage to Beaulieu. After a century as a backwater, the village had again found a purpose, though it was a purpose viewed with some suspicion and even alarm by some long-standing residents. The microcosm of Buckler's Hard was typical of events nationwide; tourism had become a matter of some importance in many parts of the country, and economic viability had to be balanced against the peace of the industrial desert. Lord Montagu and Brian Hubbard had tried to develop the village gradually, and to pay heed to all the conflicting interests. Brian Hubbard's period as the managing director saw the completion of the National Motor Museum at Beaulieu, and the realisation of the Chesterton Plan at Buckler's Hard; failing health forced him to give up the detailed running of affairs, but in his last years he still was heavily involved in all major decisions as deputy chairman of Montagu Ventures Ltd. He died in the autumn of 1979, aged 57.

By that time Edward Montagu had the assistance of a new general manager, Kenneth Robinson, who had come to Beaulieu in 1969, as assistant to Raymond Player, succeeded him in 1971, and became managing director in 1975. Robinson was one of a new breed, whose skill and expertise was in marketing, an essential for the running of an organisation for tourists and museums. Hitherto, the managers of the landed estates had been, by and large, men of the countryside, knowledgeable in farming and housing the human relationships. Robinson was able to concentrate on the business of visitors' attractions — a relatively new field at that time. Edward Montagu and Kenneth Robinson were to become pioneer experts in the management of tourism, so that their advice and guidance was sought by others, both in England and abroad.

During the 1970s, the long-term plans for Buckler's Hard were reviewed. There were several problems requiring resolution. Many individual properties required extensive repair. As they became uninhabitable, the village community diminished. In addition, the Mulberry Tea rooms were perceived as inappropriate, the Maritime Museum required modernization, the car parks were inefficient and it was difficult for visitors to gain any understanding of 18th century life in the village.

After much discussion, a combined programme was agreed which aimed to:

a) maintain Buckler's Hard village as a living community
b) restore the village street to its appearance and atmosphere in 1793
c) improve visitor enjoyment by additional interpretation of 18th century village life and improvements to the Maritime Museum
d) extend knowledge of the site through archaeological investigation

In the intervening years, considerable progress has been made. Several cottage interiors have been renovated to provide modern living standards for today's villagers. Five cottage interiors have been used to explain 18th century village life. This has involved the recreation of a Shipwright's cottage, a Labourer's cottage and the New Inn, while Henry Adams' workroom has been restored in the Master Builders House Hotel, his former home. Detailed exterior restoration and conservation of the cottages has also begun. Future plans include rebuilding and re-display of the Maritime Museum, and replacement of the cafeteria by a more appropriately located catering facility and the construction of an information centre. Thus, Buckler's Hard, after a century of drift, is now set on a definite course. By missing a beat during the industrial revolution of the 19th and 20th centuries, the village has retained its 18th century form, supplemented by new sensitively located purpose-built structures to meet the needs of the visiting public.

References

[1] Beaulieu Muniments. Steward's letters 23 Feb 1940
[2] *ibid* 13 July 1942
[3] M R D Foot *SOE in France*
[4] Buckler's Hard Archives
[5] *The Royal Enginers Journal* vol 89, September 1975, pp 195-6
[6] Minutes of Beaulieu River Sailing Club

15 Buckler's Hard: the inhabitants

AT NO TIME was Buckler's Hard a wholly shipbuilding village: the population always had an agricultural element, due to the lack of farm workers' houses at nearby Clobb Farm. From 1750 to about 1820 however the shipbuilding trades were predominant, although until 1914 there were always men in the village whose employment derived from the river — as fishermen, or in work on the sea defences.

During the halcyon days of shipbuilding, the yard was the focal point of economic and social life. A contract obtained by Henry Adams meant employment for unskilled labourers, and an influx of skilled men together with their families who perhaps became lodgers in cottages occupied by locals. At the end of each contract, the launching, with its attendant festivities, were days to remember.

When ships were being built, the construction site towered above the houses, blocking the view of the river. The accompanying noise pervaded the entire community: sounds of timber being dragged down the street, of hammers on ironwork, of the adze on timbers; and all within 100 yards of the villagers. However, apart from the curl of coal and wood smoke, they were spared the air pollution suffered in the industrial north. In any case, when the shipyard workers were busy, most of the male inhabitants of Buckler's Hard were away working on the farms, or on the river. Nor would the house-bound wives have suffered the loneliness of the modern suburban housing estate.

The first comprehensive documentary evidence on the occupations of Buckler's Hard villagers is to be found in the 1841 census, when the average number of people per housing unit was

4.63, of whom 1.53 were children. In 1841 the occupations of the adult males can be compared with those of 1851,[1]

	1841	1851
Shipbuilder (Edward Adams)	1	0
Agricultural labourers	21	21
Shipwrights	9	1
Fishermen	2	5
Innkeepers	2	1
Bricklayers	1	1
Preventive Service	1	0
Cordwainer	0	1
Sailmaker	0	1

The end of the firm of Adams, between the two censuses, clearly had a profound effect on the economy of the village.

It is reasonable to assume that during the 100 years before 1841, the proportion of villagers engaged in shipbuilding was no greater than in 1841. Indeed, the residence there of nine shipwrights, one an apprentice, was perhaps as high as in the more active period of naval shipbuilding; now they worked on a steady flow of small merchantmen which demanded a stable and indigenous labour force. However, the village had no sawyers, in marked contrast to 40 years earlier. During the heady days of naval shipbuilding, some of the workforce was temporary and itinerant, staying for one or two years only for the completion of a single contract. In April 1804, when Adams' business was exceptionally busy, a total of 35 shipwrights were employed,[2] plus sawyers and labourers, making a total of about 50 men, few of whom lived in Buckler's Hard. The contract men lived in lodgings and left when the ship was built. Some of the labourers lived at Beaulieu rails, on the edge of the New Forest, making a meagre living from husbandry, supplemented when possible by sporadic employment at Buckler's Hard.

The bankruptcy of the Adams brothers caused some distress to the Beaulieu rails men, who had to seek aid under the poor law. In 1818 relief was also given to a shipwright in Buckler's Hard.[3] But whilst naval building was taking place, some responsibility was taken by the parish of origin from which the skilled men had come. For example, when Thomas Burlace injured his leg at Buckler's Hard, of which village he was a resident, some financial

184

aid was sought and obtained from Deptford.[4]

Identification of the shipyard workforce by name before 1841 is not easy as there are few written records. But the identity of a handful of men can be gleaned from various sources. During the years 1813 to 1817 these were all shipwrights, Robert Allen, Edward and Thomas Burlace, Joseph Denham, Benjamin, John and William Fielder, Charles Glastonbury, Henry Gill (foreman of the yard in 1814), Andrew Grunsell, Thomas Payne, John Scanes, George and James Ward, Charles, Edward and John West, and James and John Williams. Of these, seven were Buckler's Hard men, the Burlaces, Scanes, Ward, the Wests, and Williams. George Hawkins was a caulker at that time, and Frederick Hurdle a carpenter. Sawyers included John Attwood, William Browne, John Harvey, James Phillips, William Sait, and James Ward. The blacksmiths, appropriately, were James, Joseph and William Smith, together with Thomas Sheath. Thomas Prescott was a labourer in the 1790's, as were George Bound and Josiah Denman between 1814 and 1818. The carter was Joseph Purse; such was his control of his charges that it was said of him, 'there never was no hollering'.

Of those engaged in shipbuilding, the shipwrights were paid most. The mere statement of a weekly wage is insufficient for a comparison to be made with our own times as there are too many variables, such as expectation, taxation, services and the like. As a rough guide to the standards of the time, the artisan earning £1 a week or over in 1800 could bring up a family in reasonable comfort, while the man with a wife and two children earning nine shillings a week was near to bare subsistence living. Further, any computation of earnings must take into account the incidence of unemployment. Until the end of the Napoleonic wars, shipwrights were in short supply and thus reasonably secure from unemployment. In 1804 the national shortage was so acute that a census was made of all the shipwrights employed in the merchant's yards.[5]

At Buckler's Hard they were paid according to productivity, based on the length of the ship, and the time taken to complete each part of it. During the summer months they worked from six in the morning to six at night with breaks for breakfast, and a midday meal; during the winter work began at dawn and ended at dusk. Average weekly earnings were some 25s to 30s compared with a national average of about £1. Carpenters, sawyers, and caulkers could earn about £1 to £1 5s but were not always continuously employed. As shipwrights served a seven-year apprenticeship, they could expect a greater chance of employment than the unskilled.

Although shipbuilding was important to the village's economy, as a source of employment it was always second to agriculture, the largest group of workers in the UK until after 1851. Around 1800 the farm labourer was much poorer than the shipyard worker; throughout the 19th century agricultural wages were lower than industrial incomes. There is little documentary evidence regarding the payment of farm workers resident in Buckler's Hard, as they were employed not by the Beaulieu estate but by tenant farmers. Some were hired by Edward Adams, in his capacity as a farmer, before 1847; one or two were employed at Clobb Farm and at other neighbouring farms. It would be reasonable to assume that they were paid according to the national average of about 10s a week in 1800, and about £1 a week by 1900. In 1800 the meagre wage would have enabled the farm labourer and his family to live on a diet mainly of bread, with an occasional piece of cheese or bacon; meat was a luxury, as was milk and tea. After about 1860, the abolition of import duties made tea the drink of the poor, and living standards of the British people rose. However the farm worker has always had perquisites, such as ground for chicken and a pig and free wood. At Buckler's Hard all the cottages had sizeable plots of land on which vegetables could be grown. In addition, the rents of the cottages were comparatively low; in 1888 the manor of Beaulieu was charging from 1s (5p) to 2s (10p) a week, according to the size of the cottage.

Those few residents who were employed by the Manor of Beaulieu, such as river defence men, had the fringe benefits of all estate workers: continuous employment, even in times of depression and, from the middle of the 19th century onwards, a small pension, with a rent-free cottage, at the end of their working life. Moreover, they were looked after when sick, with full wages and medical attention paid by the lord of the Manor. Also widows of estate workers were given a small pension. The incidence of unemployment among the male inhabitants of Buckler's Hard was not great, by nature of the village itself. A tenancy implied some connection with the manor, farms, or the shipyard, as the houses were 'tied' cottages.

The lot of those employed by the Manor of Beaulieu was at least as good as that of others in southern England. Beaulieu was comparatively quiet during the Agricultural Labourers' Revolt in 1830, unlike neighbouring Fawley, where the resident agent was tied to a cart and whipped. In 1890, during the period of nascent trade union militancy, Henry, first Baron Montagu, had to face a deputation from some of his estate workers concerning their wages. He instructed his steward to discover what those employed on neighbouring estates were paid, and was thus able to prove that those in Beaulieu and Buckler's Hard were treated fairly by current standards. From 1905 onwards, with the advent of John, second Baron Montagu, the villagers became part of the paternal estate system under which, as long as they behaved themselves, they had a job for life.

Throughout this period there were opportunities for wives and unmarried girls to find employment in unskilled or semi-skilled work. Neighbouring farmers needed servants, as did the Adams family, and the two local innkeepers. Until various acts of Parliament passed between 1833 and 1876 imposed restrictions, wives and children could supplement the family income by helping at harvest time, stacking sheaves, building ricks and gleaning. However, there was little opportunity for them to gain skills.

Unemployed Buckler's Hard residents became charges on the Poor Law overseers in Beaulieu. A Poor House was built in Beaulieu in 1793, on the site of the medieval monastic Cross House, where Pondside House stands today.[6] Throughout the first half of the 19th century, the Poor Law authorities used one of the houses in the East Terrace of Buckler's Hard for paupers or for orphans although occupants were not necessarily Buckler's Hard people. Money for the poor was obtained by a local levy on all landowners and tenants, and not from central government funds. In 1794, when the poor rate was a shilling in the £, Henry Adams paid £2 6s 5d as his contribution. Immediately after the Napoleonic Wars there was hardship in the village due to the bankruptcy of B and E Adams. During the next intense depression, the so-called 'hungry forties', coincidental with the stewardship of Henry Adams' grandson, Henry Pocock, and which included the Duke of Buccleuch's emigration to Natal scheme, no Buckler's Hard men left the country. During the 1800s and 1890s, and again in the 1920s, they escaped the worst of the downturn in the trade cycle.

Apart from working conditions, what was life like for the

inhabitants of Buckler's Hard? There is no simple answer as there was then a great gulf between rich and poor. Buckler's Hard was unusual in that it was never a separate parish; thus it had no resident squire, parson or schoolmaster to form the usual rungs of the social ladder. For the first 100 years of its history, however, the village had master shipbuilders, the nearest equivalent to 'upper class' residents. John Darley was not rich, but he paid for his son to be educated by Botley Braxstone in Beaulieu in the 1740s; William Scanes, the last of the master builders, was described in 1867 as wealthy, and had two domestic servants. But above all, Henry Adams and his sons were the prime examples of well-to-do inhabitants. Though they would have been small fish in a larger pool, they were the apex of the limited society of Buckler's Hard. They were on familiar, though deferential, terms with the gentry, and their horizons extended beyond the Beaulieu river; their circle of acquaintances was geographically wide, though limited in the main to other shipbuilders. They were to be found as subscribers to local charities, whilst Balthazar was enrolled as an officer in the militia in 1798. Their life was quite different from that of the ordinary villager.

A picture of the Adams' social life can be drawn by a detailed description of their activities in 1791, when Henry was still in control — but a year in which business was relatively slack.[7] On Saturday 8 January, Balty, Edward and Henry went shooting whilst John rode a horse along the shore at Sowley. After attending morning service at Beaulieu, the family spent the next day with the Pococks at Sowley. Later in January, the three brothers were taken by carriage to Hythe where the ferryman rowed them to Southampton. Then they walked to Northam to transact business with Mr Nowlan, a local shipbuilder. Also, Mr Marshall, the Deputy-Surveyor to the Navy Board, and Thomas Nicholls, Purveyor of the New Forest, spent a week with Henry Adams at Buckler's Hard. During the first week of February John and Balty spent the week socialising in Southampton at the Assembly Rooms and the Dog's Nose Club. Then on Saturday, 12 February, learning that five of Mr Pocock's ducks had been stolen, John Adams obtained a warrant to search the cottages at Pitt's Deep, to no avail. Balty, meanwhile, had set out for the west of England in search of timber. In March the three brothers took part in a shooting match at Beaulieu, visiting Lymington and Southampton for pleasure, and travelling to London on business with the Navy

Board. There they visited the theatre several times. The journey from Southampton to London, by stagecoach, took twelve hours with breaks for breakfast at Popham and lunch at Egham. In April, John and Edward went to Portsmouth on business, riding horses to Ashlett Creek, then crossing the Southampton Water to Warsash, whence they walked eight miles to Gosport where they stayed the night. The next day they spent in Portsmouth on business, and travelled to Fontley, near Fareham, to spend that night with Cort the ironmaster. From there, they travelled to Northam to see Nowlan before returning home after a night in Southampton. At noon on Wednesday 4 May there was the excitement of the launch of the *Beaulieu* when Henry Adams entertained 80 guests, after which the party danced until three in the morning. The next day, the ship was christened by Sir Harry Burrard of Lymington. Some 48 hours later Henry Adams gave a feast for his shipwrights. On Sunday 8 May, after attending morning service at Beaulieu where the Reverend Henry Adams preached the sermon, Edward, Balty and John sailed for Portsmouth to see the *Beaulieu* enter Portsmouth harbour. A week later, Edward Adams, accompanied by the Navy Board overseer, Ancill, travelled to Portsmouth to attend the ship's survey. On 4 June the three brothers sailed to Cowes to witness the naval gun salute in honour of the King's birthday. In the middle of June, John and Edward went to the Isle of Wight to the fair at Newport, and combined this with sight-seeing. One week later, they rode to Stoney Cross, visited Rufus' Stone, and had a picnic in the Forest. Then Balty journeyed on business to Portsmouth once more. During the first week in July Balty and John went to Bursledon, to meet Marshall, Deputy-Surveyor to the Navy Board, then to Northam to discuss business with Nowlan before returning home via Southampton. On the last Sunday in July John and Edward sailed to Lepe to take tea at the Ship inn. Edward and John spent the first week of August in Portsmouth and Southampton and were back in time to see *The School for Scandal* at Lymington theatre. The three brothers found time, later that month, to spend a few nights in Southampton, attend a whale of a party at Mr Ancill's, and another at Newtown on the Isle of Wight, where Sir Harry Burrard was the host. On the last day of August all four brothers went on a picnic at Netley Abbey. In early September Balty was again in Portsmouth on business whilst Edward and John were in Southampton. Henry Cort came to Buckler's Hard to stay with

Henry Adams where he witnessed an unfortunate accident. On Monday 12 September, three or four men were preparing to launch Edward's yacht when the vessel moved, crushing Thomas Prescott, who was working underneath. Three days later John joined a shooting party at Beaulieu and then spent two weeks in Portsmouth on business. In October Balty and Edward went to Southampton to register the new yacht, returning via Cowes. Later, Edward, John and Mr Ancill, the Navy Board overseer, were able to spare several days fishing for whiting off Calshot. On 1 November Mr Marshall came to Buckler's Hard to survey the *Santa Margarita*, then being rebuilt by Henry Adams. During the latter part of November Balty and John were in London once more where they remained until the end of the year. Whilst his sons were travelling, Henry Adams, the occasional trip to Sowley, and to London apart, stayed in Buckler's Hard. He entertained Colonel Mitford, the owner of Gilbury, and saw much of his relatives, the Warners. All in all, the Adams' men were living a full life.

Nor was the lot of the Adams' ladies less occupied.[8] Henry's youngest child, Elizabeth, was aged 17 in 1794. Britain was then at war with France, locked in a struggle which was to last until she reached her 38th birthday. How did a young lady of means spend 22 years of war?

On 7 January 1794 she walked into Lymington, the nearest town, about eight miles away, and spent 1s 10d on black gauze. Two days later she walked to Lymington again, crossing the Lymington river by the toll bridge, which cost her one penny as a foot passenger. On Sunday 12 January, with all the family, she went to church in Lymington, by carriage. She appeared to enjoy a wide ecclesiastical experience, as two weeks later she went to the French Huguenot church in Winkle Street, Southampton. She made frequent trips to Southampton with her brothers, carried ashore by sturdy porters through 200 yds of stinking mud when the tide was out. Throughout the rest of the winter and early spring, she remained in Buckler's Hard, losing a few pence at loo, a round card game, and paying threepence to have her stockings washed. She helped to entertain her father's guests, including Mr Ancill, the Navy Board overseer; and had tea with Colonel Mitford of Gilbury.

On 4 May 1794 Elizabeth accompanied her brothers to witness the Prince of Wales' review of the regiments at Lyndhurst. On 12 May she went 'with my two brothers and Mr Ancill to the launch at

Northam', i e, of the 32-gun *Lively*, built by Mr Nowlan. Then, as was her custom, she was in London from mid-May to mid-June. On 12 June she went to 'an illumination on account of the victory obtained by Earl Howe over the French' ('The Glorious First of June'). Back in Hampshire, on 20 June she watched the embarkation from Southampton of Earl Moira's troops for Ostend. One week later, Elizabeth and her brother Edward left Buckler's Hard early, and sailed to Portsmouth in his yacht. There they attended the launch of the 90-gun *Prince of Wales* . . . 'their Majesties attended and directly after embarked in barges for Spithead. They were saluted by all the ships on shore'. Elizabeth Adams then shopped in Portsmouth, where she bought a hat for 7s 6d, some ribbon for 1s 2d, and some cherries for sixpence. Hitching a lift from Portsmouth to Cowes on the frigate *Aquiline*, she rejoined Edward in his yacht, and got back to Buckler's Hard at one o'clock in the morning. In September, she visited relatives in Bristol then, in October, went to London with her brother Balty. Whilst the latter spent two months on business, Elizabeth visited relatives, the theatre and enjoyed the sights of London.

She spent 1795 in much the same way. A picnic at Netley Abbey at Easter was followed by her annual visit to London. She was at Vauxhall for a grand fete in honour of 'the Prince of Wales' nuptials', i e, of the future George IV to Caroline of Brunswick. In August she went to Cowes to see 'all the transports that were intended for the expedition against the French but which, owing to the defeat of the Emmigrants (*sic*), did not go further than Cowes'.

In 1804, now aged 27, Elizabeth sailed in a man-of-war from Yarmouth, Isle of Wight, to Jersey, where she spent the rest of the year with friends. Thus, she was in sight of the French coast at a time when Napoleon was preparing his invasion of England.

In 1814, 37 and still unmarried, Elizabeth went to London for the peace celebrations following the first abdication of Napoleon and the start of the Vienna Congress. On 20 April she saw the King of France, Louis XVIII, who made a public appearance in London. On 7 June, with hundreds of others, she stood on Westminster Bridge to catch a sight of the Czar of Russia disembarking — in vain, as Alexander had gone ashore privately down river. On 9 June she attended a firework display to mark the peace, and a week later she saw Marshal Blucher. On 18 June she watched a grand procession of sovereigns who attended a civic banquet at the Guildhall. On 20 June she wrote 'Peace was proclaimed with the usual solemnities but after the grand procession of Saturday it appeared trifling'. On 4 July she attended the launch of the *Nelson* at Woolwich. Three days later came the climax of her London visit, when she went to the thanksgiving service at St Paul's, attended by the Prince Regent, all the royal Dukes, and the members of the Lords and Commons. She returned to Buckler's Hard in October, after six months in London.

Elizabeth, who received £2,000 under her father's will in 1805, outlived the rest of her family. She moved to Beaulieu in 1822, where, together with her mother, who died in 1827, and her unmarried sister, Mary Anne, she lived in Warner's House. She saw the decline of the shipbuilding business, the death of all her brothers, and of her sister who died in 1858. Her last years were spent in sadness, with occasional visits from distant relatives. In the year of her death, 1867, one event pleased her; the last remaining public house in Beaulieu, except for the Montagu Arms, was closed. 'The other inn is to be done away with — where a sad scene of drunkenness often occurred, and caused the ruin of many poor families! Is it not disgraceful that so disgraceful a vice should be practised by those who should set a good example!' At her death, aged 90, the beneficiaries of her estate, (less than £5,000), were her nephews, Major Henry Adams of Dublin, and Charles Pocock of Dovercourt, Essex.

Henry Adams, who started as a shipwright, had climbed the social ladder as had other Hampshire builders. Richard Wyatt of Bursledon built men-of-war in the 1690's and his daughter married a baronet; Moody Janverin became the owner of Hamble House and his daughter wed John Taylor of the Inner Temple; Philomen Ewer of Bursledon, a master shipwright of the 1740's, left a fortune to his children; the Richards of Hythe became extensive landowners. On the other hand, many shipbuilders had failed. Darley and Herring, who built on the Beaulieu river, and Thomas Raymond of Southampton, all went bankrupt, as did Good, who built the *Repulse* at Buckler's Hard. But if the Adams family were able to rise socially, one reason for their success also contributed to their downfall. Henry Adams was helped, initially, by the fact that he was plying his business on a manorial estate. This meant that he and his family could not be landowners, and real estate was the one commodity which helped to perpetuate wealth. When shipbuilding declined, Henry Adams' grandchildren were forced to find a living away from the Beaulieu river. But at least for a period the Adams' family had risen above the general run, which is more than any other Buckler's Hard family were able to do.

As is usual in English social history, the life of the gentry and of the upper classes can be illustrated from their writing whereas for the mass of the population, the only sources are contained in documents relevant to misfortune. As a contrast to the Adams' family, the bare outline of the fortunes of two other men, Henry's contemporaries, will suffice. Thomas Burlace came from Deptford as a craftsman before 1775, in which year he married Arabella Burnett in Beaulieu. Employed by Henry Adams he lived most of his life in Buckler's Hard in a West Terrace cottage for which he paid £4 a year rent in 1791. Unlike so many of the poor, he had a small family, a son Edward, born in 1779 and a daughter Elizabeth born in 1776. Yet he was to die in poverty as he had the misfortune to hurt his leg in about 1812, by when he was aged 68. Unable to work, he had to apply for poor relief. But, as Deptford was his parish of origin, the Beaulieu Overseers applied to the Overseers there for the money.[9] To help themselves, Mrs Burlace, then aged 74, with her daughter, ran a dames' school at Buckler's Hard. The daughter married and left the village in 1814, by which time payment for poor relief had come from Deptford. Thomas Burlace died in 1816, aged 72, and Arabella his widow died in 1820, aged 82. Thus, after a life's work as a skilled and comparatively well-paid craftsman, the Burlaces were unable to save enough for their old age. Also, unlike the employees of the manor of Beaulieu, they obtained no pension from the owners of the estate, nor did Adams help his unfortunate workman.

The second example, Jasper Stickland, had an even starker life. One of a large family with many branches, he was born in about 1770, and made a meagre living as a general labourer, with periods on poor relief. In 1806 he was again on outdoor relief, with a wife and at least two children to support. In 1808 his third child was born. In 1809, with his brother Solomon, he stole and killed a lamb, valued at 20s, belonging to Edward and Balthazar Adams. On 5 March 1810 both were found guilty at Winchester Assizes, and were sentenced to be hanged, later commuted to transportation for life to New South Wales. Jasper and Solomon Stickland sailed from England on the *Admiral Gambier* on 5 May 1811, arriving in Syndey on 29 September. Jasper's wife, Sarah, evidently found companionship elsewhere, as she bore an illegitimate child in 1811. She lived on in Beaulieu, a burden to the Poor Law Overseers.

These examples from the period when shipbuilding was still an important feature of Buckler's Hard life, illustrate that the wealth generated by that industry did not permeate through to the lower orders. The next generation, after the acute depression of the 1820's, were to fare better. Charles Glastonbury, Edward Adams' foreman shipwright, at least was able to keep his large family of nine children above starvation level. Although he left Buckler's Hard to work on the Thames, he returned to the village where he died in 1877, aged 88. With the advent of the paternalism of Lord Henry Scott in 1867, Buckler's Hard residents who were employed by the manor were given pensions in old age and aid during sickness. This bridged the gap until national state insurance began in the present century.

Buckler's Hard residents were no worse off economically than were the proletariat of the towns. Whilst much of the north and midlands was experiencing the 'take off into an industrial society', Buckler's Hard remained part of a rural manorial estate, and escaped some of the worst effects of fluctuations in the economy. Moreover, the general social way of life of Buckler's Hard people had advantages over that of the townsman, as well as disadvantages. In the spring, summer and autumn, the villagers lived in a beautiful environment. During the winter, as the main street runs almost directly north and south, they had little protection from the cold winds. The winter months brought isolation and the various illnesses stemming from damp and cold. For most of the inhabitants, the only means of transport was on foot. The landlords of the two inns had horses, as did the Adamses, but the expense of keeping one was too much for the ordinary villager. There were no regular horse-carrier services to and from the village and, until the coming of the bicycle, the inhabitants of Buckler's Hard had to walk to obtain the ordinaries of life. If clothes, or linen, or ribbons were needed, a walk to Lymington, six miles distant, or to Hythe, and thence by ferry to Southampton was entailed. The inhabitants could reach Gilbury (or Upper Exbury) by using the ferry across the river, but there was little to attract them there. Beaulieu would have been visited frequently, for social events and for routine business. Beaulieu Fair was a gala occasion, until it was abolished by the first Baron Montagu because of the fighting and feuding which took place between the locals and the men from East Boldre. There was no church in Buckler's Hard; the chapel was not set up until 1886, using the by-then

194

disused infants' school room, and the Anglican chapel at Park, now a private house, was not dedicated until 1905. Anglicans in Buckler's Hard had to walk to Beaulieu in order to attend Sunday services, and to solemnise christenings, marriages and burials for which a farm-cart was used as a bier followed by a sombre retinue of mourners. It should not be assumed however that the Buckler's Hard villagers during the 19th century were regular churchgoers, other than for the great events in their lives, or other special holy days. A census carried out by the church of England in 1851 suggested that four out of ten of the total population of all denominations attended Sunday services. It is reasonable to suppose that Buckler's Hard was no deviant from the norm. In a rural community, work had to be done on Sundays, on the farms, or in the shipyard, during the summer months. Nonconformists — about 25% of the villagers were dissenters in 1867 — attended chapel at East Boldre, about the same distance from Buckler's Hard as was Beaulieu. Nonconformity was regarded with some disfavour on most of the landed estates in southern England as almost akin to atheism, so that no chapel was erected in Beaulieu or Exbury. The Baptist Church at Blackfield was not built until the end of the 19th century. There was no school in Buckler's Hard until the Napoleonic wars, when a dame school was set up for a short time in the West Terrace by Mrs Burlace, the wife of a shipwright. In 1847 the Duke of Buccleuch financed an infants' school in Buckler's Hard with Mrs Harding as the teacher, but this was closed by 1886. Apart from the infants, schooling entailed a daily walk to Beaulieu, where a new school was built in 1813. Before that, education was carried out in the Church by schoolmasters who were paid the usual salary of £10 a year by the lords of the Manor. Such schools were at first for boys only, but by 1825 a girls' school had been established in one of the rooms of the Beaulieu Poor House where Elizabeth, Henry's spinster daughter, was a mistress from 1823 to 1830. Compulsory education was not enforced until 1876, so that many of the children of Buckler's Hard had little formal education.

Too much should not be made of the hardships of walking, a commonplace of everyday life in those days. Many of the shipyard workers at Buckler's Hard lived in Beaulieu rails, near East Boldre, and walked to and from work daily. There was no mail box for posting letters at Buckler's Hard until 1909 — before that the nearest was one mile distant at St Leonard's. However, the lack of mobility, other than by foot, hit hardest the elderly, the sick, and the cripples who found it difficult, if not impossible, to leave the village.

For most villagers, it was a 'do-it-yourself' age. Food had to be acquired or grown. The whole family needed to spend much of their very limited free time toiling in their gardens or allotments. Bread was baked in the village, as not all the cottages had an oven. For example, in 1867, the tenant of the New inn was also the baker. There was wood in abundance, and coal could be obtained from the shipyard. It was usual, even after the shipyard closed, for colliers, en route to the Brickyard at Bailey's Hard, to unload some coal at Buckler's Hard. But in the battle for survival the villagers did not necessarily benefit from the abundance of their surroundings. Harsh game laws made poaching a transportable offence until the middle of the 19th century, whilst the fish in the river belonged to the owner.

At least Buckler's Hard was never a deserted village, nor did it become a commuter's dormitory. Three or four generations in succession remained in the village until after the 1914-1918 war. Even now, despite its role as a tourist attraction, the village has an entity and a community. Today's villagers are conscious of the heritage of the past, and perhaps mindful of the words of Francis Bacon, in his *Essay on Praise*,

'Fame is like a river, that beareth up things light and shallow, and drowns things weighty and solid'.

References

1. Enumerator's Census 1841 and 1851
2. N M M Greenwich, Further Papers and Accounts presented to the House of Commons, 25 June 1805
3. H E R Widnell *The Beaulieu Record* p 175
4. *ibid*, p 173
5. N M M Greenwich, *op cit*
6. H E R Widnell *The Poor House* Vol II (unpublished)
7. John Adams'Diary 1791
8. Elizabeth Adams' Diaries
9. Beaulieu Muniments: B/PLA 10

16 Buckler's Hard: the village and its houses

TODAY'S VISITOR to Buckler's Hard, despite the re-creation of some of its past, still needs imagination to visualise the village as it was in its shipbuilding days. The main village street runs almost due north towards the river. If one stands at the south end, at the top of the street, how does it differ from the village as it was? West and East Terraces on the left hand and right hand respectively still flank the main street, but another row of houses, at right angles to the two terraces, to the south of the present Maritime Museum, has now disappeared. This group of houses was called Slab Row as they were made of slabs of wood, ie with the bark still on. Slab Row was pulled down during the 19th century by the first Lord Montagu, largely due to the persistence of the Reverend Powles, the colourful Vicar of Beaulieu, who was disturbed at the squalid state of the houses. Today, rises in the ground, between the Maritime Museum and the south end of the street, show where the brick foundations of Slab Row once stood.

To the east of the present East Terrace, there was another row of houses known as Back Street. This had almost disappeared by 1918, when only two rather dilapidated tenements remained. This remnant was restored and extended in 1921, and was then enlarged and modernised in the 1970's. Although one writer has asserted that there was a windmill at Buckler's Hard which was used to drive saws to cut the timbers,[1] there is no evidence of its existence in any contemporary map or document. It is highly unlikely that such a highly capricious power source as wind was used for such a purpose, and it can be assumed that the sawing was done by hand. There were always sawyers resident in Buckler's Hard, and labour was comparatively cheap.

To the left of the village street, in a large open space which is now a field, stood the West Timber Yard used to store the timber which came by land, mostly oak, elm and beech, which was fashioned and cut in the saw pits, and then brought down by horses to the building site at the river's edge. As this had to be done in all weathers the village street would have been heavily rutted. It is highly unlikely that timber was stacked in the main street, for there was ample space nearer the building site. One writer has asserted that 'many complaints are on record from residents in the village that the timber was stacked so high that it shut out the light from the houses'. Unfortunately, the source is not given, and there is no evidence of this from Beaulieu Muniments. At the south end of the village street, near the present shop, there was a well, and later a pump, from which the people of the village drew their water. Behind the Master Builder's House, was a large field with stables in which the Adams' family kept their horses. At the water's edge were five launchways, and six wooden buildings used for a variety of purposes; two forges, a mould loft, a treenail house, a shed for grinding stone, and another for steaming plank. By 1845, when shipbuilding was almost dead, all those sheds were designated as 'mast and rope houses'.[2] Downstream was the East Timber Yard, which received timber brought by sea, and which was large enough to accommodate all the pieces needed on site. In the East Timber Yard there were more sawpits, and a coal yard.

The village had a blacksmith, as did every village in the 19th century, for his craft could be equated with the garage of our own day. The smithy was used not only for the shoeing of horses, but also for the making and repair of tools, both domestic and agricultural, and for ordinary household items such as pots and pans, fireplaces and crude utensils. Perhaps a child could have persuaded the smith to make him an iron hoop, with a crook, the trundling of which, over the bumps and through the puddles in the road, helped to make the daily journey to school in Beaulieu seem shorter.

The two inns were not just places where the lower orders could ruin themselves; they were the community centres of their day. In the Ship inn, the shipwrights and the caulkers were paid their wages. As the cottages were too small for entertaining, the parlours of the inns were the only rooms large enough for friendly concourse or convivial parties. Even simple pleasures, dominoes or cards or dice, were enjoyed at the inn rather than at home, crowded with children, food, and washing. An evening visit each day was the regular habit of the adult males of the village, so that the innkeepers were able to make a steady living.

The two innkeepers also acted as shopkeepers, for there was no separate shop in the village until the 20th century. Business transactions took place in the inns, as did the collection of the poor rate, or subscriptions for friendly societies, shoe clubs, Christmas clubs and the like. Legend has it that the New inn, now the Maritime Museum, became a centre for smuggling in the days of Joseph Wort. The dominance of the alehouses came to an end during the last quarter of the 19th century when Gladstone's licensing laws, and the propaganda of the temperance societies, made the upper classes aware of the evils of drink. The first Lord Montagu enforced the closure of all but one of the Beaulieu taverns, and in Buckler's Hard the Reading Room was established in 1886 so that the villagers could imbibe edifying literature rather than strong beer. Even when the Master Builder's House was first opened as an hotel, it had no licence.

The inhabitants of the village, by the standards of their day, were comfortably housed. The cottages, Slab Row apart, were built of brick at a time when there were still mud houses; originally, some of them had thatched roofs, but tiles were put on many. In some cases, the families had a room upstairs as well as down, unlike some of the cellar dwellings of the industrial north. Moreover, the stairs, though narrow by modern standards, were inside the houses, a boon in the dead of winter. No-one was more than 100 yards from the water supply — again, unlike many town-dwellers in the early 19th century. The cottages had their own privies, and there was space to bury the waste in the ground. Underground sewage is comparatively modern, and Buckler's Hard, like most of the other country villages, did not have septic tanks until the 20th century was well advanced. In our own times, standards of comfort have increased so rapidly that the young demand much more than did their parents a mere 30 years earlier. At Buckler's Hard, where the cottages have been preserved, one is looking at houses built for people seven generations removed. Amalgamations, extensions and modernisation have changed the interiors, but the outsides of the houses have remained relatively unaltered. Front gardens, side garages, entrance halls, and all the other so-called essentials of the modern housing estate cannot be created in a village built for another age.

The village is to be preserved as it is today, but paradoxically its present composition is not as it was in the 18th or 19th centuries. From the foundation of the village in the 1720s until the second quarter of the 19th century, the number of houses in the village grew. When at its maximum size it comprised the two main terraces, and Slab Row and Back Street, in addition to Bath Cottage, built in 1760 by the third Duke of Montagu for his arthritic son. Today, Bath Cottage still stands, as does one remaining house in Back Row. At the present time the houses in the main terraces are known by numbers which derive, with considerable modification, from the old tenancies of the entire manor, as follows, *West Terrace:* 74 to Master Builder's; *East Terrace:* 91 to 84. Today, the village shop is number 74, and the Maritime Museum is 91.

Building began nearest to the river, and most of the two existing terraces were constructed before the two rows which have now disappeared. In general, the houses in the West Terrace, nearest to the river, were high class houses, whilst in the East Terrace the Ship and the New inn were larger than average.

The Master Builder's House was almost certainly built originally by Alexander Morris who ran the Beaulieu brickworks for Miles Troughton; the latter intended that his son-in-law Philip Sone should live there. The house, in its original form, was first occupied by Morris in 1729. When shipbuilding began at Buckler's Hard, it was occupied by John Darley in 1747, and then by Henry Adams from 1749 to 1805. During Henry Adams' tenancy, additions were made to the house, including an extension towards the river, the present Adams' Room, a banqueting hall, and stable in the field to the west of the house. Edward Adams lived there from 1813 to 1849, his widow remaining until 1852, and William Scanes from 1858 to 1872; then Frederick Buckle occupied it from 1872 to 1883, after which the house ceased to be linked with the by then defunct shipyard. In the 19th century the house was usually known as the Shipbuilders House. By 1910 it was in a dilapidated state, and later became the home of Jim Thomas, whose official title was Lord Montagu's boatman, but who was, in effect, the harbourmaster. It was altered and converted into an hotel in 1926, renamed the Master Builder's House and was run by George Foster Pedley and his wife until 1939. After naval occupation during the war, it had other tenants, including Stephen Fry, the son of 'C B' the famous cricketer and Saints footballer; then

200

Beaulieu Estate took it back, and it was run by Montagu Ventures Ltd from 1964 to 1971, when J R Lyons and Co took it over. In 1965 a new dining room was added, running westward; in 1972, 17 new bedrooms, and a conference room named after Sir Francis Chichester, were built adjoining the hotel.

It is possible that the original mould-loft was the upper floor of the present 82 and 83, converted into dwelling units when Henry Adams erected a wooden mould loft in the shipyard. This is mere supposition.

The ground floor of number 82 is today the chapel of St Mary's, and it has been used for religious services for almost a century. Before 1847 it was a dwelling-house, inhabited for most of the time by shipyard workers. In 1847 an infants' school was set up there under Mrs Harding, but by 1886 the school was defunct, as Buckler's Hard people preferred to send their children to Beaulieu, where the standard of education was higher. The room had been used for occasional services on Wednesday evenings, and in May 1886 an altar was put in, and the room dedicated. During the 1914-1918 war the chapel was renovated, largely due to the efforts of Lady Poole, wife of Reginald Ward Poole, of Buckler's Wood, with Lord Montagu's full support.

Further embellishments were made after the war in memory of Peter Rylands, an airman who was killed in August 1918. The bell came from the old church at Bonchurch, on the Isle of Wight, and the carved panelling from Lady Cross Lodge in the New Forest. The statue of the Virgin Mary, of French origin and more than 300 years old, stands on a chopping block from Beaulieu Abbey. In 1933 Lady Poole's son David was drowned in the Beaulieu river, and a memorial cross was made in his memory, with words composed by Sir James Barrie and Winston Churchill — a truly remarkable literary partnership. The original plain altar was replaced by one from the private chapel of Ditton Park, Lord Montagu's other estate. Thus, most of the fittings in the chapel were installed in the 1920s. In 1962 the administration of the chapel became the official responsibility of the parochial church council, although building and fabric are owned by Lord Montagu.

According to local lore the chapel was once a cobbler's shop. If so, John Read, shoemaker, lived there in the 1850s. Also it is reputed to have been a smuggler's den. In her moving monograph on the chapel, Elizabeth Goudge has the following, *During the work of restoration an interesting discovery was made. Beneath the decaying floor was a cellar. Empty bottles lay on the floor and sticking to the walls were clay candlesticks made by throwing lumps of wet clay on the walls and then thrusting candles into them. Up above the honest craft of the cobbler had been carried on, and down below the more exciting but less honourable trade of smuggler.*

Geoffrey Morley (*Smuggling in Hampshire*) states that the house was the headquarters of the smugglers, and that all the cottages were delivery points. Though there is no evidence in Beaulieu archives, the village doubtless was involved. But the evidence of the cellar is unconvincing. Moreover, the Salt Officers lived in West Terrace during the period when smuggling was at its height. Number 80, opened as a shipwright's cottage display in 1981, was occupied by William Burnett up to 1767; there is some slender evidence to suggest that for a time a Salt Officer lived there; in 1781 it was let to Thomas Burlace, the shipwright who injured his leg and was forced on to the parish. He died in 1816, aged 72 (he is recorded erroneously as 'Edward' in the Beaulieu parish registers), and Arabella, his wife, died in 1820, aged 82. Their daughter Elizabeth, married Ambrose Sainsbury, probably a shipwright, and their son Edward married Martha Blaker, a shipwright's daughter. Edward went to sea and his wife had to apply for poor relief in 1818. In 1845 Number 80 was occupied by William Payne, another shipwright, but soon afterwards severed its connection with shipbuilding.

Number 81 was the residence of Edward Adams' last foreman shipwright, Charles Glastonbury, who married Frances Williams in Beaulieu in 1811. When their first child was born in 1814 he is described as a gamekeeper, yet from 1816 onwards the registers classify him as a shipwright. Glastonbury had to seek work elsewhere when Edward Adams died in 1849 but his wife remained in Buckler's Hard during his absence. Glastonbury was back in Buckler's Hard by about 1860, and he died there in 1877, aged 88, one year after the death of his wife. He was long remembered as wearing a top hat when he was foreman of the yard. Their son George, born 1821, was a shipwright in Stepney by 1844; a daughter, Elizabeth, born 1818, married a shipwright, Richard West, whilst another daughter, Mary Anne, married William Martin, a Buckler's Hard fisherman. The parish registers are confusing as Glastonbury is spelt variously, even as Glassby.

Number 78 and 79 were almost certainly built after numbers 80 and 77. The southern wall of 80 was once an outside wall, part of a passage way to the back; the roof line of 78 and 79 is lower than that of the adjoining properties; also, the external brickwork is not bonded in, suggesting that 78 and 79 were filled in later, possibly by Henry Adams for his workforce.

In the East Terrace, number 91, the present Maritime Museum, was leased by James Wort, possibly as early as 1774, and he opened a shop there. Shortly after 1791 Wort combined his shop with licensed premises, as the New inn. The inscription over the front door, *Jos. Wort 1774* remains a mystery. The house was built before 1774, and James Wort was the lessee until 1804. Perhaps the house was rebuilt in 1774, or enlarged, when it became a shop. The blocked out window is almost certainly a relic of Pitt's unpopular and unhealthy window tax. Joseph Wort took over the lease in 1804, and continued there until 1819. He was perhaps the son of James Wort, but his birth is not in the Beaulieu registers. There were several families of that name living in the neighbourhood, and at least three James Worts. In 1767 Joseph Wort, son of James and Sarah, was baptised, the only Joseph in the period; in 1768 Joseph, son of James, was buried. In 1792 a Joseph Wort married at Beaulieu, Elizabeth Ralph of Deptford. If this was the landlord of the New inn, did he spend some of his life in London? Or, was his bride the daughter of an itinerant shipwright? A Joseph Wort was buried in Beaulieu in 1819, aged 52, at about the time when Joseph Wort disappears from the rentals. This Joseph, therefore, was born in about 1767, so that perhaps the infant who died in 1768 was not the 1767 birth. It may be reasonable to assume that Joseph Wort succeeded his father as landlord of the New inn.

William Scanes, whose family included shipwrights, was the tenant by 1845, where there were stables attached. He then moved to the Master Builder's House and his nephew, Walter Scanes Snook, took over the New inn. Walter died in 1861, aged 27, and Shilley acted as a baker and a shopkeeper there. The tenancy eventually reverted to another Walter Snook, and William Snook lived there in 1918.

The New inn was presumably so called as the Ship was already well established in the present number 87. The Ship was the seafaring hostelry, where the shipwrights were entertained after a launching. The Ship was an alehouse as early as 1752, then run by Widow Palmour, who was succeeded by John Hewett 1753-1761, then by the Misses Street, and then by Thomas Floyd. Charles Hemans was the landlord during the early part of the French wars, and by 1812 it was run by Benjamin Rawlings (or Rawlence), who was still the landlord in 1845. Rawlings was followed by D T Alston, the agent for the Oyster fishery, and then William Martin, the husband of Mary Glastonbury, lived there.

Number 89, which has been converted into a display cottage, was usually occupied by labourers. As the nearby Clobb Farm had no cottages, Buckler's Hard was the usual place of residence for those who worked there. In the 1790s it was probably occupied by the Bound family, whose descendants later lived in Bath Cottage. Thomas Corbin lived in number 89 in 1804 as did William Thomas later, both labourers.

Unfortunately it is not possible to discover the identity of all the occupants of every individual house in the village from its inception. When Buckler's Hard was founded, the houses were on leasehold land for 'three lives' or 99 years. By the end of the 18th century the leases were much shorter, and by the middle of the 19th century they were annual. Although there are many extant rentals, the properties were given different numbers at different times. Moreover, the holder of the lease did not necessarily live there; for example, the Adams' family rented several houses for their workforce, some of whom were temporary residents. Also, some houses had more than one family living in them, one occupying the upper storey, and another the bottom, or even a part of a floor. In many cases permanent lodgers, unmarried men or women, lived with a family, and did not aspire to a house of their own. Even in the two existing terraces, the number of dwellings has not remained constant. Some have been joined to make larger houses, as some of the original units comprised only one room upstairs and one downstairs. For example, the present village shop comprised at least two housing units, and perhaps even three during the early 19th century, even though known as Norton's Cottage, after its first occupant, who died in 1757. Norton's Cottage was built in 1746, but has been virtually rebuilt during the present century.

A picture of the changing economic and social life of the village can be built up by taking a sounding in particular years. In 1729, five years after its foundation, Buckler's Hard comprised seven houses; the Master Builder's House, in its original and smaller form; three Salt Officers' houses, probably in the West Terrace; a blacksmith's shop and house, occupied by John Froud, in the East Terrace; another East Terrace house inhabited by the widow of Edward Fry, a Beaulieu carpenter; and the seventh house occupied by Benson, a former Salt Officer.

In 1763 there were probably 15 houses, comprising some 18 rent payers. Henry Adams, in addition to the Master Builder's House, leased four houses for his workmen, as well as a shop. Four other houses were leased by women, one of whom was the widow of the first nightwatchman, Scanes. At least one other house was rented by a shipwright, Joseph West, so that by then the village was almost equally divided by shipyard workers, farm labourers, and women.

In 1790 there were 19 leaseholders, including one house held by a Salt Officer. Henry Adams still leased some houses for his men, and other inhabitants included at least three other shipwrights, one blacksmith, two innkeepers and two widows.

In 1804 there were 21 tenancies, in addition to the Adams House and shipyard. Adams then leased three of the larger houses in the village. Other residents included at least three other shipwrights, John Blaker, Thomas Burlace, and Philip Williams, one shipwright's widow, Hester West, two innkeepers — Charles Hemans of the Ship and Joseph Wort of the New inn, a blacksmith appropriately called Richard Smith, and 11 other families. The increase in the number of tenancies was probably due to the subdivision of houses and not to new building.

In 1813 Edward Adams occupied the Master Builder's House, and half the shipyard. In addition, he leased another seven houses which provided ten dwelling units for his workmen or dependants. Balthazar Adams held the other half of the shipyard, and four houses occupied by eight families; he himself lived at Curtle Farm and not in Buckler's Hard. The shipwrights Burlace and Williams were still in the village, as was Joseph Wort at the New inn but Benjamin Rawlence had taken over the Ship.

The middle years of the 19th century saw profound changes in the economy of the village: the palmy days of shipbuilding came to an end, coincidental with the manor of Beaulieu having, from 1867 on, a resident lord of the manor. In those years it is possible to state with reasonable confidence the identity of inhabitants of particular houses in Slab Row, Back Street, and East Terrace. In West Terrace, however, there are pitfalls, as the number of houses in that row changed during those vital years: for example, at least one house was pulled down between 1845 and 1849, while there were changes in the dwelling units through amalgamation and division.

In 1845, towards the end of Edward Adams' life but while the shipyard was still active, a survey of the manor was made for the Duke of Buccleuch[3]; in 1867 Lord Henry Scott toured the houses in his new inheritance, and left a record of his visit.[4] Those years, between 1845 and 1875 embraced the death of Edward Adams, the end of the Adams' tenancy of the shipyard, the collapse of shipbuilding, and an increase in the number of people deriving employment from the Estate. The following diagrams, showing the tenant of each house, with their age and occupation where known, show the changes in the economy in those years. However, there is a high degree of continuity in the personnel of the village; there was an occupational, rather than a geographical, shift. The number engaged in shipbuilding and allied trades had declined; the sons of sawyers and the like were working as farm or general labourers, living in Buckler's Hard, and not in the growing shipyards of Southampton. The working-class tended to remain, if possible, near their tap-roots, and left the adventure of emigration to the enterprising middle-classes. Also, families moved from one house in Buckler's Hard to another, whilst adjoining houses were amalgamated or separated according to the needs of a growing or a shrinking family. Further, in some cases one family unit occupied upstairs, and another family downstairs. The present house numbers are used to denote each particular dwelling unit, although in the 19th century they were not as today. For example, number 83 was occupied by two or three farm tenants, while number 75 was then three houses. During those years Slab Row and Back Street had begun a rapid deterioration and they were to be pulled down later in the century.

By 1918, the sociological make-up of the village had undergone a profound change. The present Master Builder's House, then much smaller than today, and in need of repair, was the home of Jim Thomas, Lord John Montagu's 'boatman'. Next door, in what is now part of the hotel bar, was the reading room, with residential accommodation above it; then the chapel, again with a living unit on the upper floor. In number 81, lived Alfred Thomas, who was employed at Clobb Farm; in number 80, Mr Mackenzie, a gardener at Buckler's wood; the rest of that terrace was occupied by Ben Hendy, and by Charlie and Don Thomas, both farm workers. The remaining houses were occupied by a Mrs Adams (not related to the shipbuilder); by her daughter Mrs Pike, whose husband Charles was a Chelsea pensioner; and, in the end house lived Montagu Adams, a dentist from Portsmouth, a descendant of

Henry Adams, who persuaded Morgan, the Beaulieu Estate Agent, to let him have a weekend cottage. Two of the three houses were amalgamated in 1932; the present shop was rebuilt completely, on former foundations in 1937.

In the East Terrace, William Snook and family lived in the present Maritime Museum, and Henry Corbin, who worked at Saltern's Hill Farm, lived in the old Ship inn. The other inhabitants of East Terrace were Charlie Thomas, George Read, George Stickland, a chauffeur, Mr Hendy senior, Walter Thomas, who worked at Clobb Farm, and Mrs Bound, in the house nearest the river which was later converted into the harbourmaster's cottage. In Back Street, only one of the two remaining houses was occupied, by a Mr and Mrs Snook, both deaf and dumb. Slab Row had by then been demolished.[5]

In 1993, conservation was partially complete. Three cottages were unoccupied, awaiting full internal renovation and external restoration. Three other cottages housed 18th century displays. Two cottages were occupied through Beaulieu management and the remainder housed staff working in the hotel or on the Beaulieu Estate.

But the village has survived the vicissitudes of fortune. Today some of the older generation talk wistfully of remembering the village when people lived there. It is remarkable that the hamlet has not become one of the hundreds of lost villages of England. Today, positive steps are being taken to ensure its future as a living community. Lord Montagu will endeavour to maintain its character, and to ensure the occupation of the cottages by families connected with the manor of Beaulieu — an important consideration at a time when so many small settlements in beauty spots are becoming weekend houses for wealthy town dwellers. The past, the present, and the future are linked together in an endless chain. After two centuries of existence Buckler's Hard looks confidently towards the next two.

References

[1] A Triggs *The Windmills of Hampshire* (in *Industrial Archaeology* No 6, 1969)
[2] Beaulieu Muniments: Rentals for 1845
[3] Beaulieu Muniments: Estate Map 1845
[4] Beaulieu Muniments: Lord Henry Scott's notebook
[5] H E R Widnell *What I remember* Vol I (unpublished)

WEST TERRACE
(From the River)

HOUSE	Bedrooms	1845
MASTER BUILDER'S	9	Edward Adams shipbuilder, aged 78
83	3	Thomas Cox farm labourer, aged 34
	1	
	3	James White farm labourer, aged 24
82 CHAPEL	1	William Reynard river defences
81	1	Charles Glastonbury shipwright, aged 55
SHIPWRIGHT'S COTTAGE	3	William Payne shipwright aged, 34
79	2	Charles Carpenter labourer
78	2	Joseph Biddlecombe farm labourer, aged 29
77	2	Joseph West shipwright, aged 59
76	3	William Gregory farm labourer, aged 30
75 and 74	2	Elizabeth Scanes shipwright's widow, aged 76
	3	Henry Ward farm labourer, aged 34
		Ben Fry Bricklayer, aged 50

1849	1867	1875
Edward Adams	William Scanes	Frederick Buckle blacksmith, wife & 7 children
Thomas Cox labourer	Thomas Cox 'rough carpenter' Widow Bound	Thomas Cox shoreman and wife Charles Thomas farm labourer
William Read farm labourer	Widow Read	Charles Glassbey farm labourer, wife & 2 children
Infants' School	Mrs Stickland (upstairs) Infants' School (downstairs)	Widow Read (Senior) (upstairs) Infants' School (downstairs)
Charles Glastonbury	Charles Glastonbury former shipwright	Jasper Stickland (Junior) St Leonard's Farm wife & 6 children
William Payne	Thomas Foss labourer	Benjamin Hendy labourer, wife & 4 children
Edward Willis labourer, aged 39	Edward Willis and orphan children	Walter Willis wife & 2 children
John Read shoemaker, aged 26	Vacant	John Lowe farm labourer, wife & 3 children
Joseph West	Widow (John) Read and 5 children	William Thomas shoreman, wife & 1 child
Thomas Holman farm labourer, aged 21	Benjamin Hendy labourer	George Harding shoreman, aged 59 and wife
Mrs Scanes	Mrs Harding infant teacher	Widow Glassby
Charles House aged 39	Charles House daughter & son-in-law	William Bull labourer, wife & 3 children
Widow Fry	John Adams labourer	

EAST TERRACE
(From the River)

HOUSE	Bedrooms	1845
84A	2	George Lowe farm labourer, aged 30
84B	3	Benjamin Fielder shipwright
85	2	John West shipwright, aged 27?
86	1	William Gough
87 SHIP INN	4	Benjamin Rawlings inkeeper, aged 74
88	2	George Jones retired?
89	2	John Picket farm labourer, aged 34
90	2	Anne Carver widow
NEW INN (Maritime Museum)	?	William Scanes inn & shopkeeper, aged 42

1849	1867	1875
George Lowe	Edward Thomas labourer	Frank Bound farm labourer
Benjamin Fielder labourer	Frederick Buckle blacksmith	John Thomas farm labourer
Jasper Stickland labourer	Jasper Stickland with 4 children (two houses)	
William Thomas farm labourer		
D T Alston innkeeper & oyster agent	William Martin fisherman i/c river & oyster agent	William Martin
Joseph Biddlecombe labourer	Joseph Biddlecombe labourer	Joseph Biddlecombe pensioner
vacant	William Thomas	Henry Glasby estate worker
William Corbin labourer	William Corbin & Thomas Goff (lodger)	Charles Thomas estate worker
William Scanes	Frederick Shelley shopkeeper & baker, aged 25	Frederick Shelley shopkeeper

211

SLAB ROW

HOUSE	Bedrooms	1845
99	2	John Reynard farm labourer, aged 45
100	2	William Voss farm labourer, aged 40
101	2	William Hendy farm labourer, aged 74
102	2	William Smith blacksmith, aged 64
103	1	John Poore farm labourer, aged 44
104	2	George Harding labourer
105	1	Ben Kemmish labourer

BACK STREET
(From the River)

HOUSE	Bedrooms	1845
98	2	James Gosling retired labourer, aged 79
97	?	John Gregory farm labourer
96	2	Edward Thomas farm labourer, aged 34
95	1	George Jones labourer, aged 21
94	1	Jasper Stickland labourer, aged 34
93	?	Martha Burlace widow of Edward Burlace
BATH COTTAGE	2	John Bound labourer

1849	1867	1875
William Bull farm labourer	Ben Kemmish pensioner	Frederick Cox estate worker
Thomas Voss	John Poore labourer	William Thomas
William Hendy retired	Mrs Carpenter widow	Henry Vardy blacksmith with Buckle
Ben Hendy labourer	Ben Kemmish junior	two cottages joined
John Poore	Vacant	Mrs E Bound servant St Leonard's
George Harding	William House estate worker	William House two houses joined
Ben Kemmish	William Bull farm labourer	

1849	1867	1875
William Gregory	George Rawlings estate worker	George Rawlings shoreman
John Gregory	Vacant – probably demolished	
Edward Goff	Edward Thomas	Edward Thomas carter at Salternshill
Vacant	Thomas Corbin farm labourer	Thomas Corbin
Stephen Gregory	William Thomas farm labourer	William Thomas retired
James Bound	Vacant	Probably demolished
John Bound	John Bound	John Bound brickyard at Bailey's Hard

Appendices

APPENDIX I
Visitors' descriptions of Buckler's Hard

William Gilpin, Vicar of Boldre, 1791

❛ *We now came in sight of Buckler's Hard on the left, where the large timber yards, houses, and ships on the stocks, made a violent chasm in the landscape. A quantity of timber scattered about a yard, makes a very unpicturesque appearance. It affords a variety of parts without a whole. And yet in a timber-yard, there are sheds and other circumstances, which are not wholly void of picturesque images. In a ship on the stocks, through every stage as it advances, there is a degree of beauty, which consists chiefly in the variety of its sweeping lines.* ❜

John Bullar of Southampton, 1819

❛ *From Beaulieu, a pleasant ride may be taken to Buckler's Hard,* about two miles distant, through a beautiful road, with delightful wood scenery on the banks of the river. Buckler's Hard is a small village, entirely supported by shipbuilding, which, during many years, was carried on by the late Mr Adams. Many fine ships that now form part of the British Navy were launched at this place. At high water, the tide forms a beautiful bay, skirted with woods. * So this place is universally, though improperly called: the name of the person to whom it formerly belonged was Buckle.* ❜

(*A Companion in a Tour Round Southampton p 99*)

T W Littleton Hay, c 1870

❛ *There are now but a couple of rows of cottages, facing each other on a green slope that stretches down to the river, and at the bottom of this slope we could see the remains of the slips on which the ships were built. While we were looking, a fossilised individual bore down upon us. He was about four feet six in height, his head was surmounted with a battered white hat pushed well back till it rested on the collar of his smock-frock, and bent down his ears at the side; from beneath the brim peeped out a few silver hairs. His nose was hooked like an eagle's beak, and his small eyes, quite lashless and inflamed, and red as a ferret's, gleamed fiercely on either side of it. He wanted to know if we wished to be ferried across – as if anyone ever could wish to be ferried across, and as if he could grafity their wish – and seemed quite hurt at our disturbing the sleepy quiet of the place, with no other motive than curiosity. However, a plug of cavendish consoled him, and made him communicative. He began to serve his time in the shipbuilding* yards there in 1806, when he was 17 years old, and he "minded" when there were two 74s – the Hanover and Victorious, and one frigate – the Hussar – in the slips. Only two merchantmen were built after the peace, and then the yards were closed. He pointed to the turf-covered slope. "Had you given a guinea," quoth he, "you couldn't ha' got a clod as big as your hand in those days, Sir". The old man had been in many parts of the country shipbuilding after the Bucklershard yards were closed; but when his working days were over he had returned to Bucklershard to live on half-a-crown a week allowed him by the parish. There was something marvellously melancholy in viewing this worn-out and discarded town and the wrecked specimen of humanity who had lived past his three-score and ten years – surely he could not have "snakes in his boot," or even be "on the shoot", – and it seemed wrong somehow that such a link with the past should have, in these hard times, to drag out the remainder of his days on half-a-crown a week. He can hardly have survived this last winter. '

C J Cornish, 1903

' On the low ridge to the left is a square-built village of good old red brick, brown tiled houses; not so much a village indeed as a street, running at right angles to the river and looking like a section of old Portsea cut away and set down in the woods. And that is exactly what it is; a fragment of the great arsenal, left high and dry by time on the shores of the Beaulieu river. Here, on the green slope where the cattle feed and children play, was built of New Forest oak, Nelson's ship the Agamemnon, 64, the ship which he was commanding when he lost his right eye at the seige of Calvi, the ship which carried his flag in the battle of the Baltic, one of whose crew, at the battle of St Vincent, tucked under his arm the swords of the Spanish officers as if gathering sticks for a faggot. Those whose boding fancy foresees a time when no sign will be left of the great industries of the North but burnt-out cinder heaps, should consider the history of Buckler's Hard.

In the middle of the last century, John Duke of Montagu, Lord of Beaulieu, and owner of the great sugar-island of St Vincent, and inheritor of the rights of the Abbots of Beaulieu to a free harbour upon his river, determined to make a seaport at Buckler's Hard. It was a far-sighted scheme, in view of the American trade, which posterity has justified by the creation of modern Southampton. Grants of land at a nominal rent, and of timber delivered free, soon attracted shipbuilders to the spot, and in September, 1743, the Surprise, 24, the first battleship built on the river was launched. From that time till the end of the great war, the work grew and prospered. Frigates succeeded sloops, and battleships frigates, and each vessel after it left the slips, was taken round to be fitted and manned at Portsmouth. The Surprise went out to fight the French in May, 1750; the Vigilant, 64, 1,374 tons, in 1774; the Hannibal, 74, was launched in 1810. The Agamemnon, after carrying Lord Nelson through the battle of the Baltic, and taking her share in Trafalgar, was lost in Maldonado Bay in the River Plate in 1809; the Indefatigable, the Illustrious, the Swiftsure, line of battle-ships, and a whole fleet of frigates were launched at Buckler's Hard during the latter years of the war. Such was the skill of the builders and the resources of the place that a 74-gun ship was not longer than 30 months upon the stocks, though 2,000 oaks, 100 tons of wrought iron, and 30 tons of copper, were worked into her fabric. The whole of this great industry was created and directed by one man, Mr Henry Adams, who carried it on for 60 years, and lived till the age of 92. His sons succeeded him; and the ruin of Buckler's Hard was due, not to the failure of its resources, but to the deliberate action of the Admiralty. The Adamses were commissioned to build four ships at once, and for not delivering them by the date agreed on, were ruined by fines and litigation at the instance of the Government whom they served. Of their once prosperous yard, no sign remains but the houses they built and four grass-grown hollows in the shore which were the slipways of the battleships. In one of these, filled with water at high tide, lies the rotting skeleton of a wooden vessel, her stem and stern posts still upright, while from her back project the broken and distorted ribs, and bent bolts of copper. From a tree in the garden of what one was the home of the Adamses, there still waves, as if in mockery, a ragged Union Jack. '
(The New Forest and Isle of Wight, pp 70-74)

216

H V Morton, 1927

❛ *The port of the little kingdom of Beaulieu is some three miles south along Beaulieu River; and it is called Buckler's Hard.*

Buckler is the name of a man who lived there centuries ago, and Hard refers to the character of the river bank in this locality. Now, when you enter Buckler's Hard you feel at once the queer atmosphere which clings to a place in which men have expended great enegry; the village seems to be resting after effort. The street, as wide as Regent Street, is only 100 yards long. It ends, as if cut off suddenly, in green hummocks and mounds on which cattle graze.

Below this single street standing among fields, the ground falls gently to the banks of the Beaulieu River. The stream is wide at full tide, and at low exposes a great tract of shallow, reedy bank. Beyond the river, wood lies piled on wood to the sky-line.

When you walk beside the river you notice once again that evidence of a dead village buried under grass. Here are more green hummocks and mounds. Great timbers go down into the water, rotting and covered with weed. In the field are gigantic dips and hollows full of lush grass and flowers. In those dips and on those rotting slipways once rested the stout oak-built ships which helped to found the British Empire. This unknown, forgotten village in Hampshire was once loud with the sound of forge hammers, here thousands of great oak trees were formed into ships of the line; and into the water of Beaulieu River was launched in 1781 the Agamemnon, a 64-gun ship of 1,384 tons burden, in which Nelson lost his right eye at the siege of Calvi.

The history of Buckler's Hard is, apart from its interest as a dead village which played its part in Empire, well worth telling; for it shows how swiftly time and fate can alter a place.

Time stepped in. The wooden walls gave place to the iron, the sail to the funnel. Gradually fewer and fewer ships were launched in the Beaulieu River. Swift as had been the rise of the village, as swift was its fall. Its old name came back; and now the grass has come back; the wildfowl cries where once the caulking hammer sounded, and the heron perches on the great oak pathways from which ships of the line stepped majestically into our naval history . . . ❜
(In Search of England, pp 33-34, 39-41)

APPENDIX II

Shipbuilding Families

(a) WYATTS of Hythe area

JOSEPH ────────────────────────	JAMES
timber merchant of Hardley	Shipbuilder
(d. 1757)	(1691-1767)
│	m. Hannah King
│	│
Sarah (+3 other children)	8 children
m. John Barnes	

As well as male Wyatts, through their daughters some of their descendants had the following surnames: Etheridge, Cooper, Hawksworth, White and Barnes

(b) ADAMS of Buckler's Hard

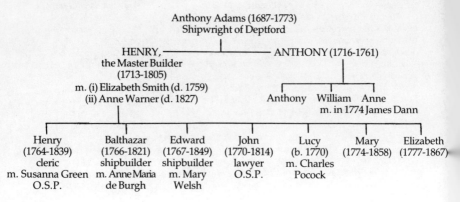

Anthony Adams (1687-1773)
Shipwright of Deptford

HENRY, ———————— ANTHONY (1716-1761)
the Master Builder
(1713-1805)
m. (i) Elizabeth Smith (d. 1759)
(ii) Anne Warner (d. 1827)

Anthony   William   Anne
m. in 1774 James Dann

| Henry (1764-1839) cleric m. Susanna Green O.S.P. | Balthazar (1766-1821) shipbuilder m. Anne Maria de Burgh | Edward (1767-1849) shipbuilder m. Mary Welsh | John (1770-1814) lawyer O.S.P. | Lucy (b. 1770) m. Charles Pocock | Mary (1774-1858) | Elizabeth (1777-1867) |

Henry Adams' grandchildren

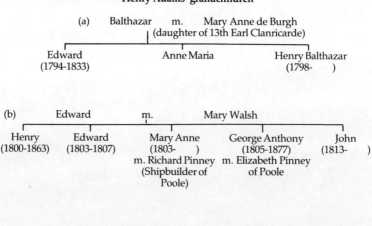

(a)   Balthazar   m.   Mary Anne de Burgh
(daughter of 13th Earl Clanricarde)

Edward   Anne Maria   Henry Balthazar
(1794-1833)   (1798-   )

(b)   Edward   m.   Mary Walsh

| Henry (1800-1863) | Edward (1803-1807) | Mary Anne (1803-   ) m. Richard Pinney (Shipbuilder of Poole) | George Anthony (1805-1877) m. Elizabeth Pinney of Poole | John (1813-   ) |

(c)   Lucy   m.   Charles Pocock

Charles Montagu   Anne   Louisa   John   Edward
(1792-   )   (1794-95)   (1797-   )   (1803-   )   (1805-   )

218

APPENDIX III

Navy Board overseers at Buckler's Hard

When naval ships were built in the merchants' yards, the Navy Board appointed shipwrights from one of the Royal dockyards to supervise the project. These overseers are not always recorded, so that this list must be incomplete.

24 August 1749 to 10 May 1749, Henry Adams, from Deptford
10 May 1749 to ?, White
October 1756 - ?, Snooks
1771 - ?, Robert Carleton
1773 - 1781, James Dann
1779 - ?, George Polyblank
1791 - 1794, John Ancill
June 1794 - November 1799, James Williams
1799 - 1804, Joseph Seaton
1804 - ?, Thomas Aylen

Many of these overseers gained high positions in the royal dockyards after leaving Buckler's Hard. Ancill became Timber Master at Plymouth; Williams the Foreman Shipwright at Sheerness; and Aylen became First Assistant at Portsmouth.

APPENDIX IV

An estimate for building of vessel of 82 tons in 1838
(Edward Adams)
(in Portsmouth City Library)

	£	s	d
60 loads square timber at £4 15s	285	0	0
2½ (loads) elm keel at £4	10	0	0
4 oak thick stuff at £13	52	0	0
oak plank	67	10	0
Memel plank (deck)	32	10	0
Cabin floor	4	0	0
Bulwarks	6	0	0
Oakum, pitch, tar, and grease	7	2	0
Paint	4	3	0
Glue, putty	1	10	0
Painters (at 3s6d a day) and glaising	1	2	6
Scuppers: joiners' nails	3	0	0
Blacksmiths and iron nails	30	0	0
Copper nails and bolts	90	0	0
Shipwrights' time 80 at £2	160	0	0
Sawyers, caulkers, joiners	100	0	0
Copper sheathing	125	0	0
	978	17	6
+Rent of yard	10	0	0
	988	17	6

(NOTE: Shipwrights employed by Edward Adams then received 4s a day, boys 1s, and sawyers 7s the pair)

APPENDIX V

Naval ships built on the Beaulieu river

The compilation of a definitive list of naval vessels built in exact location is fraught with difficulty. Records held locally are sometimes at variance with those held nationally, and the latter, compiled by Navy Board clerks, are sometimes in conflict with each other. Navy Board clerks were at times compiling lists long after the launchings, and referring to places outside their own geographical knowledge. Hence the classic entry 'Bussleton (i e Bursledon) on the Bewley river'. 'Southampton' might mean anywhere on the Southampton Water, and 'Hamble' anywhere on that river, or 'Bewley' could mean Bailey's Hard, Buckler's Hard, or Lepe. Other lists are of 'intended' building, which may or may not have taken place. The builders themselves did not keep lists or accounts over long periods; even a list drawn up by the Adams brothers of their father's and their own contribution to the Navy in the previous 60 years contains some errors.

In the Beaulieu river, there are further difficulties and many possible pitfalls. When I began working on naval building, as long ago as 1957, I spent three years in achieving just five minor modifications to all that had been written before me.

1   I proved to my own satisfaction that the *Salisbury* was almost certainly built at Bailey's Hard, and not at Buckler's Hard. Since that time, all other writers have stated definitely that the ship was built at Bailey's Hard. In the list which follows, I have added a query, as the next generation of researchers may find definitive evidence.

2   All writers before myself stated that the firm of Wyatt and Co came to Buckler's Hard from Bursledon in the 1740s. I was able to disprove this by tracing the demise of all male Wyatts from the Bursledon family, and then finding the local family who were, in fact, the builders. Again, since 1959, this has become accepted as fact.

3   As Henry Adams was a partner in the firm at Deptford, there has always been some confusion between 'Adams built' and 'Adams built at Buckler's Hard'. Before my own researches, many lists accredited to Buckler's Hard some Deptford-built ships.

4   Robert Adams, not related to Henry, built ships at Eling and Southampton.

5   In 1962, when I compiled a list of Buckler's Hard ships, I perpetrated at least two errors,

(a)   the 20-gun *Gibraltar* was included as built by Henry Adams at Buckler's Hard in 1756. *Gibraltar* is accredited to Adams in the Victoria County History of Hampshire, Volume V, in a list which contains several inaccuracies. *Gibraltar* was launched at Portsmouth Dockyard on 9 May 1754, and continued an active career until 1773. In 1756 *Gibraltar* captured a 16-gun sloop, the *Glaneur*, which was known as the *Gibraltar Prize*. There is no hard evidence that this prize was rebuilt at Buckler's Hard, but she may have been.

(b)   the 24-gun vessel launched by B and E Adams in May 1814 was named *Towey*, not *Fowey*. This error derived from the original list drawn up by a Navy Board clerk.

6   *Lively*, a 24-gun ship launched in 1756 is shown in Admiralty papers as built by
     'Janverin, Beaulieu'. As there is no evidence in Beaulieu Muniments that
     Moody Janverin, of Hamble, had a site anywhere on the Beaulieu river in 1756,
     this ship is not included. The one possibility is that Janverin built her at Lepe.

The list on page 222 therefore conflicts with others that have been published and is
based on local as well as national archives. The gunnage shown does not necessarily
mean that a ship had that exact number of guns; gunnage was an administrative
formula for the computation of the size of the crew. For example, *Mermaid*, 24 guns,
had a crew of 160; *Woolwich* (44 guns) had a crew of 280; and the 64-gun *Agamemnon*,
a crew of 500 men. Tonnage was calculated differently from the formula of today and
the figures shown as 'builder's measurements'; the breadth is the extreme
measurement, to include the tumble-home; and the length is that of the gun-deck –
as a rough approximation, the keel length would have been about four-fifths of the
gun deck.

Date of Launching	Name	Tonnage	Gunnage	Length (in feet)	Breadth (in feet)	Builder	Place
18 4 1698	*Salisbury*	682	48	134½	34	Richard & James Herring	Bailey's Hard?
27 1 1745	*Surprise*	508	24	112½	32	James Wyatt	Buckler's Hard
8 7 1746	*Scorpion*	276	14	91	26½	James Wyatt	Buckler's Hard
April 1748	*Greenwich*	1053	50	144½	41½	Moody Janverin	Lepe
7 3 1749	*Woolwich*	825	44	133½	38	John Darley & Moody Janverin	Buckler's Hard
22 5 1749	*Mermaid*	533	24	115	32	Henry Adams	Buckler's Hard
4 7 1749	*Fowey*	513	24	113½	32	Moody Janverin	Lepe
3 7 1753	*Lion* (transport)	151	4	72	22½	Henry Adams	Buckler's Hard
16 4 1756	*Kennington*	437	20	107½	30½	Henry Adams	Buckler's Hard
? 1756	*Lyme* (rebuilt)	587	28	118	34	Deptford Dockyard:- rebuilt Henry Adams	Buckler's Hard
20 5 1757	*Coventry*	599	28	118½	34	Henry Adams	Buckler's Hard
10 4 1758	*Thames*	656	32	127	34½	Henry Adams	Buckler's Hard
6 7 1758	*Levant*	595	28	118½	34	Henry Adams	Buckler's Hard
1 4 1760	*Hayling* (transport)	132	4	67	21½	Henry Adams	Buckler's Hard
21 4 1765	*Europe*	1370	64	159	41	Henry Adams	Lepe
20 7 1773	*Greyhound*	617	28	124	33	Henry Adams	Buckler's Hard
1 10 1773	*Triton*	620	28	124	35	Henry Adams	Buckler's Hard
2 11 1773	*Thetis*	686	32	126	35	Henry Adams	Buckler's Hard
6 10 1774	*Vigilant*	1347	64	159½	44½	Henry Adams	Buckler's Hard
17 12 1777	*Romulus*	885	44	140	38	Henry Adams	Buckler's Hard
Dec 1777	*Pacific* (rebuilt)	(captured from the French)					
1778	Two fireships	?	?	?	?	Henry Adams	Buckler's Hard
2 1 1779	*Sibyl* (later *Garland*)	599	28	120½	33½	Henry Adams	Buckler's Hard
13 7 1779	*Brilliant*	600	28	120½	34	Henry Adams	Buckler's Hard
24 12 1779	*Hannibal*	1054	50	146	41	Henry Adams	Buckler's Hard
10 4 1781	*Agamemnon*	1376	64	160	45	Henry Adams	Buckler's Hard
20 1 1783	*Gladiator*	882	44	140	38	Henry Adams	Buckler's Hard
August 1783	*Heroine*	779	32	131	37	Henry Adams	Buckler's Hard
July 1784	*Indefatigable*	1400	64	160	44	Henry Adams	Buckler's Hard
16 7 1787	*Sheerness*	906	44	141	38½	Henry Adams	Buckler's Hard
7 7 1789	*Illustrious*	1616	74	168	47	Henry Adams	Buckler's Hard
4 5 1791	*Beaulieu*	1020	40	147½	39½	Henry Adams	Buckler's Hard
1793	*Santa Margarita* (rebuilt)	993	38	145½	39	Henry Adams	Buckler's Hard
Sept 1794	*Cerberus*	796	32	135	36	Henry Adams	Buckler's Hard
7 4 1796	*Bittern*	422	18	110	30	B & E Adams	Buckler's Hard
12 4 1797	*Boadicea*	1052	38	148½	40½	B & E Adams	Buckler's Hard
18 12 1797	*Snake*	386	18	100½	30½	B & E Adams	Buckler's Hard
30 9 1799	*Abundance* (storeship)	673	24	140	32½	B & E Adams	Buckler's Hard
10 5 1800	*Spencer*	1917	74	181	49½	B & E Adams	Buckler's Hard
23 9 1801	*L'Aigle*	990	36	150	39	B & E Adams	Buckler's Hard
4 4 1802	*Starling*	184	12	85	22	B & E Adams	Buckler's Hard
2 5 1802	*Snipe*	185	12	80½	23	B & E Adams	Buckler's Hard
10 6 1802	*Vixen*	186	14	80½	23	B & E Adams	Buckler's Hard
6 6 1803	*Euryalus*	946	36	145	38	B & E Adams	Buckler's Hard
24 7 1804	*Swiftsure*	1724	74	173	48	B & E Adams	Buckler's Hard
10 8 1804	*Growler*	178	12	80	22½	B & E Adams	Buckler's Hard
15 12 1804	*Fervent*	179	12	80	23	B & E Adams	Buckler's Hard
2 2 1805	*Dexterous*	180	12	80	22½	B & E Adams	Buckler's Hard?
16 7 1806	*Columbine*	386	18	100½	30½	B & E Adams	Buckler's Hard
23 4 1807	*Hussar*	1077	38	154	40	B & E Adams	Buckler's Hard
20 10 1808	*Victorious*	1724	74	173	47½	B & E Adams	Buckler's Hard
May 1810	*Hannibal*	1749	74	176	48½	B & E Adams	Buckler's Hard
13 8 1813	*Medina*	460	20	116	30½	Edward Adams	Buckler's Hard
9 11 1813	*Carron*	460	20	116	30	Edward Adams	Buckler's Hard
26 11 1813	*Tay*	460	18	116	30	Balthazar Adams	Buckler's Hard
6 5 1814	*Towey*	448	24	108	30½	Balthazar Adams	Buckler's Hard

Thus, 57 naval vessels, including two fireships, were built or rebuilt in the Beaulieu river between 1698 and 1815.

The other Hampshire merchants' yards contributed the following for the same period:

Southampton	*56*
Hamble river	*51*
Hythe	*6*
Eling	*3*
Redbridge	*14*
Gosport	*2*
(Isle of Wight)	*17*

The Southampton figure, which includes the work of several builders at four sites, was inflated by 23 naval launchings between 1803 and 1814, whilst all six Hythe vessels were built in that same limited period. No single Hampshire civilian builder or firm built as many naval vessels as did Henry Adams and his sons.

APPENDIX VI
Sources of timber

It is commonly asserted that Buckler's Hard ships were built of New Forest timber. This statement is erroneous if the New Forest is defined as within the boundaries of the property of the Crown. The New Forest ends, or begins, at North Gate, on the road to Longdown and Marchwood which was opened by the Duke of Buccleuch in 1837. Timber from the New Forest was used by the royal dockyards, and especially by Portsmouth and Plymouth. The royal dockyards were the largest naval shipbuilding units, and it was right that they should have royal timber for their exclusive use.

All the crown forests were administered by an official from the Exchequer, the Surveyor General, whilst each individual forest had a Lord Warden, usually a sinecure post. Even today, the man actually in charge of the New Forest is called the Deputy-Surveyor, although there is no longer a higher official above him. During the 17th and 18th centuries the official who administered the New Forest, often a local man who knew the Forest intimately, was called the Woodward. Under him was the Purveyor, the practical man who organised the felling and the carting. Redbridge was an important entrepot for the shipping of timber from the New Forest, but royal timber cut from Castle Malwood, Boldrewood, Eyeworth, Godshill and Lady Cross was also shipped from Lymington, the Beaulieu River, Hythe and Eling. During the 18th century the timber shortage became a problem, and new plantations were made in the New Forest in 1782 and in 1808. The growing demand and the consequent shortgage led to a rise in timber prices, reminiscent of that of oil in our own time. A load of oak cost two pounds in 1660, and the price rose steadily until 1793, when it rose by 300% in the next 17 years, so that in 1810 the average cost of a load of oak was £13. Civilian shipbuilders such as Henry Adams had to rely on the great estates for a supply of compass timber, so that the woods of the manor of Beaulieu were an important factor in the development of shipbuilding on the river. But Adams was also a timber merchant, and timber bought from Beaulieu and elsewhere was not used solely for shipbuilding on the Beaulieu river. Some Beaulieu timber was used in Portsmouth and Plymouth Dockyards, and by the firm of Adams, Barnard and Company at Deptford. The ships built at Buckler's Hard were built of timber from various sources some from Beaulieu, some from other parts of England, even as far as Shropshire: some from the Baltic: and, later in the 18th century, some from the New World.

Thus, the only generalisation that can be made is that the manor of Beaulieu was, on balance, an exporter of timber, but shipbuilders on the Beaulieu river also used timber from other places.

The effects of shipbuilding on the woods of Beaulieu were not cataclysmic. The greatest tree felling operation took place in the 1720s when Dungehill Copse was partly cut down for the siting of Buckler's Hard.

From the beginning of the 17th century, the newly founded ironworks at Sowley used some 800 cords of wood a year, presumably from the woodlands near there. During the reign of Charles II there were sales of timber to the Crown in 1666, and to some Hampshire merchants, including Richard Wyatt of Bursledon between 1667 and 1672. Herring's building of one ship, at Bailey's Hard in 1698, would not have depleted the woodlands near the river. During the 18th century, when the Adams' yard was at its height, the total acreage in Beaulieu used for woodland increased marginally at the same time as that for arable farming, both increases being made at the expense of marsh and pasture. The largest scale fellings were between 1811 and 1815, at a time when Henry Adams was dead and the businesses of his two sons were in decline. The timber went to Messrs Larking and Morrice, and was not connected in any way with Beaulieu river shipbuilding. These sales were, in effect, the owners of the manor capitalising on the shortage and inflated price of timber in the Napoleonic Wars. A period of replanting then took place from 1815-1827, the greater part of it in Hartford, Newhouse, and Newlands. These plantings added some 560 acres to the woodlands. Any long-term effects of felling, for shipbuilding or other purposes, were obliterated.

Bibliography

A   MANUSCRIPT SOURCES

1   *Public Record Office*
Admiralty, Accountant General's Department
49/94 Papers relating to shipbuilding 1784-1797
49/102 Lists of ships built and repaired in merchants' yards 1801-1812
49/132,
       133, Registers of orders to yards 1658-1777
       134.
Bill Books.
Admiralty, Controller of the Navy's Department
95/12 Orders for shipbuilding 1719-1763
95/84 Ships built and repaired 1771-1783
95/85 Ships to be built 1794-1807
Admiralty, Navy Board
106 In letters
30/8/246 Part I
Register of wills proved in the Prerogative Court of Canterbury

2   *British Library*
Sloane MSS 3233 *A Survey of the ports on the south west coast of England, 1698*
Stowe MSS, 478 *Increase and decrease of the Navy 1692-1698*
Additional MSS 33722, J Skinner's Journal, 1831
Additional MSS 48978, Beaulieu Account Book

3   *Scottish Record Office Edinburgh*

4   *Greenwich National Maritime Museum*
Dimensions Book B 1660-1764
Draughts of vessels built or intended to be built
Navy Boards Letters
Parliamentary Papers 1805-1809
A key to the papers presented to the House of Commons upon the subject of the
    charges preferred against Earl St Vincent by Mr Jeffrey, MP for Poole, London 1806
Ships logs and journals

5   *Palace House Beaulieu*
Estate maps; Stewards' Accounts; Stewards' letters; Audit memoranda; Rentals;
    Expenditure vouchers; Leases.

6 *Northamptonshire Record Office*
Boughton House Papers

7 *Southampton Record Office*
Moberley and Wharton deposits
Page and Moody collection

8 *Hampshire Record Office, Winchester*
Winchester diocesan probate register

9 *Portsmouth City Library*
Edward Adams' account book

10 *Parish Registers*
The Blessed Virgin and Holy Child, Beaulieu
All Saints, Dibden
All Saints, Fawley
St John the Baptist, Boldre

B   CONTEMPORARY NEWSPAPERS AND PERIODICALS

Hampshire Chronicle 1772-1830
Hampshire Courier 1812-1814
Naval and Military Journal 1799 (then became the *Hampshire Telegraph*)
Hampshire Telegraph 1800-1812
Hampshire Advertiser (from June 1827)
The Naval Chronicle, London 1799-1818

C   PUBLISHED SOURCES

a   *Navy Records Society* (London)
Barnes G R and Owen J H *The Sandwich Papers* 1771-1782 (3 vols 1932)
Merriman, R B *The Sergison Papers* (1950)
Naish, G P B *Nelson's Letters to his wife* (1958)

b   *Southampton Record Society* (Southampton)
H S Cobb (ed) *The Local Port Book of Southampton 1439-1440* (1961)

c   *Miscellaneous*
Dom Hockey (ed) *The Account Book of Beaulieu Abbey,* (Royal Historical Society, 1975)
Dane C *The Nelson Touch – an anthology of Nelson's Letters* (London 1942)
Hardy, C *Register of East Indiamen 1707-1760*
Calendars of State Papers Domestic 1660-1704 (London 1860-1924)

D   SECONDARY WORKS

1   *Bibliographies*
Albion, R C *Naval and Maritime History* (Connecticut, USA 1963)
Anderson, R C *Eighteenth Century Books on Shipbuilding, rigging and seamanship*
    (in *Mariners' Mirror* Vol xxxiii 1947)
Callendar, A R *Bibliography of British Naval History* Part I (Historical Association
    pamphlet No 58 London 1924)
HMSO Naval Records (London 1950)
Jarvis, R C *Sources for the history of Ships and Shipping* (in *Journal of Transport History*
    Vol III No 4, Leicester 1958)
Manwaring, G *Bibliography of British Naval History* (London 1930)

2 *Local history*

Adams, R B *Hampshire Men-o'-War* (*Southern Daily Echo* 21 November 1928)
Adams, R B *The Story of Buckler's Hard* (*Notes and Queries* Vol 156, 15 June 1926)
Adams, R B *Buckler's Hard Ships* (in *Hampshire Independent*, 28 Feb 1891)
Adams, R B *The Story of Buckler's Hard* (BBC broadcast 12 March 1929)
Anon *The Cradle of Nelson's Fleet* in *Khaki* No 17, July 1916)
Albin, J *Description of a voyage from Newport to Lymington* (IOW 1792)
Arnold-Forster, D *At War with the Smugglers* (London 1970)
Bullar, J *A Tour round Southampton* (Southampton 1819)
Cobbett, J *Rural Rides* Vol I (Everyman, London 1912)
Cooke, G A *Topographical and Statistical Description of Hampshire* (London, c 1806)
Cox, J C *The Royal Forests of England* (London 1905)
Defoe, H C *The Storm* (London 1704)
Dent, H C *The Hampshire Gate* (London 1924)
Dewar, A *Voyages and Travels of Captain Nathaniel Uring* (London 1928)
Gilpin, J *Remarks on Forest Scenery and other woodland views* (Edinburgh 1834)
Godwin, G N *Buckler's Hard: a deserted shipyard* (in *Hampshire Notes and Queries*,
    Vol V, Winchester 1890)
Godwin, G N *Buckler's Hard and its Ships* (in *Hampshire Field Club Papers* Vol II
    Part I Southampton 1891)
Heywood Sumner *Guide to the New Forest* (Ringwood, 1923)
Hockey, Dom F *Beaulieu: King John's Abbey* (Woking 1976)
Holland, A J *The Tempest that became a County Legend* (in *Hampshire*, Vol I
    November 1960)
Holland, A J *The Beaulieu River: its rise and fall as a commercial waterway* (in *Mariner's
    Mirror* Vol 49, November 1963)
Holland, A J *Ships of British Oak* (Newton Abbot 1971)
Holland, C *The Birthplace of a Fleet* (*Yachting Monthly* April 1908)
Holland, C *The Story of Buckler's Hard* (in *Blue Peter* Vol iv, no 29, August 1924)
Hone, J *Birthplace of Wooden Walls* (*Everybody's Weekly* 12 July 1952)
Horrocks, J W *More about the Tauntons* (in *Hampshire Advertiser*, 1928)
Jones, Rupert J A *Centuries Changes in Lepe Shore* (in *Southern Daily Echo* 14 Sept 1928)
Jones, Rupert J A *Hampshire Men-o'-War* (in *Southern Daily Echo* 16 October 1928)
Montagu, Lord E *Beaulieu* (Beaulieu 1952)
Montagu, Lord J *Buckler's Hard and its ships* (Beaulieu 1910)
Mudie, R *History of Hampshire* (Winchester 1838)
Oakley, E R *The Smugglers of Christchurch, Bourne Heath and the New Forest*
    (London 1944)
O'Brien, F T *Early Solent Steamers* (Newton Abbot 1973)
Pannell, J P M *Old Southampton Shores* (Newton Abbot 1967)
Parsons, J D *Hampshire Men-o'-War* (*Hampshirer Advertiser* 27 October 1928)
Parsons, J D *Hampshire-built Warships* (London 1928)
Pococke, R *Travels through England 1754* Vol II (Camden Society 1889)
Ruddock, A A *Italian Merchants and Shipping in Southampton 1200–1600*
    (Southampton 1951)
Ruddock, A A *Method of Handling the Cargoes of Medieval Galleys* (*Bulletin of
    Historical Research*, Vol XIX 1949)
Thorneycroft, L B *Buckler's Hard: a forgotten little backwater* (in *Hampshire Review*
    No 11)
Uring, N *A relation of the late intended settlement of St Lucia and St Vincent* (London 1725)
Vancouver, C *General view of Agriculture in Hampshire* (London 1810)
Victoria County History of Hampshire 5 volumes (Westminster 1900-12)
Warner, R *South-west of Hampshire* (London 1795)
Widnell, H E R *Beaulieu Abbey and its estate* (in *New Forest* London 1960)
Widnell, H E R *The Beaulieu Record* (Woking 1973)
Woodward, B B *History of Hampshire* 3 volumes (London, undated)
Wyatt, S C *Cheneys and Wyatts* (London 1959)

3 *Unpublished*
Bartlett, A B *The Beaulieu river: some historical notes (1974)* (in Beaulieu Muniments)
Bartlett, A B *The Iron Works at Sowley* (1974 in Beaulieu Muniments)
Boswell, K C *Southampton and its hinterland* (Msc Thesis for University of London 1936)
Holland, A J *Shipbuilding in Hampshire 1660-1820* (MA thesis University of Southampton 1961)

4 *Ships, shipbuilding and allied trades*
Abell, Sir W *The Shipwright's Trade* (Cambridge 1948)
Albion, R G *Forests and Sea Power* (Cambridge, Mass USA 1926)
Albion, R G *The Timber Problem of the Royal Navy 1652-1852 (Mariner's Mirror* Feb 1952)
Anderson, R C *List of Men-of-War 1650-1700* (Cambridge 1939)
Anderson R and R C *The Sailing Ship* (London 1927)
Burwash, P *English merchant shipping 1460-1540* (Toronto 1947)
Charnock, J *History of Naval Architecture* (3 vols) (London 1800-1801)
Fincham, J *History of Naval Architecture* (London 1851)
Haas, J M *Methods of Payment in Royal Dockyards 1775-1865* (in *Maritime History* Vol V, Winter 1977)
Horsley, J E *Tools of the Maritime Trades* (Newton Abbot 1978)
Longridge, C N *The Anatomy of Nelson's Ships* (London 1955)
Moll, F *The History of Wood Preserving in Shipbuilding* (in *Mariner's Mirror* Vol XII 1926)
Morris, R A *Labour Relations in the Royal Dockyard 1801 - 1805* (in *Mariner's Mirror* Vol 62 November 1976)
Naish, G B P *Shipbuilding* (in *History of Technology* Oxford 1958)
Nicholls, T *Methods proposed for decreasing the consumption of timber in the Navy* (London 1793)
Richardson, H E *Wages of shipwrights in H M Dockyards 1496-1788* (in *Mariner's Mirror* Vol xxxiii 1947)
Sturt, G *The Wheelwright's Trade* (Cambridge 1934)
Sutherland, W *The Shipbuilder's Assistant* (London 1717)

5 *Naval history*
Charnock, J *Biographia Navalis* (6 vols) (London 1794-98)
Colledge, J J *Ships of the Royal Navy* Vol I (Newton Abbot 1969)
Ehrman, John *The Navy in the War of William III* (Cambridge 1953)
Gardiner, L *The British Admiralty* (Edinburgh 1958)
James, W *Naval History of Great Britain* (London 1822)
Mackenzie, R H *The Trafalgar Roll* (London 1913)
Warner, O *Nelson's Battles* (Newton Abbot 1971)

6 *Miscellaneous*
Clark, J Natal Settler – Agent (Cape Town 1972)
Foot, M R D SOE in France (MNSO 1966)

Index

Ships' names are shown in italics

232